triumphlearning™

English Language Arts

4

Coach®

Contents

CHAPTER

1 Literature

1 Diagnostic Assessment

Read the passage and answer the questions that follow.

Different

Three animal families—deer, fox, and skunk—lived in a forest. One day, the young deer, the young fox, and the young skunk were playing near the stream that ran through the forest. Their parents had told them to stay out of the stream because it had a strong current. It was on the bank of the stream that they met another young animal.

They had never seen an animal like this before. He had large front teeth and a big, flat tail. They approached him cautiously.

"I'm a fawn," said the young deer. "What kind of animal are you?"

"I'm a beaver," he answered.

"I knew you weren't a fox," said the fox. "I know all the other foxes in this forest. Why haven't we ever seen you before?"

"My family just moved to this forest," said the beaver.

"Where are you going to live?" asked the skunk.

"We don't have a house yet," the beaver said. "We have to build one."

"Don't build it next to mine!" said the fawn.

"Or mine!" added the fox.

"Or mine!" said the skunk.

"Why not?" the beaver asked. "Why don't you want me living near you?"

"Because you're different," said the fawn.

"You look strange," added the fox.

"You're not like us," finished the skunk. "We won't play with you."

The three friends scampered away, leaving the beaver staring after them.

"I couldn't play with you anyway," he called out. "I have to help my mom and dad build our house." But by now they couldn't hear him.

Soon the beaver family was hard at work. They used their sharp front teeth to cut down small trees. Then they dragged the trees into the stream. The swift current didn't bother them because beavers are very good swimmers. They piled the trees up and filled in the spaces with mud. Soon, they had built a dam across the stream. Because of the dam, a pond formed. Now, instead of a stream with a dangerous current, the forest had a pond with water that was still and calm.

The beavers built their home in the middle of this pond. Like the dam, their home was made of trees, sticks, and mud. It didn't take very long for the beaver family to finish and settle into their new home.

That very day, the fawn, the fox, and the skunk returned to the stream for the first time since the day they had met the beaver.

"What happened?" wondered the fawn. "The stream has turned into a pond."

"We did that," said the beaver, popping out of the water.

"How?" asked the fox.

"My family built a dam across the stream. Now the water is still."

"Is it safe to play in?" asked the skunk.

"Yes, because it doesn't have a current anymore," the beaver told them.

The fawn picked a stick up with its teeth, walked to the edge of the stream, and dropped the stick into the water. Instead of being swept away by the current, as it would have been only a few days ago, the stick just floated, barely moving at all. There was no current to sweep it away.

The three animals looked at the stick in the water. Then they looked at one another with wide-open eyes and mouths. Suddenly, they scampered away, leaving the beaver staring after them. But this time, they weren't running away from the beaver. They were running to ask their parents if they could play in the pond.

Soon, all three families returned. The animals' parents stood by the pond and studied the floating stick. It bobbed gently in the water, but stayed in one place.

By now, the beaver's parents had come out of their lodge and were standing next to him.

"Welcome to the forest," the fawn's father said.

"Thanks for turning the dangerous stream into a safe pond," said the fox's mother.

"Let us know if we can do anything for you in return," said the skunk's parents.

"Can we swim in the pond?" the young animals all shouted at once. Their parents nodded, and the young animals were soon splashing about in the water.

"Hey, beaver!" called out the fawn. "Come play with us!"

1. Which detail from the passage shows that the three animals are amazed at the calm water?

   A. "There was no current to sweep it away."

   B. "Then they looked at one another with wide-open eyes and mouths."

   C. "They were running to ask their parents if they could play in the pond."

   D. "The three animals looked at the stick in the water."

2. Which sentence BEST summarizes the passage?

   A. A beaver and his family make new friends by turning a dangerous stream into a safe pond.

   B. A fawn, fox, and skunk are mean to a beaver and run back to their families.

   C. A beaver and his family drag sticks across a fast-moving stream to build a home.

   D. A fawn, fox, and skunk run to their parents to ask permission to go swimming.

3. Which word BEST describes the beaver in the passage?

   A. wise

   B. honest

   C. hardworking

   D. brave

4. Which point of view is used in the passage?

   A. first-person

   B. second-person

   C. third-person limited

   D. third-person omniscient

Read the passage and answer the questions that follow.

The Magpie's Nest

One autumn long ago, in a lovely forest, the air turned very cool and crisp quite early in the season. All the different birds of the forest looked around at the changing leaves. Then they studied their own nests. Most of them had spent a very lazy summer eating bugs and berries, and they hadn't paid much attention to the condition of their homes. Their nests were drafty, and some had terrible leaks.

The birds had a meeting one afternoon and agreed that they would go and ask the magpie for advice on fixing up their nests. The magpie was a rather dull bird, and she wasn't usually included in the summer playing and fun in the forest. In fact, she hadn't even been invited to the meeting where it was agreed that she would be asked to help the others! But she had a very fine nest.

The next day, the birds flew to the magpie's nest. They all admired her nest, cooing and flattering her. Not only was her nest beautiful, they insisted, but it was also durable enough to stand up to wind and rain. Only a very smart and talented bird could make such a nest!

The magpie waited patiently. She knew the other birds just wanted her to tell them what they should do. But in the end, she decided that it would be best if all the birds knew how to build a proper nest. So, she gathered them around and said, "Please, I know how much trouble some of you have listening to others. I know how hard it is to sit still while there are so many bugs out there waiting to be chased. But it is important that you listen to everything I have to tell you—before you go to work on your nests."

"Absolutely, Ms. Magpie!" the birds all cried. "You have our undivided attention!"

"Very well," the magpie continued. "First, you need to get some mud and make a round cake with it."

"Oh," said the thrush. "Is that all? I can do that!" And she flew away to build her mud nest. This is still how thrushes make their nests today.

"No, no, there's more!" the magpie cried. "Next, you need to get some twigs and place them around in the mud."

"Oh, anybody can do that!" said the blackbird, and he flew away. Even today, blackbirds have nests made only of mud and twigs.

The magpie was becoming rather annoyed, but she continued anyway. "The next step is to add some more mud over the twigs."

"Why, a child could do that!" hooted the owl, who noisily flapped away to make a nest. Even today, if you look at an owl's nest, you can see that it is made out of some twigs and two layers of mud.

"After the second layer of mud, wrap some more twigs around the outside," the exasperated magpie added, holding her wing to her forehead.

"Okay, boss! I'm on it!" said the sparrow. And to this day, the sparrow makes exactly that kind of nest.

"Next," said the magpie, sitting down wearily, "you add some soft grass to the inside to sit on."

"Grass—got it!" said the starling, who sped off to make a rather nice nest, but not as nice as the magpie's. Even today, this is how starlings make their nests.

The magpie was about to give her final instruction when she realized there were no birds left. She was muttering to herself as she fluffed a layer of soft feathers in her elegant nest. "Fine," she said. "That's the last time I'll ever help those silly creatures!"

Never again would she agree to help the other birds build nests. That is why, today, all of the different birds make different kinds of nests.

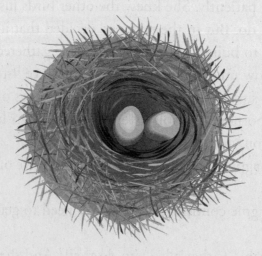

5. What is the MOST LIKELY reason the birds ask for the magpie's help with their nests?

    A. They realize winter is coming soon.

    B. They admire and respect the magpie.

    C. They hope to move in with the magpie.

    D. They need help gathering more food.

6. Which BEST states the theme of the story?

    A. Forests are cold and lonely places.

    B. You have to work hard to make friends.

    C. If you ask for advice, you must be polite and listen.

    D. Seasons will change no matter what.

7. According to the story, which bird listens the longest to the magpie's instructions?

    A. the starling

    B. the owl

    C. the blackbird

    D. the thrush

8. Why does the magpie offer to help the other birds?

    A. She wants them to like her.

    B. She wants them to stop bothering her all the time.

    C. She wants to help them learn about nest building.

    D. She wants to trick them into working on her nest.

Use "Different" and "The Magpie's Nest" to answer questions 9–10.

9. Compare and contrast the two stories. Are the themes alike or different? Use details from both stories to support your answer.

In the two stories "Different" and "The magpie's Nest" they were alike and different. One thing that they had alike is the three friends in "Different" called the bever different, and in "The Magpie's Nest" all the birds nest were different. Another thing the both storys have alike is the there friends and the birds dis respeting the bever and the magpie. One differece is that the bever wasen't being able no more and the magpie was still being included. Another different thing thay had is the magpie was old and the bever was new. They had many things alike and different.

10. Compare the beaver and the magpie. Explain how these characters are different or alike.

The beaver and the magpie are some what alike and different. They are alike because people didn't treat them right. Another way they are allike because the birds didn't let magpie play with them and the three friends didn't let the beaver play with them ether. They are differeat because the beaver was new and the magpie was old. Another differece is at the and the beaver had friends but the magpie was still included in things.

Read the poem and answer the questions that follow.

Daisies

by Frank Dempster Sherman

At evening when I go to bed
I see the stars shine overhead;
They are the little daisies white
That dot the meadow of the Night.

5   And often while I'm dreaming so,
Across the sky the Moon will go;
It is a lady, sweet and fair,
Who comes to gather daisies there.

For, when at morning I arise,
10 There's not a star left in the skies;
She's picked them all and dropped them down
Into the meadows of the town.

11. In which stanza does the poet describe the moon?

    A. stanza 1

    B. stanza 2

    C. stanza 3

    D. stanzas 1 and 2

12. Which line from the poem shows which syllables are stressed?

    A. At <u>evening</u> <u>when</u> I go to <u>bed</u>

    B. <u>At</u> eve<u>ning</u> when <u>I</u> go <u>to</u> bed

    C. At <u>evening</u> when I go to <u>bed</u>

    D. <u>At</u> evening <u>when</u> I <u>go</u> to <u>bed</u>

1 Story Details

Getting the Idea

When you read a story, you get information about people, places, and things. Stories tell about characters, such as what they do, where they live, and what they look like. A **detail** is a specific piece of information. Details help you to understand the things contained in stories. The chart below shows some different types of story details.

Type of Story Detail	Example
names of places and characters	Mario visited his aunt in Austin, Texas.
dates and time	The storm arrived on Tuesday evening.
descriptions of places	Yellow sunflowers grew in the grassy field.
things characters say and do	Keisha shouted, "Let's play tag!"
things the narrator tells you	Jake was the best player on the team.
facts in a story	He reminded her of our first president, George Washington.

To find the details in a story, it is often helpful to ask yourself some questions after reading. For example, read the following paragraph.

Eva put on her blue coat, grabbed her knapsack, and rushed out the front door. It was 7:45 a.m. She and her mom walked as quickly as they could. Ten minutes later, Eva arrived at Bellmore Elementary School for her first day of fourth grade.

By asking yourself the following questions, you can find the details in the story. What is the girl's name? *Eva*. What is the color of her coat? *Blue*. What time is it when she leaves her house? *7:45 a.m.* Where is she running to? *Bellmore Elementary School*. What grade is she in? *Fourth grade*. The author uses many kinds of details to help you understand the people, places, and things in the story.

The details in the story about Eva tell you even more. They support larger ideas that are not directly stated in the story. When you use details in the story along with your own knowledge and experience to figure out things for yourself, you make an inference. An **inference** is an educated guess about something that *most likely* or *probably* is true. For example, the passage says that Eva rushed out the front door and ran as fast as she could. Based on those details and your own experience, you can infer that she is late for school. You also read that she grabbed her coat. You can use that detail to infer that it is probably chilly outside.

Another way to better understand a story is to make a simple diagram. A **web** is a diagram that shows an important story idea and the details that help you to understand that idea. The web below is about Dorothy, a character in *The Wizard of Oz.*

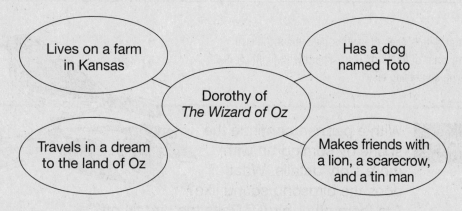

The details are shown in the four outer circles. Each detail gives you a piece of information about Dorothy, such as where she lives and where she travels in her dream. A web can be used for all types of details—characters, places, and events. A web will help you sort and organize information from a story. Seeing the details in a diagram can also help you make inferences about what you read.

Thinking It Through

Read the following sentences, and then answer the questions that follow.

Javier stood quietly and watched a small sparrow land on the branch of a magnolia tree. The brown-and-white bird tilted its head back and began to whistle a beautiful song.

What does the sparrow look like? What is the sparrow doing?

It small and it is brown-and-white. It is flying.
It land on the branch of a magnolia tree.
It was tilted its head back and began to
whistle a beautiful song

 What details does the author give about the size and color of the bird? Is the sparrow in flight, or is it doing something else?

 **DISCUSS** With a partner, continue the scene by coming up with more story details. What does the birdsong sound like? Are there other birds? Does the bird fly off?

The song sound beautiful.
Then other bird came and
they stop singing. After that
they flu away because the
saw Javier.

Coached Example

Read the passage and answer the questions.

As a child, Rochelle would sit in the living room and listen to her mother play the piano every evening. She began to take lessons as a teenager. She would practice two hours every day after school. For the first hour, she would practice her music scales. For the second hour, she would practice learning songs. Rochelle loved the smooth feel of the piano keys beneath her fingers. Each of the eighty-eight black-and-white keys had its own special sound. At night, she would often fall asleep listening to recordings of music by her favorite composers, Mozart and Beethoven. Rochelle liked to dream that, one day, she would play just like the pianists on the recordings.

1. Rochelle will MOST LIKELY continue to practice every day because

   A. she knows she can be a world-famous pianist.

   B. she loves everything about piano playing.

   C. she wants to be a better pianist than her mother.

   D. it helps her relax and fall asleep at night.

   HINT What inference can you make about Rochelle's interest in practicing the piano? Look for the answer choice that makes the most sense.

2. Which detail shows that Rochelle is dedicated to playing the piano?

   A. Rochelle loves the feel of the piano keys.

   B. Rochelle's piano has eighty-eight keys.

   C. Rochelle practices the piano every day.

   D. Rochelle loves to listen to Mozart.

   HINT Which detail supports the idea that Rochelle works hard to learn how to play the piano?

Lesson Practice

Use the Reading Guide to help you understand the passage.

Reading Guide

Read the first sentence of the passage carefully. Are there any details that describe the season? *Yes*

Which detail in the passage describes something about the ant's body? *with his six strong legs.*

Look at details the author uses to describe how the dove feels. How does the dove feel about the drowning ant? *like he need help*

Which detail tells how the ant saves the dove's life? *the ant bit the man's foot.*

The Dove and the Ant

One fall day, an ant stopped by a stream to get a drink of fresh water. Suddenly, a gust of wind came down from the sky and blew the ant into the stream. The ant struggled to stay afloat as the flowing stream swept him along. He paddled as mightily as he could with his six strong legs, but then he began to sink. Luckily, a white dove perched in a tree saw the ant sinking fast. She pitied the drowning ant and flew down to the edge of the stream. As the ant passed by, she reached out her wing.

"Grab hold, dear ant!" called the dove. The ant reached out and crawled onto the dove's wing. Soon the ant was back on dry land.

"I could never thank you enough!" said the ant to the dove. "I hope I can someday return the favor."

A few days later, the ant returned to the stream for another drink. He spied a hunter nearby pointing his bow and arrow into the trees. The ant looked up and saw that the hunter was about to shoot the dove. Quickly, the ant bit the man's foot and made him miss his aim. By doing that, the ant saved the dove's life.

Answer the following questions.

1. What time of year does the passage take place?

   A. summer

   B. spring

   C. winter

   (D.) fall

2. How does the dove help the ant in the passage?

   A. She teaches the ant how to swim.

   B. She gets the ant some water to drink.

   C. She protects the ant from the wind.

   (D.) She reaches out her wing to the ant.

3. Which detail from the passage tells that the ant is in trouble?

   A. He looks up into the trees.

   (B.) He struggles to stay afloat.

   C. He sees a hunter on the shore.

   D. He returns to the stream.

4. Which sentence from the passage BEST helps you know where the passage takes place?

   (A.) "The ant struggled to stay afloat as the flowing stream swept him along."

   B. "As the ant passed by, she reached out her wing."

   C. "The ant looked up and saw that the hunter was about to shoot the dove."

   D. "By doing that, the ant saved the dove's life."

5. What does the ant say in the passage? How do his words help you to understand his character?

   The ant says "I could never thank you enough!" said the ant to the dove. "I hope I can someday return the favor." His words help me to understand his character because he kind. It also shows me his really thank you.

Use the Reading Guide to help you understand the passage.

Reading Guide

Read the passage carefully. Which details tell where and when Chris and Nana will hike? *tnl saturday North*

Which details in the passage tell you about Nana's knowledge about hiking? *Move away from there that poison iv*

Look at the details used to describe how Chris feels. How does Chris feel during the hike? *Tired*

Which detail tells how Chris feels about Nana at the end of the story? *His grandma cares about him*

Taking a Hike

Chris excitedly told his grandmother, Nana, about the Outdoors Club he had formed with his friends. "Last month we went on a long hike," he bragged, "to prove that we are outdoor survivalists."

"I love hiking," Nana said. She must have noticed the surprise on his face because she said, "Let's hike North Trail on Saturday." Chris agreed. He could see a movie with his friends afterward.

On Saturday, they woke at dawn because Nana insisted it was the best time to hike. She wore khakis tucked into thick socks and heavy boots, a T-shirt, a thin nylon jacket, and a wide-brimmed hat. Chris looked at his shorts, T-shirt, and gym shoes and wondered if Nana wasn't overdoing it.

At the trail, Nana passed Chris a backpack, hoisting another one over her shoulders before confidently calling, "Let's go!" Chris struggled to keep pace with his grandmother. Branches along the narrow trail scratched his arms and legs. The sun beat hotly on his head. He felt relieved when Nana finally stopped for a rest. She pulled water and snacks from her backpack, telling Chris, "I packed some for you, too." He gratefully yanked the supplies from his backpack and settled against a bulky rock.

"Move away from there!" Nana shouted.

Chris leapt away from the rock. Nana pointed to plants growing along the rock's base. "That's poison ivy."

"I leaned against it!" Chris moaned.

Nana smiled and pulled a tube from her backpack. "This will help," she said.

Chris smiled back weakly. "Um, Nana? Do you think you can come to the next Outdoors Club?"

Answer the following questions.

6. Choose all of the words that describe items that Nana wore or brought with her on the day of the hike, based on evidence from the text. There is more than one correct choice listed below.

   A. gym shoes

   B. wide-brimmed hat

   C. thick socks

   D. shorts

   E. T-shirt

   F. backpack

---

7. Below are three inferences that one could make, based on the passage.

Inferences	Chris is surprised that Nana knows about hiking.
	Chris does not know much about hiking.
	After an hour of hiking with Nana, Chris respects her abilities and knowledge of hiking.

Part A

Circle the inference that can BEST be made, based on the details in the passage.

Part B

Circle two details within the passage that BEST support the inference selected in part A.

Use the Reading Guide to help you understand the passage.

Which details help you understand the setting?

How does Julia feel about summer vacation so far? Which details help you understand her feelings?

How would you describe Julia's mother? Which details help you make an inference about her character?

Nothing Exciting

The summer heat of July beat down with a ferocious intensity. Julia stood on her lawn, thinking about going back inside the air-conditioned house. But she could already hear her mother's words, "You should be outdoors. That's what summer vacation is for!" Once Julia had replied, "You mean heat and boredom?" Her mother had answered, "No, adventure and excitement!" Nothing exciting ever happened on Oak Street.

Julia looked toward her neighbor's house. She wished Sofia was home. The Allendes had left yesterday for vacation. Julia remembered her promise to pick up their mail, and she trudged toward the mailbox.

Just under the big, leafy oak tree, Julia heard something. Was that a squeak? No, it sounded more like a *meow*! She peered up through the thick branches. High above her head, she could just make out two small eyes. "Come down!" Julia cried. The kitten must have been so frightened it wasn't even blinking.

It didn't take long for Julia to convince her mother, the world's biggest animal lover, to call the fire department. And it didn't take long for the red ladder truck to arrive. Julia pointed into the dense tree branches.

"See?" she said to the firefighters as they extended the ladder. "The poor thing is so terrified it can't even move."

As one of the firefighters reached the branch where the small eyes peered out, he began to laugh. "You'll scare the kitten!" Julia warned.

"Not this kitten," chuckled the firefighter. He reached into the branches and after a tug or two, pulled out a very broken kite. The furry, golden face printed on the kite looked down at Julia with unblinking eyes.

Answer the following questions.

8. Which sentence from the passage BEST helps you understand the time of year the story takes place?

   A. "The summer heat of July beat down with a ferocious intensity." *(circled)*

   B. "Nothing exciting ever happened on Oak Street."

   C. "Just under the big, leafy oak tree, Julia heard something."

   D. "Julia pointed into the dense tree branches."

9. Which is the MOST LIKELY reason that Julia was outside at the beginning of the story?

   A. There was nothing to do indoors.

   B. Sofia was on vacation.

   C. Her mother felt Julia needed to be outdoors more. *(circled)*

   D. She wanted something exciting to happen.

10. Which detail from the passage tells why Julia looked into the tree?

    A. She was bored.

    B. She heard a noise. *(circled)*

    C. She was on her way to get the mail.

    D. She saw two small eyes.

11. How do you think Julia felt when the firefighter began laughing?

    A. upset *(circled)*

    B. happy

    C. unhappy

    D. frightened

12. How might Julia describe this event to Sofia when she returns? Use details from the passage in your answer.

    Julia might describe this event to sofia when she returns by saying "guess what?...

2 Summarize

Getting the Idea

One way to better understand a text—and to explain to others what the text is about—is to summarize what you have read. A **summary** is a brief description of a longer work, such as a story, poem, or novel. A summary can also be used for other types of writing, such as a drama. A **drama** is a play that is performed on stage.

A summary states only the most important ideas and details. If you were summarizing a movie, you would not list every single event or mention every character's name. You would tell only about the important characters and events. Read this story. As you read, think about how to summarize it.

> Yesterday, my dad and I drove to the beach to try out our new dragon kite. The sun was shining, and big clouds drifted across the breezy sky. Gulls circled and squawked overhead. We assembled the kite on the sand. "Here you go, son," Dad said as he handed me the roll of string attached to the kite and lifted the kite into the air. The red-and-black dragon rose into the sky. I held on tightly as the kite zigzagged back and forth. Suddenly, a gust of wind snapped the kite from the string. We watched our flying dragon grow smaller and smaller as it drifted out of sight.

You could summarize the story as follows:

> A father and son lose their kite when the wind snaps it from its string.

This is a good summary because it tells you the main idea and important details of the story. Less important details, such as the weather, the gulls, or the color of the kite, do not belong in the summary.

Theme

When you write a summary of a story, you must look for the most important ideas and details. Summarizing can also help you to figure out a story's theme. The **theme** is the central idea or message of a story. Some stories state their themes directly. For example, in fables and fairy tales, the theme usually appears at the end as a moral, or lesson that the author wants to teach.

However, not all stories have themes that are directly stated as morals. Some themes take a bit of work to discover. As with summarizing, to determine a story's theme, first identify the most important characters, events, settings, and ideas. Then look for a common idea or message that connects these parts. You may ask questions as you are reading to help you. For example:

- What are the main qualities of the characters? (honesty, intelligence, selfishness, humor)
- How do these qualities affect the events in the story?
- What are the actions of the characters?
- How do these actions affect the outcome of the story?
- Does the setting, or where the story takes place, affect the events of the story? How?

Read the following poem.

> The robin wakes before the sun
> And circles fast the muddy field;
> While lazy others snooze away,
> He finds his tasty morning meal.

A good summary of the poem would be: A robin finds his food in the early morning.

The theme, or main message, of the poem is: The early bird is the one who catches the worm.

Notice how the summary and theme are related. They express a similar idea.

Thinking It Through

Read the following drama, and then answer the question that follows.

The curtain opens to show the crafts workshop in a community center. Mr. Anand's pottery class has begun. Six students sit at their pottery wheels.

PABLO: (*cups his hands around a moist mound of clay, which is spinning on the wheel*) I ruined it again! Every time I try to lift up the sides, I knock it out of shape.

MR. ANAND: (*walks over to Pablo and puts his hands on the spinning clay*) You're moving your hands too quickly. Take your time. Feel the shape you want to achieve.

PABLO: (*puts his hands back on the mound of spinning clay*) Wow, slowing down really works. This vase is going to be a nice height and perfectly smooth.

Write a 1–2 sentence summary of this drama. What is the theme of this drama?

_____

_____

_____

_____

_____

 A drama is written in dialogue, which is the words the actors speak. As you summarize this drama, choose only the most important details. Think about how Pablo's actions affect the outcome of the drama.

 DISCUSS   What is the theme of this short drama? Discuss with a partner.

Coached Example

Read the poem and answer the questions.

The Guide

James walked around a bend of shore,
What lay ahead was known no more.

Strange faces shaped in windy clouds;
Dark feathers circling, cawing loud.

5   Two shells he spied beached side by side
And pleaded each to be his guide.

The small one had lived but a year
And whispered nothing in his ear.

The old one spoke of distant lands
10   And returned James to familiar sands.

1. Which sentence BEST summarizes
   the poem?

   A. James looks at birds circling in
      the sky.

   B. James watches the clouds
      changing shape.

   C. James listens to the sound of the
      ocean in a shell.

   D. James finds a shell that helps him
      find his way home.

   HINT   What are the main events that take place
   in the poem?

2. Which sentence BEST states the
   theme of the poem?

   A. With age comes knowledge and
      experience.

   B. The wind is a powerful force.

   C. Some shells last longer than
      other shells.

   D. Getting lost is fun and exciting.

   HINT   Why is the old shell able to help James?

Use the Reading Guide to help you understand the passage.

Reading Guide

Read paragraph 1 carefully. What happens to Clyde after the Civil War?

The rancher loans Big Clyde money. What does this detail tell you about Clyde's character?

Which sentences from the passage best tell you about the theme?

Big Clyde Makes Good

Big Clyde got his first job at a mill. After a few years, he decided to leave the mill and head west. While there, he worked at several different jobs. Then he returned home to become a soldier and fight in the Civil War. When the war ended, Clyde moved out west again and became a cowboy on a cattle ranch. He was one of the best cowhands on the ranch. Other cowboys admired his lassoing and herding skills. Clyde taught them many new cow-herding tricks. Then one day, during a stampede, his horse threw him off. The horse's hoof stepped on Big Clyde's foot. After that, Big Clyde walked with a limp.

Clyde became the camp cook on cattle drives. He developed a special way of seasoning smoked meat and basting it with sauce. He also created a number of tasty desserts made from simple ingredients like molasses and honey. When he became too old to ride with the cattle drives, he stayed at the ranch and tried new ways of cooking.

The rancher lent Clyde money to set up an inn, where he fed guests. The inn made Clyde and his children rich. Clyde always said, "Good luck and bad luck are the salt and pepper of life. With the right amount of both, you can make good barbecue."

Answer the following questions.

1. Which sentence BEST summarizes paragraph 1 of the passage?

    A. Clyde walked with a limp after hurting his foot in an accident.

    B. Clyde became a talented cowboy after fighting in the Civil War.

    C. Clyde impressed other cowboys with his lassoing and herding skills.

    D. Clyde's horse threw him to the ground during a stampede.

2. Which detail should NOT be included in a summary of the passage?

    A. Clyde became a camp cook.

    B. Clyde made desserts from molasses and honey.

    C. Clyde worked as a cattle rancher.

    D. Clyde opened a successful inn.

3. What is the main idea of paragraph 2?

    A. Meat can be seasoned in special ways.

    B. Camp cooks work hard.

    C. Clyde smoked and basted meat.

    D. Clyde was a creative cook.

4. Which sentence BEST states the theme of the passage?

    A. Cooks make a lot of money.

    B. Fighting in wars is dangerous.

    C. Hard times can turn into good ones.

    D. People should try many different jobs.

5. What is a good summary of the passage? Write your summary below.

    This passage was about Big Clyde and he having so many jobs. First, he had a job at a mill. Next, he head west. He had several jobs. Then he returned home to become a soldier and fight in the civil war. Then he head west and became a cowboy. One day his horse threw him off. The horse's hoof stepped on Big Clyde's foot. After, he walked with a limp. Then he opend a inn. and became rich.

Use the Reading Guide to help you understand the passage.

Reading Guide

Read paragraph 1 carefully. What is Katie planning?

How does Katie plan to make the first Drama Club meeting memorable? What does this tell you about Katie?

Which paragraph from the passage best tells you about the theme?

Big Drama

Katie loved to write dramas and act in them. Her passion led her to run for Drama Club president, and she was thrilled when she won the election. Her mind swirled with ideas of how to make the first club meeting memorable. Katie asked her close friends in the club if they had time to rehearse a scene from a play she had written over the summer. "Nobody would forget a grand scene on the main stage in the auditorium!" she said. Unfortunately, her friends said that a week wasn't enough time to prepare for such a performance.

Disappointed, Katie turned to her next big idea—club members could come to the meeting dressed as their favorite character from their favorite play. However, when Katie shared her idea with some members, they informed her that a week wasn't enough time to find costumes. They needed more notice.

Frustrated, Katie slumped in her chair. She wanted everyone at the meeting to know how much Drama Club meant to her, but so far, none of her ideas were working out. She admitted to herself that maybe her ideas were too big for the little time she had left before the meeting. Then it occurred to her that maybe grand ideas were better left for the stage. Maybe simply sharing her passion for drama and for acting in a short speech would be enough. She could even ask others to share how they felt, too. She pulled out her notebook and began writing. The meeting would be simple but still full of big ideas.

Answer the following questions.

6. Use your answer to Part A to answer Part B.

Part A

Which sentence BEST summarizes the passage?

A. Katie is nervous about being Drama Club president and does not want to plan the meeting.

B. Katie wants to impress club members with a big idea but realizes that a simple idea can have a big impact.

C. Katie believes that club members expect big ideas from her now that she is president.

D. Katie makes sure she has enough time to plan an exciting meeting with a big performance.

Part B

Which details from the passage BEST support the answer to Part A? There is more than one correct choice listed below.

A. "Maybe simply sharing her passion for drama and for acting in a short speech would be enough."

B. ". . . ideas of how to make the first club meeting memorable."

C. ". . . a week wasn't enough time to prepare for such a performance."

D. "She wanted everyone at the meeting to know how much Drama Club meant to her . . ."

E. "Frustrated, Katie slumped in her chair."

---

7. Below are three sentences that state possible themes of the passage.

	Time is needed to plan well.
Theme	Sometimes simpler is better.
	Big ideas are often difficult to complete.

Part A

Circle the sentence that BEST states the theme of the passage.

Part B

Circle two details in the passage that BEST support the theme you circled in Part A.

Use the Reading Guide to help you understand the passage.

Reading Guide

Which detail in the first paragraph helps you understand Alberto's feelings about painting a mural?

How do you know that Alberto cares about the opinions of others?

What is the central message of this passage? Which details support this message?

How do Alberto's actions at the end of the passage help you understand the theme?

A Mural for San Quito

A painter named Alberto lived in San Quito. One day, the mayor asked Alberto to paint a mural in the plaza. "I want you to capture the spirit of our village," the mayor explained. Alberto happily agreed.

After a week, Alberto's mural showed families having picnics on the white seashore. Turquoise waves washed onto the beach and left behind a soft line of foam and pink seashells. People smiled as they watched Alberto paint a row of waving sea grass. "This certainly shows the beauty of San Quito!" they whispered. Alberto's heart swelled with pride.

But a small group of frowning people had also gathered. "Who goes to the seashore?" Alberto overheard someone grumble. "Exactly," another agreed. "Where are the mountains? My family hikes there all the time." Alberto felt his heart sink. He picked up a brush and began covering the blue ocean with dark green paint. Soon the towering San Quito Mountains filled the mural. "Now, that's San Quito!" someone declared. Alberto beamed.

"I disagree," someone said. "Our street festivals best show San Quito!"

"No! Our opera hall!"

"What a joke! He should paint only the orange groves!"

Alberto became dizzy from picking up one brush and then another, laying on first the vibrant shades of San Quito's festivals and then the lavender stones of the opera hall. At last, he could take no more. He began flinging buckets of paint against the plaza wall. Streaks of orange and blue, dribbles of purple and green, sprays of yellow and red covered the wall and quickly dried in the midday sun. Alberto dropped the buckets in a noisy clatter and walked away.

"It's terrible," someone muttered. "It doesn't capture San Quito at all!"

Answer the following questions.

8. What is the main idea of paragraph 2?

   A. Alberto likes to paint pictures of families.

   B. Many people watch Alberto paint.

   C. Alberto decides to paint the seashore.

   D. Alberto is happy to hear that people like the mural.

9. Why did the author include the detail about frowning people in paragraph 3?

   A. to show that not all people are happy with the mural

   B. to describe the people of San Quito

   C. to tell about people who do not like Alberto

   D. to explain why Alberto painted the mountains

10. Which detail should NOT be included in a summary of the passage?

    A. Alberto agrees to paint a mural of San Quito.

    B. People do not agree about what Alberto should paint.

    C. Families enjoy picnics at the seashore.

    D. Alberto gives up and walks away from the mural.

11. Which sentence BEST states the theme of the passage?

    A. People should not judge the work of others.

    B. It is not possible to please everyone.

    C. Getting angry does not solve problems.

    D. Painters should listen to the opinions of others.

12. Underline the most important ideas and details in the passage. Use this information to write a good summary of the passage.

_____

_____

_____

_____

_____

3 Elements of Fiction

Getting the Idea

Fiction is writing that describes made-up people and events. Fiction includes stories, fables, fairy tales, poems, dramas, and novels. Just as an artist uses things like shapes and colors to create a painting, a writer uses a number of elements to create a work of fiction. Character, plot, and setting are the main elements of fiction.

Characters are the main actors in a story. They can be people, animals, or other creatures. Like people in real life, characters in stories have inner qualities or **character traits**. A character might be funny or serious, brave or cowardly, selfish or generous. Sometimes an author will directly describe a character's traits. Other times you must look at details, such as what a character says, does, or thinks, to figure out what he or she is like as a person. For example:

> "Next Tuesday is soccer tryouts," Coach Breyer announced at the end of gym class. "The competition will be tough."

> Alex pumped his fist in the air and dribbled his soccer ball back to the locker room. "I can't wait for those tryouts," he thought to himself.

The author does not say that Alex is very confident, but you can figure it out from the way he pumps his fist in the air. He seems eager to try out for the team.

Characters also have **motivations**, or reasons for the ways they act. Specific details provide clues about a character's motivation. Read this example.

> Each day, after school, Julie studied her multiplication tables. She thought of how proud she would feel if she got an A on the upcoming math test.

Julie's motivation for studying is that she wants to get an A on the math test. And the reason she wants an A is so that she can feel proud.

Plot is the series of events that happen in a story. A plot begins with a period of rising action. **Rising action** refers to the events in a story that lead to a conflict. A **conflict** is a problem that the main character must solve. Some stories contain more than one conflict. The **climax** is when the conflict reaches its most exciting point. It is when the character is just about to solve the problem. The final part of the plot is the resolution. A **resolution** is how the conflict or problem is solved.

Read the following passage.

> Max made a sharp turn on his skateboard as he neared the top of the hill. Suddenly, one of the wheels popped off. Max tried to balance on the wobbling board as he sped downhill. He was just about to crash into a fence when he jumped off the board and landed on soft grass.

During the rising action, Max turns and a wheel pops off his skateboard. The conflict is Max's effort to keep his balance. The climax is when Max is just about to crash. And the resolution is when Max lands on the grass.

Setting is where and when a story takes place. The setting might be stated directly, or you may have to figure it out from the details in the story. Settings may change as the story unfolds.

> The sound of the crashing waves grew fainter as I walked on. Soon the shells and pebbles gave way to the dry crunch of pine needles beneath my feet. All around, wind hissed through the branches.

It is not directly stated in the passage, but you can guess from the details that the narrator is walking from the seashore into a forest.

Thinking It Through

Read the following passage, and then answer the question that follows.

All afternoon, Louis paddled his oar against the rough waters of the river. His arms and back ached. Finally, he turned to his brother Pete in the back of the canoe. "Can you give me some help for a change?" Louis asked.

"What?" Pete said, lifting his headphones from his ears as he looked up from reading his comic book.

"Never mind," Louis said, shaking his head as he paddled on.

How would you describe Pete's character?

_____

_____

_____

_____

_____

    At the end of the story, Louis shakes his head. What does this detail tell you about how he feels?

DISCUSS What is the setting of the story? With a group, discuss whether the setting is a good one to reveal the character traits of the two brothers. Could a different setting have worked as well?

Coached Example

Read the passage and answer the questions.

Jamar lifted his violin to his chin, and then he grinned. He had never felt better prepared for a concert. The air hummed with the sounds of people taking their seats in the auditorium. From where he sat on stage, he could hear the audience rustling behind the thick velvet curtain. Jamar tried not to notice Oscar, who was sitting next to him. Oscar's twitching had started to get on Jamar's nerves. If Oscar had practiced as he should have, he'd have nothing to worry about. "Boy, I'll be glad when this is over," Oscar whispered. Jamar ignored him. He looked at his sheet music and waited for the band leader's signal to begin.

1. Where does this passage take place?

   A. in a classroom

   B. in an auditorium

   C. at a park

   D. on a roof

   HINT Which details tell you about the setting of the passage?

2. What is Jamar's motivation for ignoring Oscar?

   A. He doesn't want to get in trouble.

   B. He doesn't hear him.

   C. He wants to annoy him.

   D. He wants to focus on his playing.

   HINT What does Jamar do after ignoring Oscar?

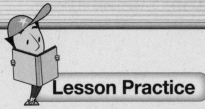

Lesson Practice

Use the Reading Guide to help you understand the passage.

Reading Guide

Where are Marla and Teddy playing and studying?

Which events lead up to Marla and Teddy making a bet?

In paragraph 5, Teddy says, "I'm not too concerned." What character trait does this detail reveal about him?

The Night Before

Marla had been studying for hours, and her eyelids felt heavy. The science test that she was taking the next day was very important, so she wanted to go over everything one more time. Unfortunately, her brain was no longer cooperating. She knew she needed a break.

Downstairs, Teddy sat playing video games. Teddy had to take the same science test. Though he was Marla's twin brother, Teddy did not share her love of studying. In fact, Teddy hated to study, and his grades showed it. Marla came in and asked what he was doing.

"I'm studying," Teddy joked.

"I can't believe you," Marla said. "You know the test tomorrow is really important, right?"

"Important to you," Teddy said. "I'm not too concerned. I bet I do better than you on the test."

"It's a bet," Marla answered. "The winner has to do the other's chores for a week."

Marla and Teddy shook hands. With that, Marla grabbed a pack of crackers from the kitchen and returned upstairs.

The next day, she went into the test feeling confident. For the next few days, she waited excitedly to find out her grade. When she got an A, she knew she had earned it, just as Teddy had earned his F and the prize of doing all her chores for a week.

Answer the following questions.

1. Which word BEST describes Marla?

   A. clever

   B. honest

   C. responsible

   D. humorous

2. Which sentence from the story describes the climax of the story?

   A. "Unfortunately, her brain was no longer cooperating."

   B. "Downstairs, Teddy sat playing video games."

   C. "Marla and Teddy shook hands."

   D. "For the next few days, she waited excitedly to find out her grade."

3. Which of the following is part of the setting?

   A. a pack of crackers

   B. a kitchen and a staircase

   C. a science test

   D. weekly chores

4. The rising action in the story is when

   A. Marla questions and challenges her brother.

   B. Teddy fails the science test.

   C. Marla grabs a pack of crackers from the kitchen.

   D. Teddy plays video games.

5. Describe the conflict in the story, and tell how it is resolved.

   _____

   _____

   _____

   _____

   _____

Use the Reading Guide to help you understand the passage.

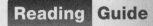**Reading** Guide

Which events lead up to Mariah's being angry with Gia?

Where are Mariah and Gia talking?

In paragraph 8, Mariah starts to cry. What character trait does this detail reveal about her?

Friday Night Dinners

"See you Friday night!"

Mariah charged into the kitchen as soon as her sister hung up the phone. "Where are you going Friday night?" she demanded.

"To a dance at school," Gia replied, adding "not that it's any of your business."

"But Friday is family dinner," Mariah said, frowning.

For twelve years, Friday night meant family cramming into the tiny kitchen, pots and pans bubbling on the stove as her aunts, mother, and grandmother prepared a feast. Then everyone would squeeze together at the table to eat, talk, laugh, and sometimes argue. Mariah loved sitting in the midst of such a big, loud crowd. "Mama won't let you go," Mariah challenged her sister.

"She already gave me permission," Gia bragged, smiling victoriously.

Mariah's frown deepened as she studied her older sister. Gia was sixteen now and talking about going away to college. Every Friday, she and Gia pushed a card table and dining table together so that everyone could fit. Then they set the tables, playfully tossing napkins at each other until their mother yelled at them. She knew her sister was growing up, but wasn't family more important than friends? Before she knew it, tears flooded Mariah's eyes.

"Mariah, it's just one dinner," Gia explained.

Mariah shrugged, wiping her eyes. "For now," she said, trying not to sound like a weepy child. "But soon you won't ever be here on Fridays."

Gia hugged her sister, laughing. "Okay, I'll stay for dinner," she said. Gia wiped the tears from Mariah's cheeks. "I can be a little late to the dance."

Mariah grinned and hugged her sister back.

Answer the following questions.

6. Read the sentence in each choice. Then match the sentence to its story element on the right.

A. Gia is planning to miss family dinner to go to a dance with friends.

1. rising action

2. climax

B. Mariah begins to cry when she thinks Gia values friends more than family.

3. resolution

C. Mariah and Gia argue about her missing family dinner.

4. conflict

D. Gia realizes family dinner is important to Mariah and decides to leave late for the dance.

---

7. Choose all phrases that describe Mariah's character traits, based on evidence from the text. There is more than one correct choice listed below.

A. values family

B. dislikes big dinners

C. enjoys big, loud events

D. upset about sister growing up

E. enjoys time with friends

F. likes spending time with sister

Use the Reading Guide to help you understand the passage.

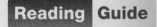

Reading Guide

How do Rani's actions show what kind of person she is?

What problem does Rani face?

What does Rani do to solve the problem?

Ready for a Storm

Mom and Rani sat on the deck of their house under a large umbrella. They overlooked the backyard where a tent was pitched. Rani had hosted a backyard campout the night before.

Mom and Rani were listening to their favorite radio station when suddenly an urgent weather bulletin came on. The announcer reported that an intense storm was headed directly for their city. The storm was bringing heavy rain and strong winds up to sixty miles an hour. People were warned to stay indoors until the storm had passed.

Mom calmly remarked, "Don't worry. Here's the plan. I'll bring the umbrella and deck furniture inside. You take the hanging plants to the shed and take down that tent. OK, Rani?"

Rani nodded, wanting to live up to Mom's expectations. Mom was already collapsing the umbrella as Rani hurried to the back fence where flowering plants hung from hooks. She staggered with the heavy pots, taking them to the backyard shed.

She grabbed a hammer and raced to the tent, noticing the dark sky and strengthening wind. She had pulled out three tent pegs when a sudden gust swept inside the tent, and it billowed up over her head. The tension of the airborne tent made it more difficult to remove the fourth peg. Rani tugged hard, but the peg wouldn't budge.

She clenched her teeth and kept trying. She wiggled the peg back and forth, enlarging the hole until the peg popped out. Rani dragged the tent into the shed just as heavy, fat raindrops hit her face.

Mom and Rani met inside the house, collapsing into the deck chairs that were now in their dining room.

"We did it!" Rani exclaimed.

Answer the following questions.

8. Where does the story take place?

    A. inside a house in the country

    B. at a campground

    C. in the backyard of a city house

    D. at a radio station

9. Which word BEST describes Rani's character?

    A. confident

    B. friendly

    C. careful

    D. determined

10. What is the rising action in the story?

    A. Mom and Rani hear an urgent weather bulletin on the radio.

    B. Mom and Rani need to get things inside before the storm comes.

    C. Mom makes a plan to prepare for the storm.

    D. Mom and Rani wait for the storm to pass.

11. Which sentence describes the climax of the story?

    A. "Rani tugged hard, but the peg wouldn't budge."

    B. "Rani had hosted a backyard campout the night before."

    C. "People were warned to stay indoors until the storm had passed."

    D. "Rani nodded, wanting to live up to Mom's expectations."

12. How is the conflict of the story resolved?

    _____

    _____

    _____

    _____

    _____

    _____

4 Point of View

Getting the Idea

When you read a story, someone is *telling* it to you. A **narrator** is the person who tells the story. **Point of view** is the perspective, or view, from which the narrator tells the story. Most stories are told in either first-person or third-person point of view.

In **first-person** point of view, the narrator is a character in the story. The words *I* and *we* are used. Read this example.

> I walked onto the pitcher's mound and faced the batter. He took a couple of practice swings and then looked straight at me, waiting for the pitch. As soon as I threw the ball, I knew it would be a strike. He swung and missed as the ball sailed right over the plate!

The narrator is a character (the pitcher) and is represented by the word *I*.

Second-person point of view is rarely used in fiction. Here, the narrator speaks directly to the reader, making you part of the passage. Read this example.

> Open the box and remove the fan. Be sure to take off the plastic wrap before you plug in the machine.

In **third-person** point of view, the narrator tells the story without actually being in it. The story uses words such as *he, she, it,* and *they*. When the narrator knows only the thoughts and feelings of a single character, the point of view is **third-person limited**. Read this example.

> Robby felt scared as the *Santa Maria* heaved back and forth in the stormy waves. He knew Captain Jones had calmly steered the ship through worse storms. Still, he felt uneasy, and he sensed the other passengers were also afraid.

The narrator is outside of the story. He knows only the thoughts and feelings of Robby. Those of the other characters—Captain Jones and the passengers—are told only through Robby's eyes.

In some stories, the narrator knows about all of the characters' thoughts and feelings. This is called **third-person omniscient** point of view. Read this example.

> Dexter lay in bed. He wanted to go outside and play in the snow, but he had a cold. His mother asked him to drink some orange juice. She was glad he was resting. She hoped he would feel better in the morning.

Again, the narrator is outside of the story. But this time, he knows the thoughts and feelings of *all* of the characters—both Dexter and his mother. Notice that the narrator uses the words *he* and *she*.

Comparing and contrasting the point of view from which different stories are told can change how you think about the narrator and characters. A story told from first-person point of view gives you a very personal look at a character's (the narrator's) thoughts and feelings. However, it is only the way one character views the story. A story told in third-person point of view might seem less personal, but you may get a broader view of the characters.

The chart below shows the different points of view and their features.

First-Person	Third-Person Limited	Third-Person Omniscient
Told by one character in the story	Told by narrator outside of the story	Told by narrator outside of the story
Narrator is *I*, *me*, *we*, *us*	Narrator uses *he*, *she*, *it*, *they*, and *them*	Narrator uses *he*, *she*, *it*, *they*, and *them*
Narrator relates personal view	Narrator knows thoughts and feelings of single character	Narrator knows thoughts and feelings of all characters

Thinking It Through

Read the following passage, and then answer the questions that follow.

I felt scared as I inched toward the edge of the diving board. The pool below seemed so far away. I took a deep breath and closed my eyes. I had done this a hundred times before, and I knew that I needed to stay calm. I raised my arms over my head, bent down, and sprung off of the board. For a moment, I felt nothing as I fell through the air. Then I plunged into the pool with a loud splash and rose back to the surface with a wide smile.

Which point of view is used in the passage? How does this point of view help you to understand the thoughts and feelings of the diver?

_____

_____

_____

_____

_____

 The narrator uses the word *I* in the passage. What does this tell you about the point of view?

 **DISCUSS** With a partner, discuss how the passage would be different if it were told from a third-person limited point of view.

Coached Example

Read the passages and answer the questions.

Cutting Wood

"Good day to make a fire," Grandpa said, looking out the window at the gray winter sky. "I'll need to cut some wood."

"Can I help?" I asked.

"Sure, Calvin," he said. "You're old enough now to handle a saw."

We grabbed our coats and walked to the garage. I felt excited when he handed me a saw and a pair of gloves. I had wanted to learn how to use a saw for some time. We walked to the woodpile outside. Grandpa placed a log on an old stump, which he used as a sort of worktable. He moved the saw back and forth across the log. Soon, the sawed half dropped to the ground.

"Now you try," he said, placing another log on the stump and handing me the saw. I pressed the blade on the log and tried to push the saw. The blade jerked and jammed in the wood.

"I can't do it," I said, feeling my excitement turn to disappointment.

"You're trying too hard," Grandpa said. "Let the tool do the work."

I relaxed my grip on the handle, and sure enough, the saw moved easily through the wood. When the log fell in half, I felt proud. "I did it!" I said.

Fishing at Night

Ned led the way through the dunes to the ocean. He knew that his grandson, Anthony, had never been to the shore at night, and he wanted to make sure that he didn't get lost on the way.

The full moon hung low over the ocean as they reached the water's edge. Ned tied a hook to Anthony's line and put on a piece of bait. He enjoyed teaching Anthony new things and felt that his grandson really loved spending time with him. He baited his own line and showed Anthony how to cast out beyond the waves. He watched Anthony struggle with his first few casts, but knew that he would get the hang of it.

A few hours later, Ned waded into the surf to net Anthony's first fish. As he handed Anthony the beautiful sea trout from the net, he remembered the excitement of catching his first fish many years ago.

He watched Anthony hold the fish up in the moonlight. He knew that his grandson would remember this day for the rest of his life.

1. Which point of view is used in "Cutting Wood"?

   A. first-person

   B. second-person

   C. third-person limited

   D. third-person omniscient

   HINT The words give you clues to the point of view. Which word is used to represent the narrator in "Cutting Wood"? Who is telling the story?

2. Which statement BEST describes the similarity between the narrators of the stories?

   A. Both narrators are characters in the stories.

   B. Both narrators tell mostly about one character's feelings.

   C. Both narrators watch the story events from outside of the stories.

   D. Both narrators know about the thoughts and feelings of all the characters.

   HINT In third-person limited, the narrator has limited knowledge of the characters' thoughts and feelings.

3. Write how Anthony feels at the end of "Fishing at Night," using the first-person point of view.

   _____

   _____

   _____

   _____

   _____

   HINT What words might Anthony use to express his feelings about catching the fish?

Lesson Practice

Use the Reading Guides to help you understand the passages.

Reading Guide

Identify the words that represent the narrator in the passage.

Is the narrator a character in the story or someone outside of the passage?

How does the point of view help you understand the passage?

Show Time

I watched with excitement as family members and relatives filed into the auditorium. Tonight was the dance recital. At last, I would get to show off all my hard work. I hoped everything would be perfect.

My dance class was doing a routine using large wooden boxes. Each dancer had to balance on top of a box and do different steps. It wasn't an easy routine, but I'd practiced it at home many times.

The first part of the show went smoothly. Then came the part with the boxes. We all stood in line, each girl on her own box, facing the audience. For my next move, I needed to place one foot on the box next to mine. At the same time, I needed to keep my other foot on my own box. It was an easy move, I always thought.

I looked out at the audience, head up, with a big smile. Oops! While my head was up, I didn't look at where I was going. I missed my partner's box and slipped! Suddenly, I was standing on the stage floor.

My face was red with embarrassment. But I remembered what our dance teacher had told us: "If you make a mistake, keep dancing so the audience will not notice." I did my best to follow her advice and finished the routine without making any more mistakes. My family said I did a great job.

The Audition

Reading Guide

Does the narrator know about the feelings of all the characters?

Which character is the narrator telling the reader mostly about?

Is the narrator represented by the word *I*? What does this tell you about the point of view?

Anita woke up with a start. Today was her audition for the Youth Symphony Orchestra. She bounced out of bed and ran to take a shower.

At breakfast, her mother asked, "Are you ready?"

Anita didn't answer as she sat down. She didn't feel hungry, but her teacher, Mr. Jackson, told her it was important to eat today. As Anita ate, she thought about her mother's question.

Her clothes were ready. The Symphony's Web site said to wear nice clothes that were comfortable to perform in. Anita had chosen the blue dress she had gotten for her sixteenth birthday last year.

Her music was ready. She had chosen four pieces by her favorite composer, Chopin. The Web site said that people auditioning didn't have to memorize their music, but Anita knew all of her music by heart.

Her mind was ready. The audition would last from five to eight minutes. "Don't think about the time," Mr. Jackson had told her. "Just think about the music. Let it flow through you. That's what Chopin would have done."

Anita had applied to the Youth Orchestra online last month. Before she sent her application, she had asked Mr. Jackson, "Do you really think I'm good enough?"

He had given her a big smile. "Anita Hernandez, you're the hardest-working student I have. You have enormous musical talent. You're going to be absolutely great!"

Thinking back on that now, Anita grinned and looked up at her mother. "Yes, Mama. I'm ready."

Answer the following questions.

1. Which point of view is used in "Show Time"?

   A. first-person

   B. second-person

   C. third-person limited

   D. third-person omniscient

2. Who is the narrator of "The Audition"?

   A. Anita

   B. Anita's mother

   C. Mr. Jackson

   D. someone outside of the story

3. Which BEST describes the narrator of "Show Time"?

   A. a character in the story

   B. someone who tells about the feelings of all of the characters

   C. a person who is not in the story

   D. someone represented by the word *her*

4. Which point of view is used in "The Audition"?

   A. first-person

   B. second-person

   C. third-person limited

   D. third-person omniscient

5. Which story gives a more personal view of the main character? Explain your answer.

   _____

   _____

   _____

   _____

   _____

Use the Reading Guides to help you understand the passages.

Reading Guide

Which words in the passage are clues about the point of view?

Does the narrator know what Miguel is thinking or feeling? What does this tell you about the point of view?

How does the point of view affect your understanding of the passage?

Mr. President

Nobody expected Miguel to run for student government. He usually sat in the back of the class, shrinking into his seat as if he wanted to be invisible. He never raised his hand, answering questions only when the teacher called on him. Because of his quiet voice, the teacher always had to ask him to speak up. So when posters appeared, announcing Miguel's candidacy for class president, everyone was surprised.

Everyone could tell that Miguel was striving to overcome his shyness by smiling in the hallway and saying hello. They also knew that the hardest part for Miguel would be the debate. All candidates had to deliver a ten-minute speech about why they were running for office. How would Miguel be able to present his ideas well since he had trouble speaking in class?

Miguel was the last speaker at the debate. The other three students had given impressive speeches. Miguel approached the podium and lowered the microphone. In a quiet yet clear voice, he said, "I am running for class president because I want to make a difference. I am too shy to deliver a fancy speech, but that doesn't mean I don't have good ideas. My *abuelo* (my grandfather) told me that you have to go out of your comfort zone to change. Giving this speech is about as far out of my comfort zone as I can get!" Miguel laughed softly, and the audience laughed with him. In the rest of his speech, he outlined his ideas, and they sounded good. Not surprisingly, Miguel won the election. His quiet confidence made him a natural leader.

The Vice President

Reading Guide

Is the narrator part of the story or outside of the story?

Does the narrator know what characters are thinking and feeling? How can you tell? What does this tell you about the point of view?

How does the point of view help you understand the characters in the passage?

The weekly student government meeting had just started when Ana rushed in, all out of breath. George raised his eyebrows at her apologetic look and said, "We started without you." He wanted to add "again" but didn't because Mrs. Harris, their faculty advisor, was attending the meeting. As president of the student body, it was Ana's job to run the meetings, but she was rarely on time. So, as vice president, George started the meetings. He wanted to be president so badly, and he thought about how much more he cared about the meetings than Ana did. *If she cared*, George thought, *she wouldn't be late*.

Sensing George's frustration, Ana took over the meeting. She knew it was important to be punctual, but between advanced chemistry and the yearbook, it was difficult to find the time to get everything done. She knew that George covered for her a lot, and she appreciated it. But Ana wished he were a little more understanding about her busy schedule. She didn't think it was a big deal for him to start without her.

As the meeting continued, George noticed how flustered Ana was. He realized that Ana often seemed frazzled. He knew that if he were president, he probably wouldn't have as much time for soccer. He wondered what Ana had to give up when she became president.

At the end of the meeting, Ana told George she was sorry for being late again. He shrugged. "It's OK. I can start the meetings when you need me to."

"Thanks, George," Ana said. "That means a lot to me."

Answer the following questions.

6. Choose all the words that are clues to the point of view in the passage "Mr. President." There is more than one correct choice listed below.

    A. I

    B. he

    C. they

    D. we

    E. you

    F. us

---

7. Read the sentences from the passages. Then match each sentence to one point of view on the right.

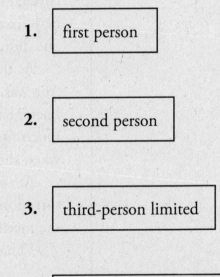

A. "He wanted to be president so badly, and he thought about how much more he cared about the meetings than Ana did."

B. "'Giving this speech is about as far out of my comfort zone as I can get!' Miguel laughed softly, and the audience laughed with him."

1. first person

2. second person

3. third-person limited

4. third-person omniscient

8. Use your answer to Part A to answer Part B.

Part A

What is the the point of view of the narrator in the passage "The Vice President"?

A. first person

C. third-person limited

B. second person

D. third-person omniscient

Part B

Which details from the passage BEST support your answer to Part A? There is more than one correct choice listed below.

A. "So, as vice president, George started the meetings."

B. "She knew that George covered for her a lot, and she appreciated it."

C. "He knew that if he were president, he probably wouldn't have as much time for soccer."

D. "He wondered what Ana had to give up when she became president."

E. "At the end of the meeting, Ana told George she was sorry for being late again."

---

9. In the box below are some features of points of view. Copy each feature into the table column where it belongs. Some features are used twice.

> Told by a narrator outside the story.
>
> Narrator uses *he*, *she*, *it*, *they*, and *them*.
>
> Narrator does not know thoughts and feelings of characters.
>
> Narrator knows thoughts and feelings of all characters.

"Mr. President" Point of View	"The Vice President" Point of View

Use the Reading Guide to help you understand the passage.

Reading Guide

Which words help you identify the point of view?

Is the narrator part of the story or telling the story from the outside?

How does the point of view help you understand the thoughts and feelings of the characters?

The Neighborhood Newsletter

"The first meeting of the Brookside Neighborhood Newsletter is called to order," Luke said, as he eyed his friends Maxine and Steven. Luke had planned the time and the place—his house—of the meeting. Luke always led the way when the three friends did things together. He felt he was the best leader.

Without too much trouble, they divided up the writing. Choosing the newsletter photographer, however, was not so easy. Luke claimed the job, but Maxine protested. She was tired of Luke getting to do all the fun stuff. She said, "I have more experience taking photos than you, Luke. I take photos for the school paper."

Steven wondered why this conflict was necessary. He suggested that both Luke and Maxine take photos and then as a group they would decide which ones to use. Luke refused to agree. He thought *his* photos would be the best, and he wanted *his* photos to appear in the newsletter.

"That's it!" Maxine shouted. "You can count me out."

Steven sided with Maxine, and they gave Luke an ultimatum. Either they go with Steven's plan for the photos or the newsletter wouldn't happen. Luke was steaming inside, but he gave in. He knew his friends would come around to his side once they saw his photos.

When the friends got down to work publishing the newsletter, they reviewed all the photos by Luke and Maxine. Luke realized that Maxine's photos were much better than his, and he reluctantly told her so. The group chose one of Luke's photos and many of Maxine's photos for the final version of the newsletter.

"That's the best way to settle things," cheered Steven.

Answer the following questions.

10. Which point of view is used in the story?

    A. first-person

    B. second-person

    C. third-person limited

    D. third-person omniscient

11. You can identify the point of view in this story because the narrator

    A. speaks directly to the reader.

    B. relates her thoughts and personal feelings.

    C. knows the thoughts and feelings of all the characters.

    D. knows the thoughts and feelings of a single character.

12. Who narrates the story?

    A. Luke in the story

    B. a person outside of the story

    C. a neighbor in the story

    D. Maxine in the story

13. What does the point of view help you understand about Steven?

    A. He wants to be a peacemaker when there is conflict.

    B. He finds it hard to make decisions.

    C. He prefers to work on projects alone.

    D. He needs to be the leader in a group.

14. If you were to rewrite this story, whose point of view would you choose and why?

    _____

    _____

    _____

    _____

    _____

    _____

    _____

    _____

    _____

5 Understanding Poetry and Drama

Getting the Idea

Prose, poetry, and drama are different kinds of writing. In **prose**, one sentence follows another. Sentences are grouped in paragraphs. Examples of prose include chapter books and newspaper articles. **Poetry** is written in lines. Lines are grouped in **stanzas**, or **verses**.

The paragraph and poem below both tell about the same topic. What differences do you see?

Prose	Poem
Last night, I tried to finish my math assignment on the couch. I was having a hard time concentrating because all I could hear was the sound of my dog snoring.	Papers strewn about my lap, A dog's snoring fills the room, Making the earth tremble. Soon it's nine o'clock, The time continues to pass. Will my homework be ready For tomorrow's class?

Poets use the sounds of words in creative ways. For example, many poems include rhyme. Words that **rhyme** end with the same sound. The rhyming words in a poem often appear in a pattern at the ends of lines. In the poem below, *green* and *between* rhyme.

> I'm **glad** the **sky** is **paint**ed **blue**,
> And the **earth** is **paint**ed **green**,
> With **such** a **lot** of **nice** fresh **air**
> All **sand**wiched **in** be**tween**.

A poem also has a **rhythm** created by the stressed and unstressed syllables in the poem. If there is a pattern to the rhythm, the pattern is called **meter**. Read the poem aloud. The stressed syllables are shown in bold print. In this poem, almost every other syllable is stressed. Lines 1 and 3 each have four stressed syllables, and lines 2 and 4 each have three stressed syllables. This pattern gives the poem its rhythm.

Like a short story or novel, a **drama** tells a story. It includes characters, a setting, and a plot. However, a drama is written so that people can put on a play. It begins with a **cast of characters** that lists the characters who appear in the play. It includes a description of the **setting**. This description tells the director, set designers, and actors what the stage should look like. A drama includes stage directions and dialogue. The **stage directions** are written in *italic* print. They tell the actors what to do. **Dialogue** is the words the actors speak.

A **scene** is a part of a drama. Read this drama about unfinished homework and a snoring dog.

CAST OF CHARACTERS
Ruben
Mom
Tag, the family dog

Scene One
In dim lights, we can see a living room. On one end of the couch, Tag, a dog, is curled up asleep. On the other end sits Ruben, in his pajamas. Paper is scattered around him, and a textbook is open. The snoring of the dog and the ticking of a clock grow louder and louder until Ruben speaks.

RUBEN: (*to himself*) If only Tag would stop snoring! Then maybe I would be able to think straight.

(*The snoring of the dog and the ticking of the clock can still be heard, but more softly. Mom enters. She is wearing pajamas.*)

MOM: Ruben! Why are you still up? It's getting late.

RUBEN: (*pushing his book and papers to the floor*) I can't figure out this math homework!

Thinking It Through

Read the following poem, and then answer the question that follows.

excerpted from

Songs of Innocence
by William Blake

Piping down the valleys wild,
Piping songs of pleasant glee,
On a cloud I saw a child,
And he laughing said to me:

"Pipe a song about a Lamb!"
So I piped with merry cheer.
"Piper, pipe that song again;"
So I piped: he wept to hear.

What characteristics of poetry can you find in this poem? Give three examples.

_____

_____

_____

_____

 Read the poem aloud. Do you hear any rhymes? Do you hear a beat, or rhythm?

DISCUSS With a partner, take turns reading the poem aloud to each other. Does it become easier to understand the more you hear it? Does it get easier to read aloud?

Coached Example

Read the drama and answer the questions.

CAST OF CHARACTERS
Jenny
Tanya

Scene One

The backdrop shows a meadow with hills and trees. Jenny enters pulling a wagon holding a giant pumpkin. Tanya enters and meets Jenny in the center of the stage.

TANYA: Jenny, where on Earth did you find that pumpkin?

JENNY: (*grinning with pride*) In my garden!

TANYA: You mean you grew that thing?

JENNY: I sure did! And I'm taking it to Grandma's house. Now that I've grown the biggest pumpkin that Hillsdale has ever seen, we're going to bake the biggest pumpkin pie that Hillsdale has ever seen.

TANYA: Ooh! I want to see that! And then I want to eat it!

(The two girls exit together.)

1. The setting of this scene could BEST be described as

    A. a city sidewalk.

    B. Grandma's kitchen.

    C. the country.

    D. a schoolyard.

     The description of the setting is given before the dialogue.

2. How does Jenny feel about the pumpkin?

    A. proud

    B. frightened

    C. embarrassed

    D. curious

     Read the stage directions as well as the dialogue.

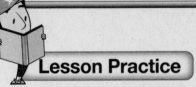

Lesson Practice

Use the Reading Guide to help you understand the poem.

Reading Guide

The lines of this poem are grouped into stanzas. How many stanzas does the poem have?

Do you see any words that rhyme in stanza 1?

Read stanza 1 aloud. How many beats do you hear in each line? Do you hear the pattern of the rhythm?

Which words rhyme in stanza 2? Do you see a pattern to the rhymes in the poem?

excerpted from

The Gardener

by Robert Louis Stevenson

The gardener does not love to talk,
He makes me keep the gravel walk;
And when he puts his tools away,
He locks the door and takes the key.

5 Away behind the currant row
Where no one else but cook may go,
Far in the plots, I see him dig
Old and serious, brown and big.

He digs the flowers, green, red, and blue,
10 Nor wishes to be spoken to.
He digs the flowers and cuts the hay,
And never seems to want to play.

Silly gardener! summer goes,
And winter comes with pinching toes,
15 When in the garden bare and brown
You must lay your barrow[1] down.

[1]**barrow:** wheelbarrow

Answer the following questions.

1. Which version shows which syllables are stressed in line 2?

   A. He <u>makes</u> me <u>keep</u> the <u>gravel</u> walk

   B. <u>He</u> makes <u>me</u> <u>keep</u> the gravel <u>walk</u>

   C. <u>He</u> makes <u>me</u> keep the <u>gravel</u> <u>walk</u>

   D. He <u>makes</u> me <u>keep</u> the <u>gravel</u> <u>walk</u>

2. Which words from the poem do NOT rhyme?

   A. walk, away

   B. row, go

   C. blue, to

   D. brown, down

3. Which stanza tells where the gardener digs?

   A. stanza 1

   B. stanza 2

   C. stanza 3

   D. stanza 4

4. The speaker thinks that the gardener

   A. works too hard.

   B. is too old.

   C. would rather be a cook.

   D. likes winter better than summer.

5. What does the speaker think that the gardener should do? Give examples from the poem.

   _____

   _____

   _____

   _____

   _____

   _____

Use the Reading Guide to help you understand the drama.

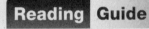

What does the description of the setting tell you about where this scene takes place?

What does the dialogue tell you about the characters?

What do the stage directions tell you about the characters' actions?

The Race

CAST OF CHARACTERS
Luis
Anna

Scene One

The curtain opens to show a bike path with trees, shrubs, wildflowers, and a park bench. A teenage boy and girl enter from stage right. They are both wearing T-shirts, athletic shorts, and running shoes. They are breathing as if they have just stopped running.

LUIS: That was a good run! You've really improved!

ANNA: (*laughs*) You're just saying that because you're my kind big brother.

LUIS: When have I ever said anything to you just to be nice?

ANNA: (*laughs again*) That's true. (*She sits down on the bench and begins to untie the laces of one of her shoes.*) But still, I'm really worried about the race.

LUIS: What for? The race is only three miles long. You run farther than that all the time. And anyway, your goal is to finish, not to win.

ANNA: (*She pulls off her shoe and pulls a stone out of it.*) For one thing, Mom and Dad will be there. For another thing, anything could happen. (*She holds up the stone.*) I could get another stone like this in my shoe! I could trip and fall and break my leg!

LUIS: You could trip and fall and break your leg crossing the street, too. Why worry about everything that could go wrong?

ANNA: (*sighs*) Why are you always right?

Answer the following questions.

6. The setting of this scene is MOST LIKELY

   A. in a big city park or in the country.

   B. in a gym.

   C. at Luis and Anna's house.

   D. at the beach near a lake or the ocean.

7. Which of the following is a line of stage directions?

   A. You're just saying that because you're my kind big brother.

   B. *She sits down on the bench and begins to untie the laces of one of her shoes.*

   C. The race is only three miles long.

   D. I could get another stone like this in my shoe!

8. How does Luis think that Anna should feel about the race?

   A. He thinks she should be scared because she needs to practice more.

   B. He thinks she should tell their parents that she is not going to run.

   C. He thinks she should tell everyone that she is going to win.

   D. He thinks she should not worry about the race.

9. Why does Anna take off her shoe?

   A. She wants to put on a different pair of shoes.

   B. She is joking around with Luis.

   C. She needs to take a stone out of the shoe.

   D. She has decided to stop running.

10. Write two lines of dialogue to continue this scene.

   _____

   _____

   _____

   _____

Use the Reading Guide to help you understand the poem.

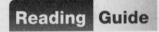

How is the text organized? What does this tell you about the genre?

Identify words that use sounds creatively.

How is rhyme and rhythm part of the text?

adapted from

Love between Brothers and Sisters
by Isaac Watts

Whatever brawls are in the street
There should be peace at home;
Where sisters dwell and brothers meet
Quarrels shou'd never come.

5   Birds in their little nests agree;
And 'tis a shameful sight,
When children of one family
Fall out, and chide, and fight.

Hard names at first, and threatening words,
10 That are but noisy breath,
May grow to clubs and naked swords,
To murder and to death.

The wise will make their anger cool
At least before 'tis night;
15 But in the bosom of a fool
It burns till morning light.

Pardon us please, our childish rage;
Our little brawls remove;
That as we grow to riper age,
20 Our hearts may all be love.

Answer the following questions.

11. Choose all the features that are part of the poem.

    A. stressed syllables

    B. stanzas

    C. stage directions

    D. rhyming words

    E. dialogue

    F. lines

---

12. Read the first two stanzas of the poem.

> **Whatever brawls are in the street**
> **There should be peace at home;**
> **Where sisters dwell and brothers meet**
> **Quarrels shou'd never come.**
>
> **Birds in their little nests agree;**
> **And 'tis a shameful sight,**
> **When children of one family**
> **Fall out, and chide, and fight.**

There are four pairs of words that rhyme. Write the word pairs on the lines below.

_____

_____

_____

_____

Use the Reading Guide to help you understand the drama.

Who are the characters?
Where are they?

How do you learn about
the characters' conflict?

What do the stage
directions tell you about
how the characters feel?

For the Love of Benny

CAST OF CHARACTERS

Frida

Fernando

Scene One

The curtain opens to show a small kitchen one would find in a typical apartment, with a table and four chairs. A teenage boy stands near the sink, filling a dog bowl with water. A teenage girl sits at the table, holding a leash. They both look angry.

FRIDA: I walked Benny yesterday!

FERNANDO: (*rolling his eyes as he places the water dish next to a food dish near the kitchen table*) For the hundredth time, you did *not* walk him yesterday! I did, right after school.

FRIDA: (*loudly*) I had dance class after school! I walked him after dinner!

FERNANDO: What? Benny only gets one walk a day. Mama said if we don't take good care of him, he's gone!

FRIDA: (*setting the leash on the table and standing*) I'm doing *my* part. I feed him *every single morning* while you are still snoring away. (*She makes snoring noises.*)

FERNANDO: Because *I* have more homework than you do, so I go to bed later than you. It's only fair, Frida.

FRIDA: Every day it is like this, you bossing me around, telling me when to walk him, when to feed him, because you are *so* busy and *so* important! Not fair!

(*A loud whine is heard off stage to the right. Both teens turn to look toward the noise, and their faces soften.*)

FERNANDO: (*softly*) I guess we have been fighting a lot lately.

FRIDA: (*sadly*) I don't think Benny likes it.

Answer the following questions.

13. Choose all the features that are part of the drama.

    A. dialogue

    B. scenes

    C. stanzas

    D. cast of characters

    E. meter

    F. stage directions

---

14. Below are three statements that could be made about poetry and dramas.

Features of Poetry and Drama	Both include specific formatting and word choices.
	Both use sentences that are short and to the point.
	Both have characters, settings, and plot.

Part A

Circle the statement that can be made about BOTH poetry and drama.

Part B

Circle one example each within the poem and the drama that BEST supports the statement selected in Part A.

Use the Reading Guides to help you understand the passages.

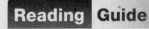

Reading Guide

How are the lines of the poem organized?

Read the first stanza aloud. Listen for the rhythm in each line.

Which words rhyme in stanza 1? Look for rhyming words in the rest of the poem.

Dangerous Creatures

In some places you'll find creatures,
Who have extremely scary features.
The best plan is to stay far away,
Or you may not make it through another day.

5   A puffer fish makes a tasty dish,
But you need to watch out for this fish.
If you fail to cook the puffer just right,
You may get sick from only one bite.

A scorpion is just a tiny thing,
10 But look out for its poisonous sting.
It's not the claws that you should fear,
But its tail will sting if you get near.

A blue-ringed octopus is so small,
It seems about the size of just a golf ball.
15 Sighting one should ring an alarm bell,
For an up-close meeting won't end well.

A king cobra can rise and spread its hood,
If you venture too close that won't be good.
This poisonous snake will attack and spit,
20 Better run, don't walk, to the nearest exit.

So don't go looking for a trophy to box in,
All these creatures can harm with toxin.
It's best to give them each a clear berth,
And enjoy a pain-free day on Earth.

Reading Guide

What clues in the drama help you identify the setting?

Why is the inclusion of the plastic bag important in the description of the setting?

How do Charlie, Grant, and the lifeguard each feel about the "jellyfish?"

How do the stage directions and the dialogue help you understand the characters' feelings?

Mistaken Identity

CAST OF CHARACTERS
Charlie
Grant
a lifeguard

Scene One

The curtain opens to show a beach. A lifeguard wearing sunglasses sits in a tall chair at the edge of the stage. Center stage, two boys stand facing each other. They are each wearing swimming trunks. On the ground between them is a clear plastic bag filled with water.

CHARLIE: (*pointing to the bag*) What is that thing?

GRANT: I'm not sure, but it might be a jellyfish.

CHARLIE: (*He bends down toward the bag.*) If I can just get a closer look, maybe I can figure out what it is. It's *clear* like a jellyfish.

GRANT: (*panicking*) Charlie, no! Don't get near it. Don't you know that a jellyfish has tentacles that can sting?

CHARLIE: The poor thing is stuck here on the sand. We need to get it back into the ocean.

GRANT: We don't have to take care of this ourselves. That lifeguard must know what to do for a stranded jellyfish.

(*Grant motions the lifeguard over urgently. The lifeguard joins the boys.*)

LIFEGUARD: (*He lowers his sunglasses as he examines the bag.*) Do you two boys need glasses? That's not a jellyfish. It's a plastic bag full of water!

CHARLIE: (*sheepishly*) Actually, we do need glasses.

GRANT: We left our glasses on the beach blanket when we went for a swim.

(*The lifeguard grins as he picks up the bag and empties it.*)

Answer the following questions.

15. In the poem, which version shows which syllables are stressed in line 5?

   A. A <u>puffer</u> <u>fish</u> makes a <u>tasty</u> <u>dish</u>

   B. <u>A</u> puffer <u>fish</u> makes a <u>tasty</u> dish

   C. A <u>puffer</u> fish <u>makes</u> a tasty <u>dish</u>

   D. <u>A</u> puffer <u>fish</u> <u>makes</u> a tasty dish

16. Which stanza in the poem tells about a spitting snake?

   A. stanza 2

   B. stanza 3

   C. stanza 4

   D. stanza 5

17. Which of the following word pairs from the poem do NOT rhyme?

   A. right, bite

   B. fear, near

   C. ball, bell

   D. berth, Earth

18. In the drama, the setting of the scene is

   A. a beach.

   B. an aquarium.

   C. a seafood restaurant.

   D. a sports field.

19. What BEST describes stage directions?

   A. tells the actors what to say

   B. tells the actors what to do

   C. tells the actors what words rhyme

   D. tells the actors what to sing

20. Select a stanza from the poem. Rewrite it as a drama. Include the features of a drama in your writing.

_____

_____

_____

_____

_____

_____

_____

_____

_____

_____

_____

_____

_____

_____

_____

_____

_____

_____

_____

_____

_____

6 Compare and Contrast Literature

Getting the Idea

When you think about the ways that passages are alike and different, you compare and contrast. When you **compare**, you look for ways in which passages are alike. When you **contrast**, you look for ways in which they are different.

When you compare and contrast, pay attention to the plot, or the series of events in a story. Look at the setting, too. Does one story take place in the city and one in the country? And of course, look at the characters. Are there similarities or differences in the appearance or personality of the characters? What problem does each character have to solve?

Theme is another basis for comparison. A **theme** is the central idea of a story. Often, it is a lesson about life. Take the story "Cinderella," for example. This fairy tale is told around the world. If you were to compare two different Cinderella stories, you would find that they share similar themes. These are: *Good things come to those who wait* and *Kindness is usually rewarded*. However, you would soon see that the stories differ in several ways.

Read this passage from a classic version of "Cinderella" that most American readers know.

> Cinderella wore old, tattered clothes, while her stepmother and stepsisters had lovely clothes and lived comfortably. But no matter how mean her stepmother and stepsisters were, Cinderella was always cheerful. Even the little animals loved to be near her. She made friends with the mice and birds, and sewed outfits for them to wear.

Now read this passage from "Yeh-Shen," a version of the story that is told in China.

> The stepmother did not like Yeh-Shen, for she was more beautiful and kinder than her own daughters. She gave Yeh-Shen the worst jobs to do. Yeh-Shen's only friend was a fish with golden eyes. Each day, the fish came out of the water to be fed by Yeh-Shen. The young girl had little food for herself, but she was always willing to share with her friend the fish.

A good way to compare and contrast the passages is with a Venn diagram, like the one below.

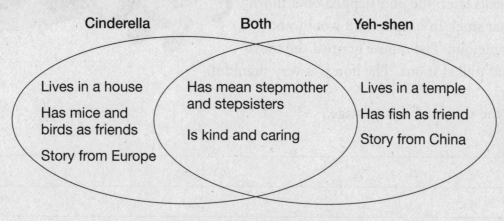

Cinderella   Both   Yeh-shen

Lives in a house

Has mice and birds as friends

Story from Europe

Has mean stepmother and stepsisters

Is kind and caring

Lives in a temple

Has fish as friend

Story from China

In this Venn diagram, the differences between the stories are shown in the outer parts of the circles. The similarities are shown in the overlapping middle part. Readers of this story in America and China—and in many other countries, too—will learn about a kind young girl who, despite her difficulties, finds true happiness. Although the specific details of the stories differ, the themes are the same.

Graphic novels are another form of literature that expresses theme. A **graphic novel** tells a story using graphics, or art, as the main focus. Speech balloons show dialogue, thought bubbles show characters' thoughts, and boxes include narration.

Thinking It Through

Read the following passage, and then answer the question that follows.

A lion used his big paw to catch a mouse. The mouse was afraid of the lion. He promised the lion that if he were set free, he would someday repay the lion. The lion laughed at him. How could a mouse ever help him? He was amused, so he let the mouse go. Many weeks later, the lion stepped on a thorn that stuck in his paw and would not come out. The mouse grasped the thorn and pulled it out. The lion was very thankful.

What is the theme of this passage?

_____

_____

_____

_____

_____

 What lesson do you think the lion learned from his experience with the mouse?

 In a group, discuss why this passage would work well as a graphic novel.

Coached Example

Read the passages and answer the questions.

Santosh's Elephant

The sun was just beginning to rise over the small village where Santosh lived. Santosh woke up with a nervous feeling in his stomach. He walked out the door of his house and headed slowly toward the forest nearby. When he arrived at the clearing, he stood there for a few moments and wiped the sleep from his eyes. While he had helped his father wash and feed the elephants many times, today would be his first time riding one by himself. He knew his father and other villagers would be traveling with him. Still, for some reason, Santosh felt anxious about the journey. Was he skilled enough to handle an elephant? His palms were moist, and there was a lump in his throat. He looked up at the female elephant that he would be riding behind his dad through the twisting jungle trail that lay ahead. She seemed to loom over him, larger than any animal he had ever seen.

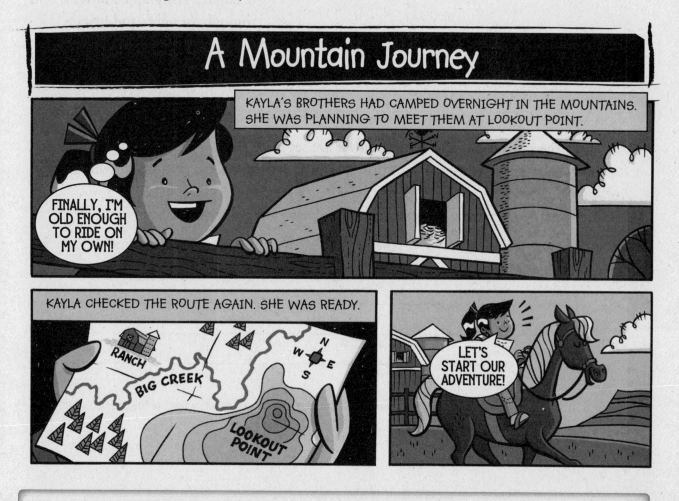

1. The themes of the passage and the graphic novel are similar because they both involve

   A. spending time outdoors.

   B. experiencing something for the first time.

   C. traveling far from home on your own.

   D. taking care of large animals.

   HINT The theme is the central idea of a story. Notice how Santosh and Kayla each react to what is planned for the day.

2. How do the story and the graphic novel show the plot?

   A. The story doesn't have a plot, only a character description. The graphic novel tells what happens in a paragraph.

   B. The story describes what is happening by using images and words. The graphic novel uses only words to describe the plot.

   C. The story tells what is happening by using words. The graphic novel uses images and words to describe the plot.

   D. The story is told through dialogue. The graphic novel is told through thoughts and images.

   HINT What makes graphic novels unique and exciting to read?

3. While the passage and the graphic novel are set in different places, they have some things in common. Compare and contrast them, using specific details in your answer.

   _____

   _____

   _____

   _____

   _____

   _____

   HINT Look for details that describe where the stories take place, the feelings and actions of the characters, and the events of the plots.

Lesson Practice

Use the Reading Guides to help you understand the passages.

Reading Guide

How does Akande respond to his wife's suggestion?

Why does Akande think it is all right to bring a cup of water to the feast?

What do you think went through Akande's mind after seeing that the lamps would not light?

The Chief's Feast
based on a fable from Nigeria

One day, a village chief announced a great midnight feast. He asked that each guest bring a cup of oil to light the many lamps arranged around the garden. Akande wanted to attend, but he had no oil to bring.

His wife suggested that he buy some oil. Akande replied, "Why would I spend my own money to attend a feast that is free?"

Akande thought, "If hundreds of people were to pour their oil into the chief's pot, could my one cup of water spoil all that oil?"

The day of the feast came. Everyone gathered at the chief's house. There was music and dancing. As each man entered the chief's house, he poured the contents of his cup into a large earthen pot. Akande poured his water into the pot and then greeted the chief.

When all the guests had arrived, the chief ordered his servants to fill the lamps with the oil. Akande was impatient. His mouth watered for the feast. At the chief's signal, just before darkness fell, the lamps were ordered to be lit. Everyone was surprised that no lamp would light. For each guest had thought that his one cup of water would not spoil a large pot of oil. And like Akande, each had brought water instead of oil. As the guests quietly ate their food in the darkness, they realized just what had happened.

The Judge's Decision
a fable from Turkey

Look for clues that tell you what each character is like. How do they behave throughout the passage?

What do you learn about the beggar by the end of the passage? What about the innkeeper?

Read each passage again, paying special attention to the theme of each one.

In the ancient city of Ankara, a beggar was given a piece of bread, but nothing to put on it. Hoping to get something to go with his bread, he went into a nearby inn and asked for some food. The innkeeper turned him away with nothing. Under the darkening sky, the beggar saw an open door and sneaked into the inn's kitchen. There he saw a large pot of soup cooking over a fire. He held his piece of bread over the steaming pot, hoping to capture a bit of flavor from the good-smelling steam.

Suddenly, the innkeeper grabbed him by the arm and accused him of stealing soup.

"I took no soup," said the beggar. "I was only smelling the steam."

"Then you must pay for the smell," answered the innkeeper.

The poor beggar had no money, so the angry innkeeper dragged him before the judge.

The judge, a man named Hodja, heard the innkeeper's complaint and the beggar's explanation.

"So, you demand payment for the smell of your soup?" asked Hodja after the hearing.

"Yes!" insisted the innkeeper.

"Then I myself will pay you," said Hodja. "And I will pay for the smell of your soup with the sound of money."

Hodja drew two coins from his pocket. He then rang them together loudly, put them back into his pocket, and sent the beggar and the innkeeper each on his own way.

Answer the following questions.

1. Both passages share a similar
   A. setting.
   B. theme.
   C. set of characters.
   D. unhappy ending.

2. How are Akande and the innkeeper alike?
   A. They have bad tempers.
   B. They are hungry.
   C. They like to steal.
   D. They want something for nothing.

3. Both passages have characters that are trying to
   A. trick someone else.
   B. embarrass someone else.
   C. share knowledge with others.
   D. learn an important lesson.

4. How are the two passages MOST different from each another?
   A. Akande has money, while the beggar has none.
   B. Akande learns his lesson, while the beggar does not.
   C. "The Chief's Feast" takes place in modern times, while "The Judge's Decision" takes place in ancient times.
   D. "The Chief's Feast" takes place indoors, while "The Judge's Decision" takes place outdoors.

5. Why do Akande and the innkeeper act the way they do? What lesson do you think each man learned?

_____

_____

_____

_____

_____

Use the Reading Guides to help you understand the passages.

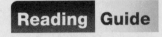

What conflict does Phaethon have with Helios?

What is the main event of the story?

Identify a theme or central idea from the story.

Phaethon's Folly
based on a Greek myth

For years, Helios brought the sun at dawn and took it away at dusk, pulling it up into the sky and down towards the sea by using his mighty chariot. Many envied the golden chariot and Helios's shining, bright horses. The horses were strong, and the sun's energy was even stronger, but Helios loved the challenge. He was custom-made for the daily journey, with the strongest arms and greatest balance, and he had earned the horses' respect over the years.

Helios's son Phaethon was jealous of his father's chariot and horses. Phaethon wanted to feel the smooth leather of the reins in his hands. He wanted to feel the sun's heat on his face in the morning and then feel it against his back at night.

Helios thought that Phaethon was being impatient and was too young to drive the chariot. "You do not yet have the physical strength to control the horses," Helios tried to explain.

But that only angered Phaethon. For weeks Phaethon argued and cried that the power of the sun was rightfully his until Helios finally gave in. Helios spent hours training his son with the horses, teaching him how to control them. But Phaethon was too confident, and he set out too soon. His journey began well, but he soon lost control. The horses ran, dipping the chariot and the sun toward the ground, burning trees, homes, and farms. Helios asked Zeus to save the world, and Zeus sent a flood to Earth to put out the fire. Zeus banished Phaethon from feeling the sun's rays forever as punishment for taking power that he had not earned.

Reading Guide

Does the graphic novel tell the full myth or just parts of it?

What is shown in the graphic novel that isn't shown in the story?

How do the visuals affect your understanding of the myth?

Phaethon's Fall

AFTER WEEKS OF PHAETHON'S BEGGING, HELIOS GAVE IN AND BEGAN TEACHING HIS SON TO DRIVE THE CHARIOT. BUT PHAETHON TOOK TO THE SKIES TOO SOON. HE COULD NOT CONTROL THE HORSES. . . .

WHOOSH!

HELIOS NEVER SAW HIS SON AGAIN, FOR HE WAS BANISHED BY ZEUS FROM THE SUN'S RAYS FOR MISUNDERSTANDING POWER.

Answer the following questions.

6. Choose all the events that are part of both the story and the graphic novel.

   A. Helios pulls the sun across the sky every day.

   B. Phaethon pulls the sun into the sky.

   C. Phaethon loses control of the horses.

   D. Phaethon pulls the sun toward Earth.

   E. Zeus punishes Phaethon.

   F. Phaethon is impatient.

   G. Zeus rewards Phaethon and Helios.

   H. Zeus causes a flood to put out the fire.

   I. Zeus lets Phaethon drive the chariot.

---

7. Use your answer to Part A to answer Part B.

   Part A

   Which statement is true only of the graphic novel?

   A. Dialogue is used to tell the myth.

   B. Visuals are used to tell the myth.

   C. Descriptive details are used to tell the myth.

   D. A narrator tells the myth.

   Part B

   How are the last sentence of the story and the second panel of the graphic novel the same? How are they different?

   _____

   _____

   _____

   _____

8. Write the words from the word box in the correct locations on the Venn diagram to compare and contrast the features of the myth in the story and in the graphic novel.

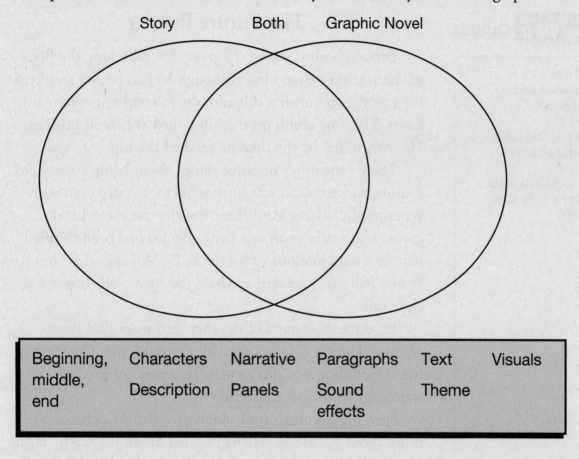

Story   Both   Graphic Novel

| Beginning, middle, end | Characters Description | Narrative Panels | Paragraphs Sound effects | Text Theme | Visuals |

---

9. Below are three statements that could be the theme of the two passages.

Theme	Power is always appealing to everyone.
	Power is always worth avoiding.
	Power is always dangerous in the wrong hands.

Part A

Circle the statement that can be made about *both* the story and the graphic novel.

Part B

Circle details within the story and the graphic novel that BEST support the statement you circled in Part A.

Use the Reading Guides to help you understand the passages.

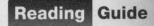
Reading Guide

What details tell
about where the story
takes place?

What plan does Benito
make for his future?

Why does Benito dread
telling his family about
his plan?

The Future Painter

Benito climbed the steep, grassy hill, watching the flock of sheep roam before him. Although he had been a shepherd for a year since turning thirteen, the job had not gotten any easier. The long climb up the hill pulled at his calf muscles. He felt winded by the time he reached the top.

There were other negative things about being a shepherd. During rainstorms, it was impossible to stay dry even with waterproof clothing. And there was the one day when a coyote had made a run at a lamb. Benito had been terrified that he would lose one of his flock. By blowing an air horn, Benito had just managed to chase the coyote off. It was a close call.

Yet there were parts of the shepherd work that Benito enjoyed. He was able to spend all day outdoors. The view from the hilltop was spectacular. He never got tired of watching hawks soar overhead.

Spending so much time alone gave Benito a chance to think about his future. He had grown up on the family farm. He felt that he could walk these hills blindfolded. His family hoped he would stay on the farm and help manage it when he got older.

Benito had given the idea a lot of thought. Although he enjoyed being outdoors and felt protective of the sheep, he wanted to leave the farm. This was not where Benito wanted to spend the rest of his life. He dreaded the day he would have to tell his family his real dream. He wanted to go to art school and become a painter.

Reading Guide

What details tell about where the story takes place?

Read each story again. How are the central ideas or themes similar?

Which events in the plots of the two stories are similar?

The Future Teacher

Shen wiped his sweaty brow as he slumped against the counter in the hot kitchen. His mom and dad had encouraged him to work at their restaurant since he was twelve, and he was still at it four years later. He had started out with small jobs, moving up to more challenging work as he grew older. By now Shen was doing some of the cooking.

Shen was his parents' only child, and he knew they wanted him to take over the restaurant. They always said the family business should stay in the family. His parents had opened the restaurant when they came to this country. They had put all their energy into making it a success. Shen's mother joked that the restaurant was their first child, born before Shen came along.

Shen's aunt worked in the restaurant, too. She encouraged Shen to think about his future. She told him he could be whatever he wanted. Shen wasn't so sure. His parents counted on him to take over, but every day Shen imagined becoming a teacher.

Shen's aunt saw that he was not thrilled by the restaurant work. When she found out Shen's wish to become a teacher, she insisted that Shen tell his parents. He would not. He felt he owed it to his parents to stay in the family business.

One day, as Shen cooked a duck, his hand slipped as he tried to slide the bird from the pan to the serving platter. The duck fell to the floor, and, off-balance, Shen stepped right on top of it. This was the last straw. Shen thought of his aunt's advice and vowed to speak to his parents that night about his plan to become a teacher.

Answer the following questions.

10. Which statement BEST describes the theme of the two stories?

   A. Follow your dreams.

   B. Don't rock the boat.

   C. Always tell the truth.

   D. Be considerate of others.

11. How are Benito and Shen alike?

   A. They decide to do as their parents ask.

   B. They enjoy the work they are doing now.

   C. They have future plans that do not match their parents' plans.

   D. They need some advice to follow their plans.

12. How are Benito and Shen MOST different from each other?

   A. Benito has a brother on the farm, and Shen has an aunt who works with him.

   B. Benito never thinks about his future, while Shen always thinks about his future.

   C. Benito learned his job from his brother, and Shen learned his job from his parents.

   D. Benito spends a lot of time alone, while Shen always has family around.

13. Which event happens in both stories?

   A. The sons give up on their future plans.

   B. The parents make plans for their sons' futures.

   C. There is cooking to be done.

   D. There is a long hill to climb.

14. How are the settings in the two stories different?

    A. "The Future Painter" takes place in the country, and "The Future Teacher" takes place in the city.

    B. "The Future Painter" takes place indoors, and "The Future Teacher" takes place outdoors.

    C. "The Future Painter" takes place in the woods, and "The Future Teacher" takes place in a school.

    D. "The Future Painter" takes place on a sheep farm, and "The Future Teacher" takes place in a restaurant.

15. What is the biggest challenge that both Benito and Shen face? Use examples from each passage to support your answer.

_____

_____

_____

_____

_____

_____

_____

_____

_____

_____

_____

_____

_____

_____

_____

_____

_____

1 Cumulative Assessment

Read the passage and answer the questions that follow.

excerpted and adapted from

The Secret Garden
by Frances Hodgson Burnett

When Mary Lennox was sent to Misselthwaite Manor to live with her uncle, everybody said she was the most disagreeable-looking child ever seen. It was true, too. She had a little thin face and a little thin body, thin light hair and a sour expression. Her hair was yellow, and her face was yellow because she had been born in India and had always been ill in one way or another. Her father had held a position under the English government and had always been busy and ill himself. And her mother had been a great beauty who cared only to go to parties and amuse herself with happy people. She had not wanted a little girl at all, and when Mary was born, she handed her over to the care of an Ayah (a nanny). The Ayah was made to understand that if she wished to please the Mem Sahib (Mary's mother), she must keep the child out of sight as much as possible.

When Mary was a sickly, fretful, ugly little baby, she was kept out of the way. And when she became a sickly, fretful, toddling thing, she was kept out of the way also. She never remembered seeing anything but the faces of her Ayah and the other native servants. They always gave Mary her own way in everything, since the Mem Sahib would be angry if she was disturbed by her daughter's crying.

By the time she was six years old, she was as mean and selfish a little girl as ever lived. The young English governess who came to teach her to read and write disliked her so much that she gave up the job within three months. When other governesses came to try to fill it, they always went away in a shorter time than the first one. So if Mary had not chosen to really want to know how to read books, she would never have learned her letters at all.

One frightfully hot morning, when she was about nine years old, she awakened feeling very upset. She became more upset when she saw that the servant who stood by her bedside was not her Ayah.

"Why did you come?" Mary said to the strange woman. "I will not let you stay. Send my Ayah to me."

The woman looked frightened, but she only stammered that the Ayah could not come. When Mary threw herself into a passion and beat and kicked her, she looked only more frightened and repeated that it was not possible for the Ayah to come to Missie Sahib (Mary).

There was something mysterious in the air that morning. Nothing was done in its regular order, and several of the native servants seemed missing. Those whom Mary saw slunk or hurried about with ashy and scared faces. But no one would tell her anything, and her Ayah did not come. She was actually left alone as the morning went on, and at last, she wandered out into the garden and began to play by herself under a tree. She pretended that she was making a flower bed. She stuck big scarlet hibiscus blossoms into little heaps of earth, all the time growing more and more angry and muttering to herself the things she would say and the names she would call her Ayah when she returned.

1. Which word BEST describes Mary?

   A. worried

   B. angry

   C. happy

   D. moody

2. Which point of view is used in the passage?

   A. first-person

   B. second-person

   C. third-person limited

   D. third-person omniscient

3. Which detail from the passage shows that Mary probably does not have many friends?

   A. "There was something mysterious in the air that morning."

   B. "But no one would tell her anything, and her Ayah did not come."

   C. "One frightfully hot morning, when she was about nine years old, she awakened feeling very upset."

   D. "She had a little thin face and a little thin body, thin light hair and a sour expression."

4. Which sentence BEST summarizes the passage?

   A. A young girl's mother leaves her at home alone.

   B. A rich young girl is mean to people and learns that no one likes her.

   C. A bossy little girl becomes upset when she finds her nanny is missing.

   D. A young girl wakes up to find herself alone and goes outside to plant flowers.

Read the passage and answer the questions that follow.

excerpted and adapted from

Little Lord Fauntleroy

by Frances Hodgson Burnett

The Captain had a small house on a quiet street, and his little boy was born there. His wife was very sweet, and their little boy was like both her and his father. Though he was born in so quiet and cheap a little home, it seemed as if there never had been a more fortunate baby.

In the first place, he was always well, so he never gave anyone trouble. In the second place, he was so sweet and charming that he was a pleasure to everyone. And in the third place, he was so beautiful to look at that he was quite a picture. Instead of being a bald-headed baby, he started in life with soft, gold-colored hair. It curled up at the ends, and went into loose rings by the time he was six months old. The boy had big brown eyes and long eyelashes and a darling little face. And his legs were so sturdy that at nine months, he suddenly learned to walk.

His manners were so good, for a baby, that it was delightful to meet him. He seemed to feel that everyone was his friend. When anyone spoke to the boy when he was in his carriage on the street, he would give the stranger a sweet, serious look and follow it with a lovely, friendly smile. This meant that there was not a person in his neighborhood who was not pleased to see him and speak to him. Not even the grocery man at the corner, who was thought to be the meanest creature alive. Every month of his life, the boy grew more handsome and interesting.

When the boy was old enough to walk out with his nanny, he would drag a small wagon about. He wore a big white hat set back on his curly yellow hair. The boy was so handsome and strong and rosy that he attracted everyone's attention. His nanny would come home and tell his mamma stories of the ladies who had stopped their carriages to look at and speak to him. And how pleased they were when the boy talked to them in his cheerful way, as if he had known them always.

His greatest charm was this cheerful, fearless way of making friends with people. I think it arose from his having a very confident nature and a kind heart. It made him very quick to understand the feelings of those about him. Perhaps this had grown on him, too, because he had lived so much with his father and mother, who were always loving and considerate and tender. He had never heard an unkind word spoken at home; he had always been loved and caressed and treated tenderly, and so his childish soul was full of kindness and warm feelings. He had always heard his mamma called by pretty, loving names. So he used them himself when he spoke to her. He had always seen that his papa watched over her and took great care of her, and so he learned, too, to be caring toward her.

5. People on the street are nice to the boy because he is

    A. friendly and kind.

    B. lonely and quiet.

    C. needy and demanding.

    D. worried and sad.

6. What detail from the story BEST tells the reader where the story takes place?

    A. The boy lives in a small house on a quiet street.

    B. The boy has brown eyes and long eyelashes.

    C. The nanny tells stories about people who speak to the boy.

    D. The boy visits the grocery man on the corner.

7. The boy speaks sweetly with his mother because

    A. he wants her to spend more time with him.

    B. he sees others acting nicely toward her.

    C. he doesn't know how to be mean to others.

    D. he hopes for gifts in return for his kindness.

8. Which BEST states the theme of the passage?

    A. Be grateful for what you have.

    B. It is best to think things through.

    C. Good things come to those who wait.

    D. Treat others as you would like to be treated.

Use "The Secret Garden" and "Little Lord Fauntleroy" to answer questions 9–10.

9. Compare the characters of Mary and the boy. Explain how they are different or alike.

_____

_____

_____

_____

_____

_____

_____

10. Compare and contrast the two passages. Are the themes alike or different? Use details from both passages to support your answer.

_____

_____

_____

_____

_____

_____

_____

Read the poem and answer the questions that follow.

My Little Neighbor
by Mary Augusta Mason

My little neighbor's table's set,
And slyly he comes down the tree,
His feet firm in each tiny fret
The bark has fashioned cunningly.

5 He pauses on a favorite knot;
Beneath the oak his feast is spread;
He asks no friend to share his lot,
Or dine with him on acorn bread.

He keeps his whiskers trim and neat,
10 His tail with care he brushes through;
He runs about on all four feet—
When dining he sits up on two.

He has the latest stripe in furs,
And wears them all the year around;
15 He does not mind the prick of burs
When there are chestnuts to be found.

I watch his home and guard his store,
A cozy hollow in a tree;
He often sits within his door
20 And chatters wondrous things to me.

11. Which line from the poem shows which syllables are stressed?

    A. He <u>does</u> not <u>mind</u> the <u>prick</u> of <u>burs</u>

    B. <u>He</u> does <u>not</u> mind <u>the</u> prick of <u>burs</u>

    C. He <u>does</u> not <u>mind</u> the prick <u>of</u> burs

    D. <u>He</u> does <u>not</u> mind <u>the</u> prick <u>of</u> burs

12. In which stanza does the poet talk about the squirrel's appearance?

    A. stanza 1

    B. stanza 2

    C. stanza 3

    D. stanza 5

CHAPTER

2 Informational Texts

Read the passage and answer the questions that follow.

Mark Twain: Master of American Literature

Mark Twain is one of the world's most famous authors. He was born Samuel Clemens on November 30, 1835, in a small town in Missouri. About four years later, the Clemens family moved to Hannibal, Missouri, on the banks of the Mississippi River. Hannibal was a growing port city. It was a frequent stop for steamboats arriving from New Orleans or St. Louis. Samuel Clemens liked to describe Hannibal as *drowsing*. He thought of the town as a place that was sleepy and never fully awake. In Hannibal, where he lived for ten years, Samuel and his friends watched the steamboats come and go every day. He vividly recalled those days for his readers in such books as *The Adventures of Tom Sawyer* (1876), *Life on the Mississippi* (1883), and *The Adventures of Huckleberry Finn* (1885).

In 1847, when Samuel was not yet a teenager, his father died. Soon after, Samuel left school to become a printer's apprentice for a local newspaper—this was his first experience with the newspaper business and writing. Later, he moved to St. Louis, Missouri, where he worked as a printer. He also traveled to New York and Philadelphia during this time, where he wrote for a number of newspapers.

In 1857, Clemens moved back to Missouri where he began a new career as a riverboat pilot on the Mississippi River. Clemens became a pilot's apprentice, or "cub," for the well-known pilot Horace Bixby. Over the next two years, Clemens became familiar with the length of the river between St. Louis and New Orleans. He eventually earned his own pilot's license. He would also take his famous pseudonym, or pen name, from his experience working on the river. *Mark twain* is a riverboat pilot's term that means two fathoms—or 12 feet. When the water was mark twain—12 feet deep—it was safe to <u>navigate</u>.

Clemens believed he would never need another career. But all riverboat traffic along the Mississippi stopped in 1861, when the Civil War began. Clemens's career as a riverboat pilot ended. The trips of early 1861 were the last he would ever make. The steamboat business never recovered. Clemens went up the river as a passenger on the last steamboat to make the trip from New Orleans to St. Louis. He would have been quite sad had he known that his days as a riverboat pilot were over.

"I loved the profession (job) far better than any I have followed since," Clemens later said, "and I took a measureless pride in it."

Clemens headed out for the West in the summer of 1861, in search of a new career. Silver had recently been discovered in Nevada, and along with many others, Clemens hoped to become rich. When he did not, Clemens started writing for local newspapers again. He went to San Francisco in 1864. Around this time, he began using the pen name Mark Twain. This was when he first realized he wanted to be an author.

In 1870, Clemens married Olivia Langdon. He had published his first book, *The Innocents Abroad*, the year before. In all, Mark Twain wrote 28 books along with numerous short stories and letters.

Mark Twain died on April 21, 1910. People around the country were saddened. Newspapers wrote, "The whole world is mourning." By that time, Samuel Clemens was no longer a private citizen. He had become Mark Twain, one of the best authors the United States ever produced.

Mark Twain Timeline

1835
Born Samuel Clemens
in Florida, Missouri

1863
First uses the pen name
"Mark Twain"

1830   1840   1850   1860   1870   1880   1890   1900   1910

1839
The Clemens
family moves
to Hannibal,
Missouri

1859
Becomes a
fully licensed
steamboat pilot

1883
*Life on the
Mississippi*
published

Dies
April 21, 1910

1. What is the main idea of this passage?

   A. Mark Twain and Samuel Clemens were the same person.

   B. Mark Twain wrote many books.

   C. Mark Twain lived a long and interesting life.

   D. Mark Twain was from Missouri.

2. What is the MAIN text structure the writer uses in this passage?

   A. chronological order

   B. compare and contrast

   C. cause and effect

   D. problem and solution

3. Which of these sentences from the passage is an opinion?

   A. "He had become Mark Twain, one of the best authors the United States ever produced."

   B. "He eventually earned his own pilot's license."

   C. "When he did not, Clemens started writing for local newspapers again."

   D. "Hannibal was a growing port city."

4. How does the timeline help readers to better understand the passage?

   A. It gives readers information that the passage does not.

   B. It lists all the books that Mark Twain ever published.

   C. It provides a fact for every year of Mark Twain's life.

   D. It provides the exact dates when certain events occurred in Mark Twain's life.

5. What does the word *navigate* mean?

   A. to work on a ship

   B. to steer a boat

   C. to measure water

   D. to learn how to sail

Read the passage and answer the questions that follow.

excerpted and adapted from

Life on the Mississippi
by Mark Twain

The Boys' Ambition

When I was a boy, there was but one lasting ambition among my friends in our village on the west bank of the Mississippi River. That was, to be a steamboat pilot. We had ambitions of other sorts, but they were only brief. When a circus came and went, it left us all burning to become clowns. Now and then, we had a hope that we could be pirates. These ambitions faded out, but the ambition to be a steamboat pilot always remained.

Once a day, a ship arrived from St. Louis, and another from Keokuk. Before these events, the day was filled with anticipation. After them, the day was a dead and empty thing. Not only the boys, but the whole village, felt this. After all these years, I can still picture that old time now, just as it was then. The town is "drowsing" in the sunshine of a summer's morning. The streets are empty, or pretty nearly so—one or two clerks are sitting in front of the stores, asleep. The great Mississippi—the magnificent Mississippi—is rolling its mile-wide tide along, shining in the sun. Then a film of dark smoke appears. A worker cries out, "S-t-e-a-m-boat a-comin'!"

A Cub-Pilot's Experience

The *Paul Jones* was now bound for St. Louis. My pilot, Mr. Bixby, agreed to teach me the Mississippi River from New Orleans to St. Louis for five hundred dollars, payable out of my first wages. I undertook the project of "learning" twelve or thirteen hundred miles of the great Mississippi with the easy confidence of youth. If I had really known what I was about to require of myself, I would not have had the courage to begin. I thought that all a pilot had to do was to keep his boat in the river. I did not think that that could be much of a trick, since the river was so wide.

The boat backed out from New Orleans at four in the afternoon, and it was "our watch" until eight. Mr. Bixby "straightened her up," and steered her along past the other boats. Then he said, "Here, take her. Shave those steamships as close as you'd peel an apple."

I took the wheel, and felt my heartbeat quicken. It seemed to me that we were about to scrape the side off every ship in the line, we were so close. I held my breath and began to claw the boat away from the danger. I had my own opinion of the pilot who had known no better than to get us into such danger, but I was too wise to express it. In half a minute, I had a wide margin of safety between the *Paul Jones* and the ships. And within ten seconds more I was shoved aside in disgrace. And Mr. Bixby was going into danger again and criticizing me for my lack of courage. I was stung, but I had to admire the easy confidence with which my chief loafed from side to side of his wheel. Mr. Bixby trimmed the ships so closely that disaster always seemed near.

When he had calmed down a little, he told me that the easy water was close ashore and the fast-moving current was outside. Therefore, we must hug the bank going upstream to get the benefit of the easy water. And we must stay well out going downstream to take advantage of the outside current. In my own mind, I decided to be a downstream pilot and leave the upstreaming to people with no common sense.

6. How did Samuel Clemens MOST LIKELY feel about his pilot, Mr. Bixby?

   A. a combination of wonder and love

   B. a combination of dislike and annoyance

   C. a combination of fear and respect

   D. a combination of loyalty and trust

7. According to the passage, what happened just BEFORE Mark Twain took the wheel of the boat for the first time?

   A. Mr. Bixby said, "Here, take her."

   B. Mark Twain's heart started pounding.

   C. Mr. Bixby commented on Mark Twain's lack of courage.

   D. Mr. Bixby calmed down.

8. Which is the BEST summary of the whole passage?

   A. A young boy dreams of becoming a steamboat pilot.

   B. A young man travels from New Orleans to St. Louis.

   C. A young boy grows up on the Mississippi.

   D. A young man fulfills his childhood dream of becoming a steamboat pilot.

9. The passage from *Life on the Mississippi* is a primary source. What other primary sources could you use to find out more about Mark Twain?

   _____

   _____

   _____

   _____

   _____

**Use "Mark Twain: Master of American Literature" and *Life on the Mississippi*
to answer question 10.**

10. Compare the two passages. How does information in the second passage give you a
better understanding of information in the first passage?

_____

_____

_____

_____

_____

_____

_____

_____

_____

7 Text Details

Getting the Idea

When you read **nonfiction**, you learn factual information about people, places, and things. Think about the many types of information contained in textbooks, encyclopedias, and newspaper articles. Informational texts tell about people, animals, plants, and many other things—what they are, what they do, what they look like. Details are specific pieces of information in a passage. They help you understand what the passage is about. Details can be descriptions, names, dates, and even actions.

All informational texts contain details. The chart below shows some of the different kinds of details you should look for when reading nonfiction.

Type of Text Detail	Example
names of people and places	Abraham Lincoln was born in Hardin County, Kentucky.
dates and time	Lincoln was born on February 12, 1809.
descriptions of places	Lincoln's family moved to a part of Indiana that had many bears and other wild animals.
things people say and do	In his Gettysburg Address, Lincoln said that "government of the people, by the people, for the people, shall not perish from the earth."
facts	Abraham Lincoln was the sixteenth president of the United States.

One way to identify important details in a text is by asking yourself questions after you read. Read this passage.

> In 1541, the Spanish explorer Hernando de Soto became the first European to see the Mississippi River. More than a hundred years later, the French explorer René-Robert de La Salle led an expedition to the Mississippi River. La Salle claimed all the land bordered by the great river for King Louis XIV of France and named the area Louisiana.

Now, think about what you just read. There are several questions you could ask to help you understand the passage. For example, how did Louisiana get its name? The passage tells you it was named after King Louis XIV. Was this the first time Europeans had been in the area? The answer is no. The passage says that Hernando de Soto, an explorer from Spain, was the first European to see the Mississippi River. As you can see, the writer uses many types of details in the passage to help you understand what happened, who was involved, and when things occurred.

Some of the details in the passage support ideas that are not mentioned specifically. Using text details and your own prior knowledge to make a guess is called making an **inference**. For example, the writer did not state the exact date of La Salle's expedition to the Mississippi, but enough information is given for you to make a reasonable guess at the date. The writer says that de Soto explored in 1541, and that La Salle explored more than a hundred years later. So, you can infer that La Salle made his journey around the middle of the 1600s.

Here's another inference to try. The writer says that Hernando de Soto was the first European to see the Mississippi. You already know that Native Americans lived all over North America before the Europeans arrived. The writer does not say it, but you can infer that Native Americans were living where de Soto explored, and that he most likely met some of them. By putting all the text details together and making inferences, you can get a fuller picture of what the passage is about.

Thinking It Through

Read the following passage, and then answer the question that follows.

Michigan and Florida are in different parts of our country. Florida is in the south. It is warm in most of Florida most of the year. Sometimes it is very hot. This allows farmers to grow crops such as oranges and coconuts. Michigan is in the north. It has four seasons with great ranges in temperature. It is hot in the summer, and cold and snowy in the winter. Autumn is a beautiful time in Michigan. The leaves on the trees change colors and then fall to the ground. Many fruits are grown in Michigan from spring to fall, such as blueberries, apples, and cherries.

The passage states that Michigan and Florida have different weather. How does the climate affect what grows in these areas? Use details from the text to support your answer.

_____

_____

_____

_____

_____

 What does the author write about the weather in each state, and the seasons during which certain crops can grow?

Coached Example

Read the passage and answer the questions.

Some sea creatures are among the world's greatest travelers. Pacific salmon are hatched in rivers, but they return to the sea to grow to full size. After a few years, they journey hundreds of miles to return upstream to the place where they were born. There, they hatch eggs.

The European eel travels even farther and goes in the opposite direction. Unlike the salmon, which hatch in freshwater rivers, this eel comes to life in the salt water of the northern Atlantic Ocean. The very young eels travel 4,000 to 5,000 miles to Europe. They take two years to make the trip. In the freshwater of European rivers, they grow slowly. It can take them thirty years to grow to full size! When they are ready to hatch eggs of their own, they make the journey across the Atlantic in the other direction.

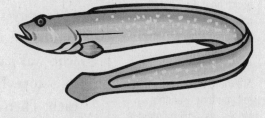

1. What sentence from the passage BEST supports the idea that Pacific salmon are among the world's "greatest travelers"?

   A. "The very young eels travel 4,000 to 5,000 miles to Europe."

   B. "After a few years, they journey hundreds of miles to return upstream to the place where they were born."

   C. "When they are ready to hatch eggs of their own, they make the journey across the Atlantic in the other direction."

   D. "In the freshwater of European rivers, they grow slowly."

   HINT   Read the text closely, keeping in mind that you are looking for detailed information about salmon.

2. The European eel MOST LIKELY lays its eggs in

   A. European rivers.

   B. Pacific rivers.

   C. salt water.

   D. freshwater.

   HINT   Use details in the passage to infer where the eels most likely end up when it is time for them to lay their eggs.

Use the Reading Guide to help you understand the passage.

Reading Guide

Read paragraph 1 of the passage carefully. Are there any details that describe when Grandma Moses was born?

Which details tell something about how the art collector might have affected Grandma Moses's life?

Read the last paragraph. Are there any details that tell you that Grandma Moses was still painting in the final year of her life?

Grandma Moses: A Great American Artist

Grandma Moses was born Anna Robertson in Greenwich, New York, in 1860. As a child, she loved to draw. At the age of twelve, Anna left home to work as a maid on a farm. When she was twenty-seven years old, she married Thomas Moses, who worked on the same farm.

As she got older, Anna took up embroidery. At the age of seventy-six, because of arthritis, she gave up embroidery and began to paint. Two years later, in 1938, an art collector who was passing through her town saw some of her paintings in a store. He bought them all for three dollars to five dollars each. Then he went to the artist's home and bought more.

In 1939, Grandma Moses showed her paintings in an exhibition of new artists at the Museum of Modern Art in New York City. An exhibition devoted to her paintings was held in 1940.

By 1943, there was a huge demand for her artwork. A self-taught artist, Grandma Moses worked from memory, portraying a way of farm life she knew from experience. She painted her New England landscapes from the top down. As she said, "First the sky, then the mountains, then the hills, then the trees, then the houses, then the cattle, and then the people."

During her life, Grandma Moses painted more than one thousand pictures, twenty-five of them after her one hundredth birthday. Grandma Moses died in 1961. She was 101 years old.

Answer the following questions.

1. According to the details in the passage, Grandma Moses was born in

    A. 1860.

    B. 1939.

    C. 1940.

    D. 1961.

2. Which detail from the passage tells why Grandma Moses started painting?

    A. She lived to be 101.

    B. She had her first one-woman show in 1940.

    C. She got arthritis and could not embroider.

    D. She liked to paint New England landscapes.

3. How did the art collector change Grandma Moses's life?

    A. He taught her how to paint.

    B. He brought her to a doctor.

    C. He told her that she should go to art school.

    D. He bought all her paintings.

4. Which detail from the passage describes Grandma Moses's landscape painting methods?

    A. She painted from left to right.

    B. She painted from right to left.

    C. She painted from the top down.

    D. She painted from the bottom up.

5. How do you know that Grandma Moses enjoyed painting up until the end of her life?

    _____

    _____

    _____

    _____

Reading Guide

Which details tell something about why Fleming was so interested in antibiotics?

Which details show that Fleming's experiment did not turn out as he expected?

Read the last paragraph. Are there any details that tell you whether Fleming worked alone to complete his work on penicillin?

Alexander Fleming: Infection's Enemy

Serendipity means the accidental discovery of something valuable or useful. Alexander Fleming had a serendipity experience when he was searching for medicine to cure infections. Born in 1881 in Scotland, Fleming graduated from medical school in England in 1906. He worked in hospitals in France during World War I. Fleming saw many soldiers die— not from war wounds, but from infections that could not be controlled. After the war, Fleming made it his mission to find medicines that would cure these infections.

In 1928, Fleming returned to England to begin experimenting. He put various bacteria into dishes. As time passed, he noticed fungus growing in the dishes. A fungus is an organism that lives off of dead or decaying matter. Fleming believed that the fungus had ruined his experiments. Then he noticed one dish didn't have any bacteria around its fungus. For some reason, this fungus prevented the bacteria from growing. He worked to identify and collect the fungus, which was from the Penicillium group.

In 1929, Fleming shared his discovery, calling the new medicine penicillin. Fleming weakened this fungus so that it worked safely as an antibiotic. An antibiotic is a medicine used to kill harmful bacteria and cure infections. While some doctors doubted penicillin's effectiveness, Fleming continued to grow penicillin. Other scientists in Europe and the United States helped. By 1945, penicillin was being produced in large quantities. Today, there are many antibiotics that cure infections, thanks to Fleming's accidental discovery.

Answer the following questions.

6. Read paragraph 1 from the passage.

> Serendipity means the accidental discovery of something valuable or useful. Alexander Fleming had a serendipity experience when he was searching for medicine to cure infections. Born in 1881 in Scotland, Fleming graduated from medical school in England in 1906. He worked in hospitals in France during World War I. Fleming saw many soldiers die— not from war wounds, but from infections that could not be controlled. After the war, Fleming made it his mission to find medicines that would cure these infections.

Underline the details that support this inference: Fleming's experience working in hospitals during World War I shaped the future of his medical career.

---

7. Copy details from the passage about Fleming's life from the box into the correct location on the timeline.

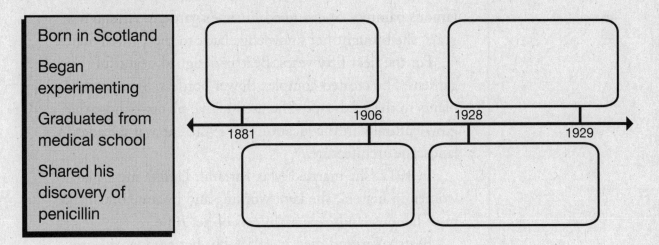

Born in Scotland

Began experimenting

Graduated from medical school

Shared his discovery of penicillin

1881   1906   1928   1929

Reading Guide

As you read, look for important details. Which are important and which are not?

Look closely at the details about Farrand's early life. They can help you make inferences about how she grew up.

What event helped steer Beatrix Farrand toward garden design?

Beatrix Farrand: Art in Nature

Beatrix Jones was born in New York City on June 19, 1872. Her family had vast gardens wherever they lived. When she was five, she followed her grandmother through her rose garden and listened as her grandmother identified the name of all the roses. She showed Beatrix how to trim away the dead blooms, too.

As Beatrix grew older, she became more interested in gardening. Then, in the early 1890s, she met Charles Sprague Sargent, who would change her life. Sargent was in charge of a large garden in Boston called the *Arnold Arboretum*. Sargent suggested that she study garden design, but she had to learn all the skills on her own.

Sargent had her work in the arboretum. In those days, many designers would add or take away land to make a design. Sargent taught Beatrix how to use an existing slope in her designs. He told her to study great art paintings. He told her to observe nature's beauty. Then he told her to travel. She went to Europe and looked at paintings by famous painters. She studied Europe's gardens. After a few years, she brought her knowledge back to the United States.

For the next fifty years, Beatrix designed beautiful gardens. She created complex flower borders. She matched plants to the landscape. She used native plants—those that grow naturally in the location. By 1900, she was a leader in landscape architecture.

In 1912, she married Max Farrand. Unlike most married women in her era, she kept working and became one of the most famous landscape architects of her time.

Beatrix Farrand died in 1959, but her gardens live on. Many have been restored, so that people today can still enjoy her artistic genius.

Answer the following questions.

8. How are women today different than those in Farrand's era?

    A. Women do not go to college.

    B. Women work after they get married.

    C. Women have more children.

    D. Women do not travel as much.

9. What can you conclude about Beatrix Farrand?

    A. She was a good painter.

    B. She had no time for marriage.

    C. She was a very friendly person.

    D. She was born into a wealthy family.

10. What effect did Charles Sprague Sargent have on Farrand's life?

    A. He was the reason she began to study the art of designing gardens.

    B. He became the reason why she traveled all over Europe.

    C. He taught her how to use flowers in garden designs.

    D. He introduced her to people who then hired her.

11. Which detail distinguishes Farrand's garden designs?

    A. She uses the same colors in all designs.

    B. She copies garden designs from Europe.

    C. She uses roses in all her gardens.

    D. She fits the plants into the existing landscape.

12. How do you know that Beatrix Farrand was one of the best landscape architects of her time?

_____

_____

_____

_____

_____

8 Main Idea, Supporting Details, and Summary

Getting the Idea

The **main idea** of a passage is what the passage is mostly about. It is the most important point that a writer makes in the article. The main idea can often be stated in one sentence. For instance, the main idea in a paragraph about bicycle safety may be to wear a helmet.

Recognizing main ideas is important. To figure out the main idea of a text, it is often helpful to ask questions. For example, you might ask yourself: What point does the writer focus on most? Are any points repeated? Are any points stressed with strong language?

Writers need more than a main idea to make their point about a topic. A **supporting detail** is a fact, example, or other piece of information that strengthens or backs up the main idea. Think about the paragraph about bicycle safety. If the main idea of a paragraph is to wear a bicycle helmet, a supporting detail might be that bicycle helmets are designed to protect riders' heads.

Read this passage. Then try to figure out the main idea and supporting details.

The manta ray is one of the most graceful animals in the ocean. Although it is very large—about twenty feet across at the widest point—it gets around easily. With its large, triangular wings, the manta ray can move fast. It pushes itself through the water easily. When other sea creatures try to attack it, it rarely gets caught. The manta ray travels smoothly and safely through the sea.

Making a diagram is a good way to identify the main idea and supporting details. Look at this diagram about the manta ray. The main idea is at the top, and the supporting details are below it.

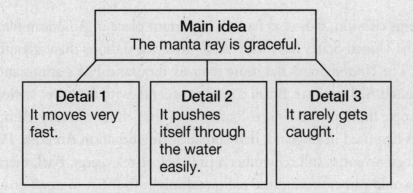

Summary

Another way to understand informational texts is to summarize what the author has written. Your **summary** should state only the main idea and the most important supporting details. Read this passage.

> Population is all the people living in a certain area. The world's population is uneven. Some places, such as the United States, are densely populated. That means a lot of people live there. The climate makes it easy for people to live and work. Other places are less populated and have few people. One example is northern Canada. The cold climate makes it difficult for people to live there.

Here is a good summary of the passage.

> The world's population is uneven. Some places have a lot of people, while other places have fewer people.

When you read, first look for the main idea, and then look for the important details. The title of a passage might give you a clue to the main idea, so that is a good place to start.

Thinking It Through

Read the following passage, and then answer the question that follows.

Since its creation, radio has had an important place in American life. Today, the United States has more radio broadcast stations than any other country. The United States has more than six thousand FM stations and almost five thousand AM stations. Brazil comes in second, with far fewer stations. Many people think of the United States when they think of radio. Although radio was first used in England, daily broadcasting began in America. People now in their seventies still remember a time before television. Back then, families would gather around the radio each night to listen to news or stories.

What is the main idea of this passage?

_____

_____

_____

 Reread the first sentence of the passage. Does the rest of the passage support it? Try to state the main idea of the passage in one complete sentence.

 With a partner, discuss the passage. Identify a detail that is not important in supporting the main idea.

Coached Example

Read the passage and answer the questions.

Libraries are amazing places. Every library has books on thousands of subjects. Each book is full of information, and each piece of information is something to learn. In fact, some people call libraries "temples of learning." People can learn about almost anything at the library. Music fans can learn about different kinds of music. Farmers can learn about planting crops. Doctors can learn about medicine. Lawyers can learn about the law. Each book has its place on a shelf. This is because libraries are extremely well organized. Libraries also have helpful and knowledgeable librarians on staff. These librarians are there to answer readers' questions and to help solve problems. It's easy to see why so many people, young and old, like to spend time at the library.

1. The main idea of this passage is

   A. libraries have many books.

   B. libraries are well organized.

   C. libraries are amazing places.

   D. each book has its place.

   HINT Look for a big, general idea, rather than a small detail.

2. Which statement from the passage is a supporting detail?

   A. "Every library has books on thousands of subjects."

   B. "In fact, some people call libraries 'temples of learning.'"

   C. "Libraries are amazing places."

   D. "It's easy to see why so many people, young and old, like to spend time at the library."

   HINT Supporting details strengthen the passage's main idea.

Use the Reading Guide to help you understand the passage.

Underline the main idea in the passage.

What did both babies and adults do while they slept?

Remember that a good summary gives the main message of a passage.

Eugene Aserinsky and the Dreaming Brain

Have you ever wondered what happens to our brains during sleep? Do our brains just shut off and rest throughout the night, or do they remain active?

In 1953, a scientist named Eugene Aserinsky asked these same questions. To find the answers, he decided to do an experiment. He closely observed a number of babies during sleep to see if their eyes moved beneath their lids. He noticed the babies had very slow eye movements when they first fell asleep. Then he noticed something very interesting. At certain times during sleep, the babies' eyes began to move very rapidly. They seemed to move as if the baby was awake and playing outside. Eugene called these periods of sleep "Rapid Eye Movement," or "R.E.M." for short.

Aserinsky then decided to try the same experiment with adults. He found the same thing. Adults also had rapid eye movements. These movements lasted between three minutes to nearly an hour. Aserinsky decided to awaken the adults when their eyes were moving rapidly. He asked them what they were seeing. The adults reported that they were dreaming. Aserinsky also awakened the adults when there was no eye movement. During these times, the adults did not report any dreams.

This experiment showed that sleep has different stages. During some stages, the brain is active. During others, it is not. Before Aserinsky's discovery, scientists believed that sleep had only one stage. Aserinsky forever changed the world's view of sleep.

Answer the following questions.

1. Aserinsky watched various subjects sleep because he wanted to know

    A. why people sleep for hours at a time.

    B. what happens while people are asleep.

    C. what people dream about while sleeping.

    D. why people sleep without dreaming.

2. According to the passage, babies and adults

    A. have very different sleep patterns.

    B. do not dream while asleep.

    C. both experience Rapid Eye Movement.

    D. have slow eye movements when dreaming.

3. What is the main idea of this passage?

    A. Babies dream more than adults.

    B. People always dream while sleeping.

    C. Scientists want to know what happens when people sleep.

    D. The human brain has different stages of activity when asleep.

4. What caught Aserinksy's attention when watching babies sleep?

    A. He noticed that they did not move much.

    B. He watched their eyes move as if they were playing.

    C. He found that they slept without dreaming.

    D. He did not see any movement beneath their eyelids.

5. Write a brief summary of the passage in your own words.

    _____

    _____

    _____

    _____

Use the Reading Guide to help you understand the passage.

Reading Guide

What is the main idea of the passage?

How did the villagers try to keep the land dry?

What are the mills at Kinderdijk?

The Mills at Kinderdijk

Most of the land in Holland is about 22 feet below sea level. Around 750 BCE, what is now the village of Kinderdijk (pronounced KIN-der-deek) was underwater. However, people were determined to make the land suitable for homes and farms. The villagers tried several methods of managing the water.

First, people dug long, deep holes to carry overflowing water from rivers away from the future site of the village. This method worked until about 1270 CE, when the rising sea threatened to flood the village. Villagers then built a dike, a long wall surrounding the village, to block water. People opened gates in the dike walls to let the excess water flow safely into the rivers. But the dike wasn't strong enough to hold the water forever. Around 1560, water pressure built up, and water seeped into the village. Another solution was needed.

In 1726, windmills were built to drain the excess water. A windmill has four large blades at the top connected to a waterwheel at the bottom. As the blades turn, the energy of the wind is used to move the water. Water is funneled into the bottom of the windmill, where the wheel scoops the water and redirects it to rivers or over dry farmland. All nineteen original windmills remain in Kinderdijk today, but now two steam power pumps help redirect the water. Tourists can visit the windmills and learn more about how they operated.

Answer the following questions.

6. Below are three possible main ideas for this passage.

Main Ideas	The villagers at Kinderdijk used several methods to manage the water.
	The villagers built holes and dikes to protect Kinderdijk.
	Windmills were built to drain extra water from the village.

Part A

Circle the main idea that is supported by details in the passage.

Part B

Circle three details in the passage that BEST support the main idea you circled in Part A.

---

7. Choose the three statements that work together BEST to create a summary of the passage.

   A. The people of Kinderdijk have tried different ways to control the flooding.

   B. Steam power pumps are the best method for water relocation.

   C. Flooding made Kinderdijk unlivable for many years.

   D. Windmills were built to relocate water, and they remain in use today.

   E. A dike is a long wall surrounding a village.

   F. People can visit the windmills and see how they work.

Use the Reading Guide to help you understand the passage.

Reading Guide

What point does the writer focus on?

What details support that point? Find a detail that is not important in supporting the main idea.

What clues to the main idea do you get from the title of the passage?

Turtle Worlds

All turtles have shells, which are tough and protect the turtle's soft body underneath. When turtles spot danger, they defend themselves. Some pull their head and legs inside their shells, while others stay in their shells and bite or scratch.

All turtles have a lot in common, but they are different, too. They are all reptiles. Turtles' favorite activity is to soak up sunshine on a log or rock. Turtles live in different places, and they eat different things. Most turtles are master swimmers and love the water, while some turtles, called *tortoises*, prefer dry land.

Wood turtles live near the water but not in it. They eat worms, tadpoles, insects, and berries. The wood turtle has an unusual way of hunting worms. It stamps its feet on the ground, and the worm pops up!

The map turtle got its name from the design on its shell, which looks like the rivers on a map! Map turtles live near slow-moving rivers and lakes. Some eat clams, crayfish, and snails, while others eat bugs, worms, and plants.

Since most turtles love water, you might not think that they would live in the desert. Yet, that is where the desert tortoise calls home. It can go a year without drinking any water! It gets most of its water from flowers, cacti, grasses, and berries.

The snapping turtle got its name for its hard bite. It can grow up to 2 feet long and weigh 75 pounds. Snapping turtles enjoy lakes, river, and ponds, and you can see them swimming on the water or walking on the bottom. If you see any turtle, just watch it. Snap a photograph, or draw it. Then leave the turtle where it is happiest—in the wild.

Answer the following questions.

8. What sentence in paragraph 2 expresses the main idea of the passage?

   A. "All turtles have a lot in common, but they are different, too."

   B. "Turtles' favorite activity is to soak up sunshine on a log or rock."

   C. "Turtles live in different places, and they eat different things."

   D. "Most turtles are master swimmers and love the water, while some turtles, called *tortoises*, prefer dry land."

9. How do desert turtles survive in a place with little water?

   A. Desert turtles don't need to drink water.

   B. Desert turtles must wait a year to get a drink.

   C. Desert turtles get much of their water from the things they eat.

   D. Desert turtles use their shells to save water.

10. What sentence could BEST begin paragraph 6?

    A. One turtle that loves to live in and near the water is the snapping turtle.

    B. Many people like the snapping turtle.

    C. Beware of all turtles!

    D. Some turtles prefer swimming in salt water.

11. What main idea does the author use to end the passage?

    A. Turtles are dangerous.

    B. Leave turtles in the wild.

    C. Watch turtles move.

    D. Turtles like to be alone.

12. Write a brief summary of the passage in your own words.

    _____

    _____

    _____

    _____

9 Relationships between Events

Getting the Idea

Most of the informational passages you read are written in a certain order, or sequence. For example, take the events leading up to America becoming an independent country. Our country's first conflict with Britain came before the second event for a reason, and the second event came before the third event for a reason. Finally, the problems became so great that America declared its independence from Britain.

Chronology is another word for historical sequence. When history writers put events into **chronological order**, they are placing those events in the order in which they happened. But listing a series of events in chronological order is not enough—it is only telling the reader what happened. To truly teach the reader something about history, the writer should also tell *why* something happened.

Read this passage.

> Yellowstone was our country's first national park. Congress passed a bill creating it in 1872. Then, Congress opened more parks in other areas of the country. People saw that an agency was needed to run the growing park system. The National Park Service was created in 1916.

The paragraph tells the events that led up to the creation of the National Park Service. The events are in chronological order. The paragraph also tells you why the National Park Service was needed.

Events in a science text are related to each other in a similar way. They must also happen in a certain sequence, or order. Read about the process of photosynthesis on the following page.

Green plants make their own food using a process called photosynthesis. First, plants take in sunlight. Plants use the energy from the sun to break down the water and carbon dioxide. The plant also takes in water from the soil and carbon dioxide from the air. Plants use the sugar as food. Finally, they release the oxygen into the air. Then, these materials are put together in a new way to make sugar and oxygen.

Sound confusing? That's because the steps in the process are out of order. The sequence needs to be fixed in order for the text to make sense. The plant needs to take in water and carbon dioxide *before* it can break them down. And if you see the word *finally*, it signals an event that should come last. Time-order words such as *first, next, then,* and *finally* can help you understand the sequence of events.

Now read the correct version of the passage.

Green plants make their own food using a process called photosynthesis. First, the plant takes in sunlight. The plant also takes in water from the soil and carbon dioxide from the air. Next, plants use the energy from the sun to break down the water and carbon dioxide. Then, these materials are put together in a new way to make sugar and oxygen. Plants use the sugar as food. Finally, they release the oxygen into the air.

Now the passage makes sense. You can understand the steps in the process. Pay attention to the order of events and steps in a process when you read about history or science. Doing so will help you to better understand what you read.

Thinking It Through

Read the following passage, and then answer the questions that follow.

Many Native American groups in North America planted Three Sisters gardens. The "three sisters" were corn, beans, and squash. These three crops were planted together in the same small plot of earth to help them grow. This "cooperation" among crops is still used today. First, corn seeds are planted in a small mound. When the corn is about six inches high, it is time to plant the beans. About a week after the beans have sprouted, it is time to plant the squash. The corn provides a stalk for the beans to climb up. And the beans provide nutrients, or food, for the soil. As the squash grows, its leaves spread out, which prevents weeds from competing for the available nutrients and sunlight.

Which of the vegetables should be planted first? Why?

_____

_____

_____

_____

HINT   What do the beans need for support?

 **DISCUSS**   In a small group, come up with a list of everyday things that you do, in school and at home, that require steps in a process. Share them with the class.

Coached Example

Read the passage and answer the questions.

In 1920, Earle Dickson was working for a medical supplies company called Johnson & Johnson. Dickson's new wife, Josephine, was just learning how to cook. She often cut her fingers while making meals. So, Earle came up with a plan. He got some tape and gauze and a pair of scissors. He cut small rectangles of gauze and stuck them on pieces of tape. After that, whenever Josephine got a cut, she could easily use a ready-made bandage.

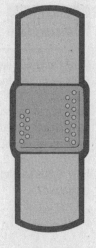

Soon after making his homemade bandages, Dickson showed them to the managers at his company. They liked the idea so much that by 1921, they were selling the bandages. They also promoted Dickson to vice president of the company. By 1924, Johnson & Johnson was manufacturing boxes of Band-Aid® brand adhesive bandages for Americans to buy and keep in their medicine cabinets.

1. What did Earle Dickson do right before showing the bandages to Johnson & Johnson?

   A. He became vice president.

   B. He came up with a plan.

   C. He cut pieces of gauze and put them on tape.

   D. He taught his wife how to cook.

   HINT Look for clue words that help you figure out the sequence of events.

2. Why did Earle Dickson decide to make bandages at home?

   A. He couldn't get them at work.

   B. His wife frequently cut herself.

   C. He wanted to impress his co-workers.

   D. He was working on various inventions.

   HINT Review the passage for details on why Dickson came up with the idea.

Lesson Practice

Use the Reading Guide to help you understand the passage.

Reading Guide

What happened before the Chunnel project reopened?

Think about why so many companies wanted the Chunnel to get built.

How is this passage organized?

The Chunnel

The Channel Tunnel, or "Chunnel," is a unique railway tunnel. It is 31.4 miles long—and 24 miles of it are underwater!

The idea behind the Chunnel was first thought of around 1802. England and France wanted to figure out a quick way to travel between the two countries without having to take a boat. Engineers thought of digging a tunnel beneath the English Channel, the sea that separates England from France. Construction workers started to dig into the earth, but no real progress was made. The project lay quiet for years.

Then, in 1984, the undersea railway project reopened. England and France hoped private companies would work together to pay for the huge cost to build the Chunnel. Many companies were interested. They knew a tunnel would provide a cheaper way to move goods than by ship, airplane, or truck. The Eurotunnel Group, a group of two hundred banks and other companies, was formed. The group gave England and France its blueprints for the Chunnel. By 1986, England and France gave the Eurotunnel Group their approval. Two years later, construction finally began.

The Chunnel took fifteen thousand workers seven years to complete. On May 6, 1994, the queen of England and the president of France held an opening ceremony for the Chunnel. The Chunnel is considered one of the seven wonders of the modern world. High-speed trains carry vehicles, equipment, and people. Nearly seven million passengers take the two-hour journey from London to Paris and Belgium every year.

Answer the following questions.

1. People first hoped the Chunnel could be built because they wanted

   A. a fun way to travel.

   B. an easy way to get to France.

   C. a way to travel besides by boat.

   D. a cheap way to move goods.

2. According to the passage, what happened BEFORE 1984?

   A. The Chunnel was on hold.

   B. The Chunnel was half finished.

   C. The money for the Chunnel was collected.

   D. The governments gave approval for the Chunnel.

3. Why did so many companies want the Chunnel built?

   A. Travel by boat was slow.

   B. Moving goods would be less expensive.

   C. Building the Chunnel was cheaper than a new road.

   D. Airplanes had not yet been invented.

4. What happened LAST?

   A. Construction workers began to dig.

   B. The Eurotunnel Group was formed.

   C. An opening ceremony was held.

   D. Fifteen thousand workers constructed the Chunnel.

5. Explain how dates in the passage helped you understand how long it took between major events in the construction of the Chunnel.

   _____

   _____

   _____

   _____

   _____

Use the Reading Guide to help you understand the passage.

Reading Guide

How does the organization of the passage help you understand the process of mummification?

Which step comes before wrapping the body in linen?

Why was mummification an important process in ancient Egypt?

Making Mummies

Ancient Egyptians believed in many gods and had traditions to please their gods, even after death. The Egyptians believed that preserving the body of a deceased person honored the gods and ensured that the person's spirit would find its body and take it to the next life. To preserve bodies, Egyptians used a process called mummification.

Wealthy Egyptians, such as pharaohs, were mummified. It is not surprising that only wealthy Egyptians were mummified. The mummifying process had many steps, took a lot of time, and was expensive.

First, the brain was removed. Egyptians used a metal hook to pull the brain out through the nose.

Next, most organs, including the liver, stomach, lungs, and intestines, were removed. They were put in containers representing the gods that were believed to protect each organ. (Why wasn't the heart removed? Egyptians believed that the heart was needed in the next life because it was responsible for thoughts and feelings.)

Then the body was filled and covered with salt to remove all liquid from it. After forty days, the salt was removed. The body was then filled with linen and sand and was painted with resin, a liquid that hardens the skin.

Finally, the body was wrapped in linen cloth. Objects meant to protect the body from evil spirits were added before a second layer of linen was applied. A mask was placed on the body's head before the mummy was laid in a sarcophagus, a decorated stone coffin. The containers of organs were put inside the tomb with the mummified body.

Answer the following questions.

6. The following are details from the passage that describe the steps in the process of mummification. In each box, write the number 1, 2, 3, 4, or 6 so that the events are in the correct order.

 Salt is applied for forty days to remove all liquids.

 The body is filled with linen and sand, and resin is applied.

 Organs are taken out and placed in containers.

The brain is removed, using a metal hook.

5 The body is wrapped in linen twice.

 A mask is placed over the head.

7. Read paragraphs 4 and 5 from the passage.

> **Then the body was filled and covered with salt to remove all liquid from it. After forty days, the salt was removed. The body was then filled with linen and sand and was painted with resin, a liquid that hardens the skin.**

> **Finally, the body was wrapped in linen cloth. Objects meant to protect the body from evil spirits were added before a second layer of linen was applied. A mask was placed on the body's head before the mummy was laid in a sarcophagus, a decorated stone coffin. The containers of organs were put inside the tomb with the mummified body.**

In these paragraphs, underline the time-order words that give clues to the order of the mummification process.

Use the Reading Guide to help you understand the passage.

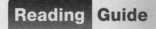

Reading Guide

What was Frederic Tudor's dream?

What steps did he take to realize his dream?

Think about how Tudor improved his business. What role did Nathaniel Wyeth play?

What happened as a result of Wyeth's help?

The Ice King

A chilled glass of ice water is refreshing on a summer day. But about 250 years ago, ice water would not have been an option unless you lived in a climate that was cold even in the summer. How did ice come to be so readily available any time of the year?

In the early 1800s, Massachusetts businessman Frederic Tudor had a dream. He wanted to cut ice blocks from the frozen winter ponds of Boston and ship them to warmer climates. He reasoned that people would be eager to have ice available to them at any time and any place.

Tudor first worked to figure out how to harvest the ice. He hired workers to cut the thick pond ice with saws. The ice blocks were then packed in sawdust to help keep them from melting as they were being transported.

Next, Tudor began creating a market for his ice by giving it away. He felt that once people became used to having iced drinks, they would be steady customers. He also showed restaurant owners how to make ice cream and persuaded hospitals to use ice when treating patients with high fevers.

Tudor's business began to take off, but he needed to find better ways to harvest the ice. In 1826, he hired Nathaniel Wyeth. Wyeth used horse-drawn plows to cut the ice into large intersecting grids. Workers then retrieved the 300-pound ice blocks from the pond and stored them in an icehouse until they were transported.

By 1833, Tudor was able to ship ice halfway around the world. News reports told of the crowd's excitement in Calcutta, India, when the ship filled with ice docked. Finally realizing his dream, Frederic Tudor became known as the "Ice King."

Answer the following questions.

8. Tudor expected that people would buy his ice because they

    A. liked that it was free.

    B. needed it to keep their food cold.

    C. wanted to impress their friends.

    D. enjoyed having it available year round.

9. According to the passage, what happened AFTER the ship docked in India?

    A. Wyeth figured out how to cut the ice.

    B. Workers packed the ice in sawdust.

    C. News reports were written about the event.

    D. Restaurants began making ice cream.

10. Tudor convinced hospitals to use his ice

    A. to make ice cream for patients.

    B. to treat patients with fever.

    C. to help patients enjoy their stay.

    D. to cool the hospital rooms.

11. Which event happened LAST?

    A. Tudor shipped ice to India.

    B. Workers cut the ice with saws.

    C. Tudor hired Nathaniel Wyeth.

    D. Ice was stored in an icehouse.

12. Explain the major events that contributed to Tudor's success.

_____

_____

_____

_____

_____

_____

_____

10 Reading in the Subject Areas

Getting the Idea

When you are reading a textbook, you will probably come across words you do not know. Each subject you study in school—science, social studies, history—uses its own special keywords and terms. Often, new terms will appear in bold print or highlighted another way. That means that you can find the word's meaning in the book's **glossary**. A glossary is a section at the back of a textbook that includes an alphabetical list of all the new words in that book and their definitions.

Read the following passage.

> During the Revolutionary War in America, **muskets** were not very accurate. American and British soldiers stood in long lines and fired large numbers of lead balls at one another. Army leaders hoped that the deadly shots would make holes in the enemy line.

The word *muskets* appears in bold print. That means it will be defined in the book's glossary. For example, the entry might look like this:

musket a heavy shoulder gun carried by foot soldiers

Sometimes, you may come across a word you do not recognize that is not in bold print. That means it is not in the glossary. So, you can use a **dictionary** to look for a definition. Think of a dictionary as a huge glossary, containing many more words. Often a dictionary will list the definitions for all the different meanings of a word, whereas a glossary might have only the definition that fits the meaning of the word as it is used in a book.

Sometimes, a word can have more than one meaning, depending on the kind of text where it is used. In a science book, the word *conductor* means a material that electricity flows through easily. In a text about music, a conductor is a person who leads an orchestra.

Here's another example from a science textbook.

> Igneous rocks are produced by heat or by a volcano. Igneous rocks can be classified by their texture and <u>composition</u>. Many kinds of igneous rocks contain the minerals quartz and plagioclase.

Now read this passage from a language arts textbook.

> Learning how to write a thoughtful <u>composition</u> can be a difficult process. However, if you follow all the steps and you understand what you are supposed to do, composition writing can be simple and fun.

The word *composition* appears in both passages, but it does not have the same meaning in both. Using the context in which the word appears in each passage, you should be able to choose which definition is the right one in each case. Look at the dictionary entry below.

> **com·po·si·tion** *noun* **1.** the act or process of composing **2.** the general makeup of a material **3.** a piece of writing, especially a school exercise in the form of an essay **4.** a written piece of music

Using what you know, which definition tells you what *composition* means as used in the science passage? The answer is definition 2. Definition 3 tells you what the same word means in the language arts passage.

Thinking It Through

Read the following passage, and then answer the questions that follow.

       The Oregon-California Trail was an important part of American history. The trail was a 2,000-mile route from Missouri to Oregon and California that allowed the early <u>pioneers</u> to travel to the western United States. The first large wave of pioneers followed the trail in 1843, when roughly 1,000 settlers made the journey at one time.

What does the word <u>pioneers</u> mean in this passage? Where would you look in a textbook containing this passage to find out?

_____

_____

_____

   Which words in this passage help you understand the meaning of the word *pioneers*?

DISCUSS   With a partner, find a word in the last sentence that would have a different meaning if you read it in a science text about hurricanes. What would the word mean in the science text?

Coached Example

Read the passage and answer the questions.

Clouds start with warm, moist air near Earth's surface. The moisture in the air is in the form of water vapor, or water in the gas state. The warm air rises. As the air rises, it cools.

High in the sky, the air becomes so cool that the water vapor <u>condenses</u>, or changes from a gas to a liquid. The water vapor forms tiny droplets of liquid water. If the air is very cold, the water vapor forms ice crystals. Clouds are made up of billions of droplets or ice crystals, sometimes both.

<u>Cloud droplets</u> form around tiny specks of dust or soot. Cloud droplets are too tiny to fall to Earth. For rain to fall, larger, heavier drops of water must form in clouds. Raindrops form when droplets bump into each other and stick together. It takes millions of droplets to make one raindrop.

1. When water changes from a gas to a liquid, it is called

   A. freezing.

   B. condensation.

   C. melting.

   D. crystallizing.

   HINT Find the keywords *gas* and *liquid* in the passage. What does the passage say about them?

2. Cloud droplets do not fall as rain because they are too

   A. hard.

   B. large.

   C. small.

   D. sticky.

   HINT Reread the description of how cloud droplets form.

Use the Reading Guide to help you understand the passage.

Reading Guide

Look at the underlined word in paragraph 1. Information in paragraphs 1 and 3 will help you understand its meaning.

What kind of information is being described in paragraph 2?

Think about the word *colony*. Would it have another meaning in a history book?

Amazing Honeybees

Humans have kept honeybees for thousands of years. In modern times, beekeeping isn't just a popular hobby, it is a major industry. Honeybees pollinate plants. This helps the plants to produce seeds. We harvest many of these plants for food.

A hive can have up to thirty thousand bees in the winter. In the summer, there can be as many as eighty thousand bees living in one hive! That's a remarkable number of bees! There is only one queen bee for each bee colony. The queen bee is the mistress of the hive, and all the bees follow her lead. The queen can lay two thousand eggs a day. Most of the eggs will grow into worker bees. They take care of the hive. Each worker bee has a specific job. Some become nursemaids and take care of the babies. Others have jobs such as food finders, hive builders, or guards. Some of the eggs will grow into drone bees. The drone bees mate with the queen bee and will become the fathers of future baby bees. Bees work together to keep the hive functioning smoothly.

When beekeepers work with bees, they must wear special clothing. This protective clothing helps prevent bee stings. Beekeepers wear a helmet with a strong net that is pulled down over the face. They always wear jackets with long sleeves to protect the arms. Bees can also climb up unprotected legs. Most beekeepers use pieces of string to tie the bottoms of their pants around their ankles.

Answer the following questions.

1. Look at the dictionary entry below.

   col·o·ny *noun* **1.** a group of people who settle in a new land **2.** a group of the same kind of animals or plants that live together **3.** a territory that has been settled by people from another country and is ruled by that country **4.** a group of people having the same interests

   Which definition tells you what <u>colony</u> means as used in the passage?

   A. definition 1

   B. definition 2

   C. definition 3

   D. definition 4

2. Which of the following is NOT a job of a worker bee?

   A. guarding the hive

   B. laying eggs

   C. taking care of babies

   D. building the hive

3. What does the word <u>beekeeping</u> mean?

   A. keeping bees as pets

   B. selling beehives

   C. raising and caring for bees as a business

   D. running an industry

4. The drone bees

   A. mate with the queen.

   B. guard the queen.

   C. lead the other bees in the hive.

   D. leave the hive in winter.

5. What is protective clothing? Which words in the passage help you understand its meaning?

   _____

   _____

   _____

   _____

Use the Reading Guide to help you understand the passage.

Reading Guide

Look at the underlined words in paragraph 1. What do you think the words mean in this passage?

In paragraph 2, notice the words and sentences around the words *nomadic* and *bison*. Which clues help you understand the meaning of each word?

If this passage were in a textbook, the underlined words would be defined in the glossary at the back of the book.

The Plains Indians

The Plains Indians lived in the area of the United States known as the Great Plains. These Native American groups had a strong connection to the land—a connection so deep that it was felt throughout every part of their culture. The people had to gather, grow, or hunt all their food. Some groups farmed the land and grew crops such as beans, maize, and pumpkins.

The people were nomadic, moving constantly as they collected wild fruits and vegetables and hunted wild animals. They followed herds of bison across the plains. Bison are large, strong, and fast, so they were not easy to hunt. But they were valuable because they provided most of a tribe's basic needs: food, clothing, and shelter. The Plains Indians never killed more bison than they needed. They were grateful for the bison and used every part of it—nothing was wasted. The meat was eaten. The skin was used to make shelter, clothing, shields, shoes, and pouches. Bison fat was turned into soap.

Because the Plains Indians moved all the time, they needed a type of shelter that could be put up and taken down quickly. They built a tepee by leaning long poles together and covering the poles with bison skin. A fire was built in the center of the tepee. There was a hole at the top of the tepee to let the smoke out. The hole could be adjusted depending on which way the wind was blowing.

Answer the following questions.

6. Look at the dictionary entry below.

   cul·ture *noun* **1.** an interest in the arts, such as music and painting **2.** the growth of bacteria in a laboratory for scientific purposes **3.** the beliefs and way of life of a group of people **4.** the process of growing new kinds of animals or plants

   Which definition tells you what <u>culture</u> means as used in the passage?

   A. definition 1

   B. definition 2

   C. definition 3

   D. definition 4

7. What is <u>maize</u>?

   A. a kind of animal

   B. something to eat

   C. a piece of clothing

   D. an item used for travel

8. What does the word <u>nomadic</u> mean?

   A. hard-working

   B. quiet

   C. staying in one place

   D. moving from place to place

9. The bison provided the Plains Indians with

   A. shelter and clothing.

   B. long poles for shelter.

   C. food, clothing, and shelter.

   D. hunting tools.

10. What is a tepee? Which words in the passage help you understand its meaning?

   _____

   _____

   _____

   _____

Use the Reading Guide to help you understand the passage.

Reading Guide

What is the subject area of this passage: science, language arts, or social studies?

What words in the last sentence in paragraph 1 help you understand the underlined word?

Would you find the word *predator* in a social studies book? Why or why not?

The Uncommonly Common Octopus

The common octopus is anything but common. Octopuses have unusual physical characteristics. An octopus has a large lightbulb-shaped head with eyes and a mouth, and eight long arms called <u>tentacles</u>. The octopus uses two rows of round suckers on each arm to move around the sea floor and to grasp food. The common octopus is a carnivore. It eats mostly crabs and other <u>crustaceans</u>, breaking the shells with a saw-like organ in its mouth.

The common octopus has special methods to protect itself from predators such as sharks, dolphins, and eels. The octopus hides on the sea floor, living in holes and caves. Because it is an <u>invertebrate</u>, it doesn't have a backbone. It can fit inside small areas at the bottom of the sea. Octopuses can also change their skin pigment to match the environment. But that's not all. They can also use specially developed muscles to change the texture of their skin. So an octopus near the rocky sea bottom would have skin that is the color and texture of the rocks around it, making it difficult to find. If threatened, octopuses can also emit a black liquid cloud. The liquid paralyzes the <u>predator</u>, giving the octopus a chance to get away.

The common octopus may be well known, but it is not a typical sea creature. Its appearance is strangely unique, and its defense methods are certainly special.

Answer the following questions.

11. A student is writing a report about the common octopus. Read this paragraph from the report and the directions that follow.

> **The octopus has developed special skills that help it survive. It can change the color and texture of its skin. It can shoot a paralyzing black liquid. It can fit in small holes at the bottom of the sea. These skills give it an advantage against _____.**

Which word BEST completes the last sentence?

A. tentacles

B. predators

C. crustaceans

D. invertebrates

---

12. Use your answer to Part A to answer Part B.

Part A

Which word and meaning would you NOT expect to find in the glossary of a science book about underwater life?

A. habitat—natural conditions and environment in which a plant or animal lives

B. prey—animal hunted by another animal

C. adapt—adjust to something, such as in appearance

D. civilization—a highly developed society that has a social organization

Part B

Which sentence best states the reason for the answer to Part A?

A. The word relates to land animals and not underwater life.

B. The word relates to people and not underwater life.

C. The word relates to weather and not underwater life.

D. The word relates to plants and not underwater life.

E. The word relates to outer space and not underwater life.

Use the Reading Guide to help you understand the passage.

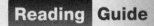

Reading Guide

What does the word *Anasazi* mean? How is it connected to the Ancestral Pueblo?

Look at the underlined words in paragraph 1. What do you think the words mean in this passage?

In paragraph 2, notice the words and sentences around the word *dwellings*. Which clues help you understand what a *dwelling* is?

The Mysterious Anasazi

Many years ago, an entire <u>population</u> mysteriously disappeared. Known as the Ancestral Pueblo or the Anasazi ("Ancient Ones"), they were Native Americans that lived from about 100 BCE until they vanished around 1300 CE. Researchers have studied the Pueblo, using <u>artifacts</u> to piece together their <u>culture</u> and learn more about how they lived.

The history of the Ancestral Pueblo covers many time periods. The fifth period is called Pueblo III. During Pueblo III, from the 1100s to the 1200s, the people settled in large villages. They carved rooms into cliffs to make homes called cliff <u>dwellings</u>. Along the canyons and cliff walls, the Pueblo also built large, separate buildings. These structures had multiple rooms—some as many as 1,000 rooms—and were the center of village life.

Many of these people moved to other nearby areas to hunt and gather food to survive. Although the Anasazi participated in hunting and gathering, the Pueblo III period was a time for communities. The Pueblo relied on <u>agriculture</u> then, growing crops for food and storing excess crops. In addition to agriculture, the Pueblo created pottery, baskets, and arrowheads.

Around 1300 CE, the Pueblo disappeared, leaving everything behind. Many believe that they moved south to find a steadier climate. The area they abandoned had crop-damaging periods of rain and drought. Perhaps they left everything behind to make travel easier so they could begin again on their new land. Others believe the Pueblo were forced to leave by other tribes who wanted to hunt on the same land.

Answer the following questions.

13. Read paragraph 3 from the passage.

> Many of these people moved to other nearby areas to hunt and gather food to survive. Although the Anasazi participated in hunting and gathering, the Pueblo III period was a time for communities. The Pueblo relied on <u>agriculture</u> then, growing crops for food and storing excess crops. In addition to agriculture, the Pueblo created pottery, baskets, and arrowheads.

Circle the words in the paragraph that help you understand the meaning of the underlined word.

14. Read this description of the Anasazi from a student report, and answer the question that follows.

> _____ such as pottery, baskets, and arrowheads teach us about Pueblo culture. The arrowheads, for example, tell us they were hunters. We also learn from the dwellings that the Pueblo left behind. Their dwellings tell us that they lived in large communities along canyons and cliff walls.

Which word BEST completes the first sentence?

A. Agriculture

B. Culture

C. Artifacts

D. Populations

Use the Reading Guide to help you understand the passage.

Reading Guide

What do plants need to survive?

Look at the underlined word in paragraph 1. What clues help you understand how the word is used in this passage?

What is the subject area of this passage? How do you know?

In what other subject area might the word <u>drought</u> be used?

Do Plants Talk?

Plants are living things that have certain needs. These needs must be met for a plant to survive. A tiny seed can grow into a large plant with the right amount of water, air, nutrients, and sunlight. Studies are now beginning to show that plants can also help themselves survive! They <u>communicate</u> with each other. Over the last few decades, plant experts have been making strides in better understanding how and why plants transmit and receive information.

Scientists have shown that when harmful insects chew plant leaves, the plants emit a chemical warning into the air. Healthy plants nearby detect the plant's distress signal and perceive it as a threat. They quickly respond by releasing a chemical defense to <u>repel</u> any insects that may be about to attack.

Another experiment using pea plants showed that signals are sent through the root system as well. One pea plant was given very little water to simulate <u>drought</u> conditions. In response, this plant began to close up to conserve water. Nearby, five other pea plants had root systems in close contact with the pea plant that was suffering drought. These five plants had an adequate water supply, but they began to close up, too. It seems that these plants anticipated a lack of water because a nearby neighbor was experiencing drought.

These experiments, and others like them, have led plant experts to conclude that on some level, plants can communicate important information to other plants. And just as important, they are able to receive messages and interpret their meaning.

Answer the following questions.

15. Which clue from the passage BEST helps you understand the meaning of <u>communicate</u>?

 A. "have certain needs"

 B. "help themselves survive"

 C. "making strides in better understanding"

 D. "transmit and receive information"

16. What does the word <u>repel</u> mean?

 A. threaten

 B. resist

 C. surrender

 D. assist

17. When a plant is attacked by insects, it

 A. turns toward the sunlight.

 B. closes up to conserve water.

 C. releases a chemical distress signal.

 D. sends a message through its root system.

18. Which word would most likely NOT be included in the glossary of a science book about plants?

 A. seed

 B. nutrients

 C. information

 D. root

19. Think about the meaning of <u>survive</u>. How is this word connected to the passage?

_____

_____

_____

_____

_____

_____

_____

_____

_____

_____

11 Text Structures

Getting the Idea

When you read, it is helpful to understand how the writer arranges the information. The way an article or passage is organized is called its **text structure**. There are a number of ways in which writers can organize information.

Chronological Order

Chronological order is the order, or sequence, in which events happen. History texts are often written using chronology. Read the following passage.

> New Mexico has an interesting history. First, Native Americans lived in the area now known as New Mexico. Then, in the late 1500s, the region was ruled by Spain. Next, in the early 1800s, the region became part of Mexico. After that, it came under U.S. control. Finally, in 1912, New Mexico became our forty-seventh state.

Notice the keywords such as *first, then, next, after,* and *finally*. They help you track the events. The dates not only help you to understand the sequence, but also how much time passed between each event.

Compare and Contrast

When you **compare**, you show how things are alike. When you **contrast**, you show how things are different. Read the following passage.

> Oranges and apples are alike in several ways. They are both fruits, and they both have seeds inside and grow on trees. Apples have a skin that you can eat, but oranges have a rind that you cannot eat. Oranges and apples grow in different climates. Orange trees grow in warmer states like Florida, while apples grow in cooler states like Washington.

The keywords *alike, both, but,* and *different* help you to understand the similarities and differences between the fruits. Other keywords you may see are *like, unlike, while, either, same, although,* and *opposite*.

Cause and Effect

A **cause** is why something happens. An **effect** is what happens as a result of a cause. For example, if you accidentally drop a glass and it falls to the floor, the glass will break. The cause is dropping the glass. The effect is the glass breaking. Read the following passage.

> The scientist Isaac Newton was the first person to explain why tides occur. Tides are the rise and fall of large bodies of water, such as oceans. Tides are caused by the moon's gravity. The gravitational pull of the moon causes the oceans to bulge out toward the moon.

Science texts often use cause and effect to explain *why* things happen in nature. Look for keywords such as *why, cause, because, therefore, as a result*, and *effect*.

Problem and Solution

Problem and solution is a text structure in which the problem, or issue, is presented first. Then, the writer tells how the problem was solved. Read the following passage.

> Central Park, in New York City, was built in the mid-1800s. Over the years, the park began to decline. By the 1970s, Central Park had become dirty and unsafe. Part of the problem was that the city did not have enough money to run the park. Then, in 1980, a group of citizens formed the Central Park Conservancy. The group raised private funds to restore the park and keep it in beautiful condition.

The writer starts off by telling you the problem: the decline of the park. Then you learn how a group of concerned citizens solved the problem.

Thinking It Through

Read the following passage, and then answer the question that follows.

Dolphins and porpoises are alike in many ways. Both are mammals that live in the ocean. They have a similar body shape, including a tail fluke. Both animals breathe through a blowhole at the top of their body. But there are many differences between these creatures. Porpoises are smaller than dolphins. Dolphins are usually about six to twelve feet long, while most porpoises are only about four to seven feet long. A dolphin's nose is often described as a pointed "beak." But a porpoise's nose is shorter and rounder, more like a snout. The teeth of a porpoise are flat, while dolphin teeth are usually shaped like cones.

What is the text structure of this passage? Use examples from the passage to explain your answer.

_____

_____

_____

HINT The passage focuses on two kinds of animals. Look for keywords that give you a clue to the text structure.

Coached Example

Read the passage and answer the questions.

Many years ago, the Colorado River flooded almost every spring. In the late 1800s, farmers had settled the land along the lower Colorado River. The floods caused major damage every year. This was a big problem for the farmers who worked near its banks. People tried to control the river. They built irrigation canals and levees to control the water. Nothing worked.

In the early 1900s, the U.S. government found a solution. It would build a dam on the river. This huge structure would stop the flooding and help create a year-round water supply for the people in the area. The government announced in 1931 that the dam would be built. The dam would be 726.4 feet high. The Hoover Dam was completed in 1935. It is located along the border of Arizona and Nevada.

1. In this passage, the MAIN text structure the writer uses is

   A. chronological order.

   B. problem and solution.

   C. comparison.

   D. cause and effect.

    What situation is described in the beginning of the passage? What do you learn later in the passage?

2. How did the government finally stop the Colorado River from flooding every spring?

   A. It built a dam.

   B. It built an irrigation canal.

   C. It built new farms nearby.

   D. It built a bridge.

   HINT Reread the passage. Which solution finally worked?

Use the Reading Guide to help you understand the passage.

Reading Guide

Look for cause and effect keywords that help you understand the reasons leading up to the Boston Tea Party.

How do the dates in the passage help you follow the order of events?

A passage can have more than one text structure. When you read about history, you learn what happened, when it happened, and why it happened.

The Boston Tea Party

The Boston Tea Party was a major event in our country's history. It is a symbol of the American Revolution.

Massachusetts was still a British colony in 1773. That year, the British government passed the Tea Act. The law said only one British company, the East India Company, could sell tea to the colonies. Americans would have to buy that tea—and they'd have to pay a tax on it, too! Many colonists were so angry, they flatly refused to buy the British tea.

The East India Company lost a lot of money because the colonists would not buy their tea. Still, the British continued to send tea to the colonies. Three British tea ships docked in Boston Harbor in 1773. Many colonists wanted the tea sent back. They did not want to pay any taxes. But the British demanded payment.

The Americans stood up for their rights. On the night of December 16, 1773, around one hundred men boarded the three ships. Many belonged to a group called the Sons of Liberty. Some were dressed as Native Americans. The men worked quietly. They dumped 342 crates of tea into the harbor. About forty-five tons of tea were thrown overboard. This event was called the Boston Tea Party.

The British government passed new laws the following year to punish Massachusetts. These were called the Intolerable Acts. The word *intolerable* means "very difficult to live with or accept." One act banned the loading of any ships in Boston Harbor.

Answer the following questions.

1. What is the MAIN text structure the writer uses in this passage?

   A. chronological order

   B. compare and contrast

   C. cause and effect

   D. problem and solution

2. What was the main cause of the Boston Tea Party?

   A. the Intolerable Acts

   B. the Tea Act

   C. the lack of tea

   D. the American Revolution

3. What was one effect of the Boston Tea Party?

   A. the Intolerable Acts

   B. the Tea Act

   C. the colonists' refusal to buy British tea

   D. the formation of the East India Company

4. Which event happened LAST?

   A. Colonists boarded three ships docked in Boston Harbor.

   B. The British government said only the East India Company could sell tea to the colonies.

   C. Colonists dumped forty-five tons of tea into Boston Harbor.

   D. Colonists formed a group called the Sons of Liberty.

5. Choose a text structure that the writer uses in the passage. Use examples from the passage to show how this text structure is used.

   _____

   _____

   _____

   _____

   _____

   _____

Use the Reading Guide to help you understand the passage.

Reading Guide

Look for clues to the text structure. Is the information organized mostly chronologically, by cause and effect, or by problem and solution?

What will plastic currency prevent?

What effect does plastic currency have on using money?

The Case for Plastic Money

Governments make currency, or the money used in specific countries. People consider the physical appearance of money very carefully. Why? Even with the most advanced technology and creative design, paper money can be reproduced. One of the biggest problems that governments face with paper currency is counterfeits, or fake money. Many counterfeiters set up printing presses and duplicate real money. Canada has discovered a new solution that goes beyond appearance to the materials used to make currency: plastic money. Safety features, such as holographic images and special ink, can be placed in the plastic money to prevent counterfeiting.

There are some negative effects of using plastic money. The material costs twice as much as the cotton used for paper money. However, plastic money is more durable. Plastic money should last much longer than paper money because it won't rip and is easier to clean. Plastic money is also recyclable, just like plastic bottles and containers. Switching to plastic money also means that ATMs will need to be updated to fit the wider plastic currency. The benefits outweigh the negatives when governments consider how much money is lost due to counterfeiting. Plastic money may not be easy to fold and slip into your pocket, but it is much safer and more durable in the long run.

Answer the following questions.

6. Use your answer to Part A to answer Part B.

    Part A

    What is the problem that plastic money solves?

    A. Ink is difficult to find.

    B. Currency is printed by governments.

    C. Paper money is easy to counterfeit.

    D. Recycling is not easy to do.

    Part B

    Which detail from the article BEST supports the answer to Part A?

    A. ". . . counterfeiters set up printing presses and duplicate real money."

    B. ". . . paper money can be reproduced."

    C. "Safety features . . . can be placed in the plastic money to prevent counterfeiting."

    D. "Governments make currency . . ."

    E. ". . . problems that governments face with paper currency is counterfeits . . ."

---

7. Read a portion of paragraph 2 from the passage.

    There are some negative effects of using plastic money. The material costs twice as much as the cotton used for paper money. However, plastic money is more durable. Plastic money should last much longer than paper money because it won't rip and is easier to clean. Plastic money is also recyclable, just like plastic bottles and containers. Switching to plastic money also means that ATMs will need to be updated to fit the wider plastic currency.

    Underline the sentences in the paragraph that state the negative effects of creating plastic money.

Use the Reading Guide to help you understand the passage.

Reading Guide

What do the dates help you understand about the main text structure?

What caused Eiffel to build the tower?

What sequence words does the writer use in paragraph 2?

The Eiffel Tower

In 1886, the French government was planning ahead for the World's Fair in Paris. The fair would be held in three years' time. The government held a design competition. They wanted an iron tower to serve as a grand entrance. Gustave Eiffel entered and won the competition. His design was chosen from more than 100 plans. Eiffel's tower featured four legs set apart at the base. The legs drew closer together as they rose, until they met at the top.

Eiffel began work on the tower in 1887. First, all 18,000 parts of the tower were made in Eiffel's factory. Then, the parts were bolted together into larger pieces. Next, these pieces were transported to the building site by horse-drawn wagons. The pieces were raised into place by steam-powered cranes. Finally, 2.5 million rivets replaced the bolts.

Eiffel faced a technical hurdle along the way. The tower's four pillars had to rest on solid ground to have a stable foundation. But two of the pillars were so close to the Seine River that they would need extra support in the marshy ground. Eiffel had a plan. He had two giant watertight containers sunk below water level. This allowed workers to work below the level of the river. They broke up and removed soil, creating space for sturdy foundations of cement and stone.

After more than two years of construction, the Eiffel Tower opened on March 31, 1899. The tower was scheduled to be torn down twenty years after its opening. But Eiffel thought ahead to save his tower. During construction, he built a science lab in the tower for important research. The tower was also used to transmit telegraphs.

Answer the following questions.

8. What is the MAIN text structure the writer uses in the passage?

   A. cause and effect

   B. chronological order

   C. problem and solution

   D. compare and contrast

9. What was the effect of the government's design competition?

   A. Eiffel submitted the winning design.

   B. The government received too many design entries.

   C. Eiffel opened a factory to construct iron parts.

   D. The date of the World's Fair was changed.

10. Which event happened LAST during the construction of the tower?

    A. Pieces were moved to the building site.

    B. Rivets replaced bolts to hold the tower together.

    C. Steam-powered cranes raised the larger pieces.

    D. Parts were made in Eiffel's factory.

11. What problem did Eiffel have to solve during construction of the tower?

    A. The tower was not tall enough.

    B. The tower had too many parts.

    C. He needed more horses to transport pieces to the site.

    D. He had to build two pillars on unstable ground.

12. Choose a text structure that the writer used in the passage. Use examples from the passage to show how this text structure is used.

    _____

    _____

    _____

    _____

    _____

    _____

    _____

12 Primary and Secondary Sources

Getting the Idea

Sources are materials that provide information. You use sources to gather facts and details about topics you wish to learn or write about.

A **primary source** was written at the time of an event by someone who was there. A primary source is also called a firsthand account. For example, a letter from a soldier who fought in a war is a primary source. The soldier is writing about things he personally experienced. An autobiography is another example. Benjamin Franklin told the story of his life in his autobiography. Other examples are diary entries, interviews, quotes (a person's exact words), and eyewitness accounts. One way to identify a primary source is to look for the word *I*. This word means that the writer of the source is reporting his or her own thoughts and experiences.

Read this passage.

> When I arrived at the scene, about fifteen people had already gathered near the half-beached whale. Two scientists waded into the water, trying to lead the thirty-foot creature off the bottom and back out to sea. After two hours, the whale began to flap its tail and fins. The scientists gave it a final push, and off it went.

The passage is an eyewitness account by a newspaper reporter (*I*) on the scene. The reporter is telling about an event that he or she actually observed or witnessed. Therefore, it is a primary source.

Not all primary sources are written works. A photograph can also be a primary source, since it gives direct information about something. Because primary sources are original accounts, their information is usually accurate and reliable.

A **secondary source** is an account of an event that was *not* witnessed by the writer. In fact, the writer most likely used information from several primary sources to write his or her account. Secondary sources are useful and important, but they are one step further away than primary sources are from the events they describe. Some examples of secondary sources are encyclopedia articles, magazine articles, textbooks, and biographies.

Read this passage.

> Kay Harris moved to Greenlawn, New York, in 1996. She took a daytime job in an art supply store. During this time, Kay developed an interest in painting. After work, she would stay up all night painting in her kitchen. Her paintings showed bold splashes of lines and colors. Kay told her friends and family that she was painting images from her imagination. For the next five years, Kay created more than one thousand paintings.

In this secondary source, the writer is not an eyewitness to the events described. The writer simply gives information collected from primary sources. The writer may have interviewed people who knew Kay Harris or read other accounts of Kay Harris, such as her personal diary. Because secondary sources often collect information from more than one primary source, they can be good general sources of information.

The chart below shows examples of primary and secondary sources.

Primary Sources	Secondary Sources
eyewitness account	textbook
diary entry	encyclopedia article
interview	magazine article
quote	book review
autobiography	biography
letter	almanac
photograph	atlas

Thinking It Through

Read the following passage, and then answer the questions that follow.

On May 29, 1953, Edmund Hillary and Tenzing Norgay became the first people to climb Mount Everest, the tallest mountain in the world. Many adventurers had attempted to climb Everest before, but none had reached the top. Hillary and Norgay planned their climb very carefully. They had the support of a great team, and they also used the best equipment. All of these things helped them to succeed.

Edmund Hillary once said, "People do not decide to be extraordinary. They decide to accomplish extraordinary things." He proved this on Mount Everest. It was truly an amazing achievement.

Does this source provide mainly primary or secondary information? Explain. What part of the source is a primary source?

_____

_____

_____

_____

_____

 **DISCUSS** In a group, discuss what primary sources can provide that secondary sources cannot provide. What can a secondary source supply readers that a primary source could never provide?

Coached Example

Read the passages and answer the questions.

Interview with Rusty Williams

Interviewer: When did you begin playing the guitar?

Williams: My father gave me a guitar for my sixth birthday. It was love at first sight. I've been playing ever since.

Interviewer: Who was your first guitar teacher?

Williams: His name was Ronnie Jones. He was a fine teacher and showed me all of the basics. After Ronnie, I studied with Brian Wall and Debbie Ray. They taught me how to play blues and jazz. After that, I learned by listening to records.

Interviewer: Who are some of your favorite guitarists?

Williams: Well, I would say Jimi Hendrix, for sure. I also love Joe Pass.

Interviewer: What are your plans for this year?

Williams: I'm playing ten concerts in Texas and California. Then, I'm recording some new songs I've written for my upcoming album, *Blues Out West*.

Interviewer: Good luck with those new songs. I'm a fan, so I can't wait to hear them!

Williams: Thanks!

Rusty Williams

Born on August 15, 1928, in Hazlehurst, Mississippi

American guitarist, singer, and composer who combines jazz and blues to create a unique guitar style

Rusty Williams began playing guitar at age six after receiving a guitar from his father as a present. Williams studied with local guitarists in his youth. He then began listening to the records of Jimi Hendrix and Joe Pass. His first song, *Trembling Blues*, used many of Hendrix's guitar styles. Later, Williams developed his own style, which is a mix of blues and jazz. His album, *Blues Out West*, has sold more than one million copies since it was released in 2008.

1. The first passage is a primary source because it

   A. tells about a famous person.

   B. uses a person's actual words.

   C. contains historical facts.

   D. provides useful information.

    HINT Look for words such as *I* to figure out whether a source is primary or secondary.

2. How are the two passages alike?

   A. Both provide an account of someone's life.

   B. Both report eyewitness events.

   C. Both include quotes from famous people.

   D. Both are based on secondary sources.

   HINT What is the topic of both passages?

3. Which passage could have been used as a source for the other passage? Explain.

   _____

   _____

   _____

   _____

   _____

   _____

   HINT Which source reports experiences in Williams's own words? What makes that source valuable to someone writing about him?

Lesson Practice

Use the Reading Guides to help you understand the passages.

Reading Guide

What is the topic of this passage?

Look for words in the passage that give you a clue to whether it is a primary or secondary source.

Where would this passage most likely be found?

excerpted and adapted from

Ralph Waldo Emerson's Essay of May 9, 1862

Henry David Thoreau was born in Concord, Massachusetts, on July 12, 1817. He graduated from Harvard College in 1837. He worked briefly at a pencil-making factory. Soon after, he began his endless walks and many studies. Each day, he learned about some new plant or animal or creature in nature.

In 1845, he built himself a small house on the shores of Walden Pond. He lived there two years alone, growing a garden, chopping wood, and studying nature.

No truer American lived than Thoreau. He loved his country deeply. He had more common sense and wisdom than most people.

Mr. Thoreau loved the fields, hills, and waters of his native town, and he made them known and interesting both to fellow Americans and to people all over the world.

He knew the country like a fox or a bird, and passed through it as freely on paths of his own. He knew every track in the snow or on the ground, and what creature had taken this path before him.

His interest in a flower or a bird lay very deep in his mind. He sensed everything around him, almost as if he had an extra pair of eyes or ears. He saw things closely, as if under a microscope. His memory was a photograph of all he saw and heard. Every bit of nature was a thing of beauty to him.

Reading Guide

Who is reporting the events in this passage?

What does the word *I* tell you about this source?

Is the author of this passage directly observing nature? Is he using his personal observations to describe what he sees?

excerpted and adapted from

The Journal of Henry David Thoreau

The surface of the water reflects the sparkling light of the sun. The red maples will blossom in a day or two. A couple of large ducks fly low over the water. At first, I see patches of white underneath, but that is just the bright light of the sun bouncing off the water. The black ducks rise at once high in the sky. They often circle about to gather their troops.

The golden-brown tassels of the alder trees hang down from their branches. The tassels are very rich in color now. One or two buttercup flowers on Lee's Cliff, fully out, surprise me like a flame bursting from the ground. I see the white and yellow lily flowers are also blooming. There are two kinds of elm trees that grow here: the common elm and the slippery elm. The common elm has all of its new leaves out and open. The slippery elm will open its new leaves in about two days of pleasant weather.

As I was going along the road by Meadow Mouse Brook, I saw a great bird on the oaks. It was just starting to lift off. It was mostly a dirty white with broad wings with black tips and black on other parts. I am not sure whether it was a white-headed eagle or a fish hawk. It rose and circled, flapping several times, till it got under way. Then, it moved off steadily in its flight over the woods northwest.

Answer the following questions.

1. Information in the first source could BEST be used for

    A. writing a report about Thoreau's life.

    B. learning about Thoreau's personal feelings.

    C. writing an eyewitness account of Thoreau.

    D. gathering quotes made by Thoreau.

2. The second source provides the reader with

    A. details from an interview.

    B. general information.

    C. historical facts.

    D. personal observations.

3. Which statement BEST describes how the two sources are similar?

    A. Both explain or describe primary sources.

    B. Both describe the scene of an event.

    C. Both provide information about a specific person.

    D. Both gather information from secondary sources.

4. Which statement BEST describes how the two sources differ?

    A. Only the second source describes direct observations.

    B. Only the second source uses other sources.

    C. Only the second source gives accurate information.

    D. Only the second source could be used to learn more about a topic.

5. Which passage could have been used as a source for the other passage? Explain.

_____

_____

_____

_____

_____

Use the Reading Guides to help you understand the passages.

Reading Guide

What is this passage about?

Is this a primary source or a secondary source?

What clues tell you what kind of source this is?

From 1892 to 1924, immigrants arriving at Ellis Island were inspected to determine if they could enter the United States. The following is from an inspector's report written in 1912.

excerpted and adapted from

Our Immigrants at Ellis Island
by Mrs. Francis E. Clark

Five Bulgarians—Paul Popoff, Petros Popoff, Thomas and John Dimchefski, James Strumnitz

They have come over to get a higher education; they have saved up enough money to get a start, and they mean to work their way through Harvard College. They have all had a good high school education at Samokov, in Bulgaria, and can speak English pretty well. Each one has about twenty-five dollars. They all look strong and well, and promise to make good citizens, and are marked "O.K." and sent to the railway station.

An Irish Woman—Bridget Maloney

She comes from the north of Ireland. Her ticket was sent to her by her daughter, who is at service in New York. She expects to meet her daughter. She is sixty years old and has no money, but she is sure her daughter will come. She is marked "T.D." (Temporarily Detained) and sent to the detention room.

An English Boy—Timothy Donalds

He is thirteen years old, and has come over to live with his uncle, who is in San Antonio, Tex. He had two hundred dollars, but it was stolen from him in the steerage while he was seasick. He has only $1.37 left, but is sure his uncle will send for him. He also is marked "T.D." and sent to the detention room. Later, a telegram comes from his uncle, and he is marked "O.K." and sent to the railway station.

Ellis Island

Reading Guide

What is this passage about?

Is this a primary source or a secondary source?

What clues tell you what kind of source this is?

From 1892 to 1924, about seventeen million immigrants—people coming to live in the country—arrived in New York by boat. First, they entered the immigration station called Ellis Island. Many immigrants came to the United States with hopes for a better life—freedom, better jobs, better homes. Immigration officials, who were called inspectors, had important jobs. Their job was to make sure that immigrants were healthy. Traveling by boat for many months meant that immigrants could have contagious diseases. Inspectors made sure that immigrants wouldn't spread diseases to other people.

Inspectors also made sure that immigrants were able to support themselves or be supported by relatives. They asked immigrants questions to make sure they were able to work and could find work. If immigrants came to live with relatives, inspectors made sure that the relatives knew they were coming. If female immigrants came to get married, inspectors made sure their future spouses were expecting them. Inspectors often had to detain immigrants, or keep them in a special area in the immigration center. Immigrants were detained until they were healthy or until their family or fiancées were able to contact the immigration offices. Some immigrants had to be sent back to their home countries to prevent health issues or financial issues.

Answer the following questions.

6. Use your answer to Part A to answer Part B.

    Part A

    Which detail is a clue that "Our Immigrants at Ellis Island" is a primary source?

    A. Information about inspectors is given.

    B. It provides specific details about immigrants' lives.

    C. There are facts about Ellis Island's use as an immigration station.

    D. The introduction states that the passage is from an inspector's report.

    Part B

    Which detail from the source BEST supports the answer to Part A?

    A. "From 1892 to 1924, immigrants arriving at Ellis Island were inspected to determine if they could enter the United States."

    B. "The following is from an inspector's report written in 1912."

    C. "They have all had a good high school education at Samokov, in Bulgaria, and can speak English pretty well."

    D. "She is sixty years old and has no money, but she is sure her daughter will come."

    E. "Later, a telegram comes from his uncle, and he is marked "O.K." and sent to the railway station."

---

7. Choose all of the secondary sources that could have been used to write "Ellis Island." There is more than one correct answer choice.

    A. autobiography   F. diary entry

    B. magazine article   G. letter

    C. atlas   H. almanac

    D. biography   I. photograph

    E. encyclopedia   J. textbook

8. Write the words from the word box in the correct locations on the Venn diagram to compare and contrast the firsthand account and the secondhand account.

Information about Ellis Island

Descriptions of immigrants

Information learned firsthand

Eyewitness accounts

Information from several sources

Facts about Ellis Island

Information about inspectors

Dates of immigration

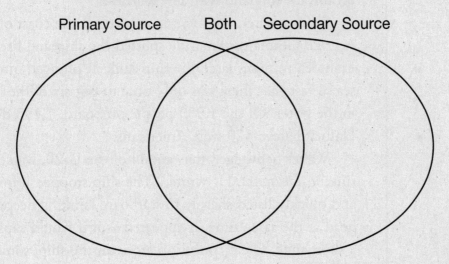

Primary Source   Both   Secondary Source

Reading Guide

Does this passage provide mainly primary or secondary information?

What words are clues to whether this is a primary or secondary source?

What does this passage supply to readers that another type of source could not?

The Sinking of the *Lusitania*

The year was 1915, and England and Germany were at war. In the New York harbor, sailors were readying the ship *Lusitania*. The English boat was preparing for a trip across the Atlantic. People who would soon board the ship weren't concerned about the war. The ship was a passenger ship, not a war ship. Why would the Germans sink it? Even if there were trouble, the ship carried 24 lifeboats.

On May 1, their ship left. On the same day, the German government printed a warning in the newspapers. It said that travelers in the war zone should "travel at their own risk." Few of the *Lusitania* passengers saw the notice. They sailed off toward England with few worries.

Six days later, the *Lusitania* sailed off the coast of Ireland. A U-20 German submarine spotted the ship and fired. Eighteen minutes later, the ship sank. It plunged into the sea so fast that there was only time to put six of the lifeboats in the water. Of the 1,959 people on board, 1,195 died. Unfortunately, 120 were Americans.

Walter Schweiger, the captain of the U-20, watched the sinking *Lusitania*. He wrote, "The ship stopped immediately and quickly listed sharply to starboard, sinking deeper by the head at the same time. It appeared as if it would capsize in a short time. Great confusion arose on the ship; some of the boats were swung clear and lowered into the water."

America was outraged. President Woodrow Wilson protested, and the Germans responded. In September, they agreed to warn a ship before firing on it to make sure passengers got off safely. Americas' anger toward Germany continued. Two years later, America joined England and declared war.

Answer the following questions.

9. The writer

    A. witnessed the event.

    B. did not witness the event.

    C. wrote a diary entry.

    D. did not describe the event.

10. What does this passage contain that would not be known by Captain Walter Schweiger?

    A. how the ship sank

    B. what happened to the lifeboats

    C. what passengers on the *Lusitania* thought

    D. how the passengers reacted to the torpedo

11. What sentence contains information from a primary source?

    A. "In the New York harbor, sailors were readying the ship *Lusitania*."

    B. "It said that travelers in the war zone should 'travel at their own risk.'"

    C. "Of the 1,959 people on board, 1,195 died."

    D. "President Woodrow Wilson protested, and the Germans responded."

12. Paragraph 5 contains a primary source because it

    A. tells about a person who sank the boat.

    B. describes what happened in the past.

    C. includes details from a historical event.

    D. uses a person's words who viewed the event.

13. What kind of primary source would give the reader a more detailed account of the sinking of the *Lusitania?* Give two reasons why.

_____

_____

_____

_____

13 Opinion and Evidence

Getting the Idea

Authors of informational texts make claims about many things. A **claim** is a statement that something—an idea, event, or observation—is true. For example, an author states: "Babe Ruth was the most talented baseball player of all time." The author is stating this idea as if it is true. However, it may or may not actually be true.

An **opinion** is a personal belief that cannot be proven true. No one can *prove* that Babe Ruth was the best baseball player; some people may disagree. When stating an opinion, authors often use words like *good, bad, pleasant, awful,* and *should* to express their feelings. Authors may also use phrases such as *I think, I believe,* and *in my view* to let you know that they are stating a personal opinion. Read this passage.

> Bigelow Park is the most beautiful park in our state. Its wildlife, lakes, and bike paths are more wonderful than any other park has to offer. It also has the best swimming pool and roller-skating rink. There is no better way to spend an afternoon than at Bigelow Park.

Words such as *better, best, most, beautiful,* and *wonderful* tell you that the author is stating opinions. These are the author's own feelings about Bigelow Park, and no one else's. Read the chart below.

Examples of Opinions
The dinner that Ted cooked tasted awful.
I feel that my mom made the right decision.
People should exercise every day to stay healthy.
In my view, the umpire made a bad call.

Authors use evidence to back up their claims. **Evidence** is information used to support a point or claim. One effective type of evidence is fact. A **fact** is a statement that is always true. Unlike an opinion, you can prove a fact in an encyclopedia or other reliable source. See how evidence affects the claim about Babe Ruth:

> Babe Ruth was the most talented baseball player of all time. In 1927, he hit 60 home runs in a single season, a record that lasted for 34 years. When he retired in 1935, Ruth had hit a total of 714 home runs. This major-league record lasted for 39 years.

The facts about the home runs and records are powerful evidence. They can be verified in a book. Together, they make the author's opinion about Babe Ruth believable and strong.

Another type of evidence writers use is an eyewitness account. An **eyewitness account** is someone's firsthand description of an event. For example:

> The tornado was the worst storm that ever hit Norwood. "I've never seen a storm damage so many houses," said Mayor Peter Olson.

The writer uses an eyewitness account (Peter Olson's statement) to support his claim about the tornado.

Finally, a writer could use an expert opinion. An **expert opinion** is the opinion of an expert or someone who knows a great deal about a topic. For example:

> Rain forests are valuable places that should be protected. Scientists at Costa Rica University say that our planet would suffer greatly if the rain forests were cut down.

The writer uses an expert opinion (the opinion of scientists) to support the claim that rain forests should be protected.

Thinking It Through

Read the following passage, and then answer the questions that follow.

> Riding a bicycle without a helmet is dangerous. In 2007, nearly 52,000 people were injured in bicycle accidents. More than sixty percent of serious bicycle injuries are head injuries.

What claim does the writer make? What kind of evidence does the writer use to support this claim?

_____

_____

_____

_____

 A claim is often stated at the beginning of a passage. Do you see information in the passage that can be proved?

 **DISCUSS** With a partner, come up with three opinions and three facts about bicycle riding. Share them with the class.

Coached Example

Read the passage and answer the questions.

Seagulls are annoying birds. They are a nuisance and a pest to everything around them. Have you ever heard their squawking and crying? It's enough to drive a person crazy. They are even annoying to look at. Their feathers are messy, and their splotchy gray and brown color is ugly.

Last week at the beach, I saw an entire flock of seagulls attacking a man and woman who were eating lunch. They waved and yelled at the diving gulls. The gulls kept diving at them. The screaming birds stole their french fries and hamburgers. When the gulls were finished with their stolen meal, they picked from the garbage pails and littered the beach with trash. This is not the first time I've seen this happen.

1. Which sentence from the passage is an opinion?

   A. "Seagulls are annoying birds."

   B. "The screaming birds stole their french fries and hamburgers."

   C. "The gulls kept diving at them."

   D. "This is not the first time I've seen this happen."

    Which answer choices describe events that actually happened? Which answer tells how the writer feels?

2. What kind of evidence does the author use in the passage?

   A. expert opinion

   B. scientific facts

   C. eyewitness account

   D. personal views

    The writer tells about his experience at the beach.

Use the Reading Guide to help you understand the passage.

Reading Guide

Look at paragraph 1. What does the writer claim about highways?

Opinions express an author's feelings or beliefs about something.

Note that Carl Yates works for the National Highway Service.

Highway Problems

Highways have changed the way Americans live. While highways may have improved travel in some ways, they have also caused many problems.

Highways are bad for the environment. Today, more than 244 million cars travel on our highways. Cars burn gasoline for their fuel. Burning gasoline creates air pollution. An average car burns 581 gallons of gasoline each year. Now, think about those 244 million cars traveling on our highways. Think about all of the gasoline they are burning. Do you get the picture? Highways create pollution.

Highways are dangerous. Cars travel at high speeds on highways, and it is easy for accidents to happen. Carl Yates, who studies highways for the National Highway Service, explains that highway traffic offers drivers little room or time to react to mistakes. Yates also points out that many highways have poor road surfaces and lack proper safety signs. This also causes accidents, he says.

Highways are noisy and upsetting. For example, last week I was stuck in traffic for three hours on a local highway. Drivers were honking their horns and flashing their lights. The air was filled with the smell of car exhaust. The noise and smell gave me a headache for hours. This happens often when I travel on highways. I like highways when they are empty, which is never!

Answer the following questions.

1. Which sentence from paragraph 2 is an opinion?

   A. "Highways are bad for the environment."

   B. "Cars burn gasoline for their fuel."

   C. "Today, more than 244 million cars travel on our highways."

   D. "An average car burns 581 gallons of gasoline each year."

2. What kind of evidence does the writer use in paragraph 2?

   A. expert opinion

   B. firsthand account

   C. facts

   D. personal beliefs

3. The writer mentions Carl Yates in paragraph 3 to

   A. support a claim.

   B. provide facts.

   C. retell an account.

   D. express a feeling.

4. What kind of evidence does the writer use in paragraph 4?

   A. personal views

   B. eyewitness account

   C. proven facts

   D. judgments

5. What is the writer's claim in paragraph 4? What kind of evidence could the writer add to paragraph 4 to strengthen this claim?

   _____

   _____

   _____

   _____

   _____

   _____

Use the Reading Guide to help you understand the passage.

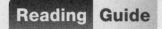 **Guide**

What is the author's opinion?

What words are clues that tell you it is an opinion?

Identify evidence that supports the author's opinion about buying local.

What kind of evidence is the information from the USDA?

Buy Local!

From April through November in a typical U.S. town, trucks pull up each Wednesday in the town center. A three-block area is transformed into a farmer's market. You can buy anything from berries and tomatoes to homemade salad dressing. Buying fruits, vegetables, and other foods from these local farmers is the best choice for the environment, for consumers, and for the community.

Buying local produce means that the food is grown near consumers. According to Local Harvest, an organization that promotes buying local, most produce is harvested about a week before it is delivered to grocery stores. Produce travels an average of about 1500 miles before being sold. When people buy local, the food is fresher since it doesn't have to sit in a truck or train for a week. If you can't make it to the farmer's market, another way to get local produce is to sign up for a Community Supported Agriculture program. You pay for a share of the harvest and can pick up a box with a wide variety of produce.

The U.S. Department of Agriculture (USDA) calls the farmer's market a "local food system." Although the USDA doesn't regulate, or set rules for, buying local, it does support the practice. Farmer's markets support local farmers economically and may also support local stores. Consumers who shop at a farmer's market may also visit nearby stores. This boosts the economy of small shops. A farmer's market is a step in the right direction for the health and financial stability of a community.

Answer the following questions.

6.   Read paragraph 1 from the passage.

> **From April through November in a typical U.S. town, trucks pull up each Wednesday in the town center. A three-block area is transformed into a farmer's market. You can buy anything from berries and tomatoes to homemade salad dressing. Buying fruits, vegetables, and other foods from these local farmers is the best choice for the environment, for consumers, and for the community.**

Underline the sentence in the paragraph that states the author's opinion.

---

7.   Choose all the sentences that are evidence supporting the author's opinion. There is more than one correct answer choice.

   A. "You can buy anything from berries and tomatoes to homemade salad dressing."

   B. "Consumers who shop at a farmer's market may also visit nearby stores."

   C. "According to Local Harvest, an organization that promotes buying local, most produce is harvested about a week before it is delivered to grocery stores."

   D. "A farmer's market is a step in the right direction for the health and financial stability of a community."

   E. "Although the USDA doesn't regulate, or set rules for, buying local, it does support the practice."

   F. "Farmer's markets support local farmers economically and may also support local stores."

Use the Reading Guide to help you understand the passage.

Reading Guide

How does the author feel about art education?

What experts does the author mention in the passage?

Which evidence comes from a personal view?

Which evidence comes from an eyewitness account?

The Arts in School

Not every school offers education in the arts. But there are many benefits for students who are involved in the arts—music, art, theater, and dance. Arts education should be available in every school in America. I am glad that my school has an arts program.

Arts programs help students do well overall in school. When students learn skills in the arts, they transfer them to other subjects. A report by Americans for the Arts backs this up. It followed students who were involved in the arts on a regular basis. The report said that these students are four times more likely to win a writing award than those who do not participate. Christine Marmé Thompson supports this idea, too. She is a college professor who teaches art education. Thompson says that the arts should be a core school subject for American students.

Arts programs teach hard work and persistence. Students won't learn to play an instrument unless they practice. They won't learn to perform a role in a play unless they spend time rehearsing. I was invited to dance at the school assembly. There were many complicated steps I had to learn, but I kept at it every day. Over weeks, I learned the dance and performed well.

Students also develop social skills through arts programs. They must learn to work together, whether they are in a band, choir, or drama group. Not only do students learn to respect how others think and work, but they must compromise to reach a common goal.

It should be the goal of every school in America to offer arts education. Taking part in the arts helps students not only while they are in school but throughout their whole lives.

Answer the following questions.

8. Which sentence from the passage states the author's opinion?

   A. "Arts programs teach hard work and persistence."

   B. "When students learn skills in the arts, they transfer them to other subjects."

   C. "A report by Americans for the Arts backs this up."

   D. "Arts education should be available in every school in America."

9. Read the following sentence.

   The report said that these students are four times more likely to win a writing award than those who do not participate.

   What kind of evidence does the sentence contain?

   A. eyewitness account

   B. scientific fact

   C. personal view

   D. firsthand account

10. Why does the author include Christine Marmé Thompson in paragraph 2?

    A. to support a claim

    B. to express a feeling

    C. to prove a fact

    D. to make a judgment

11. Which sentence is an example of a personal view?

    A. "She is a college professor who teaches art education."

    B. "It followed students who were involved in the arts on a regular basis."

    C. "Over weeks, I learned the dance and performed well."

    D. "Arts programs help students do well overall in school."

12. What is the author's claim about arts programs and social skills?

_____

_____

14 Charts, Diagrams, and Timelines

Getting the Idea

Authors of informational texts often use graphics to convey information. **Graphics** are visual tools such as charts, graphs, diagrams, and timelines. These visuals help you to better understand a text; they may even give you extra information that is not in the text.

A **chart** is a graphic that organizes information. Look at the chart below. It uses columns and rows. An author might use this chart about different countries in an article comparing countries of the world.

Country	Capital	Flag Colors	Language
Sweden	Stockholm	blue, yellow	Swedish
France	Paris	blue, white, red	French
Poland	Warsaw	red, white	Polish

Each column of the chart has a **heading** in bold print at the top. The headings tell you what the information in each column is about. To find the capital of France, go to the "Country" column, find France, and then follow the row to the "Capital" column.

A **diagram** is a simple drawing with labels to make something easier to understand. A diagram may show the different parts of an object. For example, an author might use the diagram on the right to help you to better understand a text that describes the different fins of a fish. The fins help the fish to swim. The fish moves its tail (caudal) fin back and forth to move forward in the water. The dorsal and anal fins, at the top and bottom of the fish, help the fish keep its balance as it swims. And the pectoral and pelvic fins help the fish to steer.

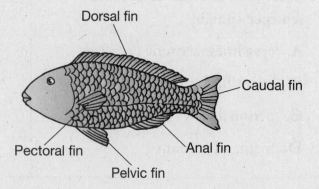

A diagram may also show how something works, how to put something together, or how to play a game. For example, an article that tells about an eruption of a volcano might include this diagram about how volcanoes work:

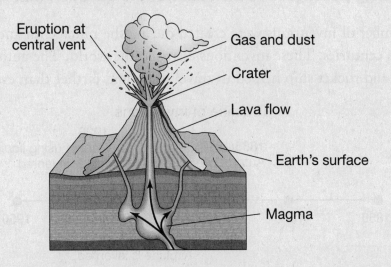

Eruption at central vent

Gas and dust

Crater

Lava flow

Earth's surface

Magma

Look closely at the diagram. It shows how magma beneath the surface of Earth rises up and causes a volcano to erupt. You can read a description of a volcano in a text, but seeing it in a diagram helps you to understand the process even more.

Another kind of graphic tool is a timeline. Authors writing about history and science often use a **timeline** to show the dates when important events happened. Timelines make it easy for you to see the order in which events take place. For example, an author writing about dinosaurs might include the following timeline to show when different dinosaurs lived.

Dinosaur Timeline

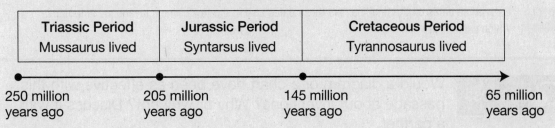

Triassic Period	**Jurassic Period**	**Cretaceous Period**
Mussaurus lived	Syntarsus lived	Tyrannosaurus lived

250 million years ago 205 million years ago 145 million years ago 65 million years ago

Time (in millions of years) is shown at the bottom of the timeline. The names of the time periods and dinosaurs appear above. Most timelines show time moving from left to right, or past to recent.

Thinking It Through

Read the following passage, and then answer the question that follows.

A number of inventions were created during the nineteenth and twentieth centuries. These inventions changed the world. The automobile, airplane, and rocket ship helped us travel faster and farther than ever before.

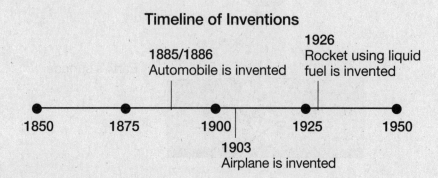

Timeline of Inventions

1885/1886
Automobile is invented

1926
Rocket using liquid fuel is invented

1850   1875   1900   1925   1950

1903
Airplane is invented

How does the timeline help you to better understand the text?

_____

_____

_____

_____

_____

 Look at the dates on the timeline. Are those dates also in the text? Which invention came first? Which came next?

DISCUSS Would a diagram or a chart have been as effective with this passage about inventions? Why or why not? Discuss it with a partner.

Coached Example

Read the passage and answer the questions.

Most ants live in nests. It is the job of the worker ants to build the nest. The worker ants dig tunnels below the earth. The tunnels lead to rooms called chambers. Each chamber of the nest has its own special purpose. One chamber is built especially for the queen. Another is built for her to lay her eggs. Other chambers are used for storing food. Newborn ants have their own nursery chamber. A single ant nest may be home to millions of ants!

Ant Nest

1. What additional information can a reader learn by looking at the diagram?

   A. Ant nests have tunnels.

   B. Some ant nests are built underground.

   C. Ant nests have resting chambers.

   D. Some ant nests are built as mounds.

   HINT Look at the different types of rooms labeled in the diagram.

2. The diagram BEST helps readers understand

   A. the role of the ant queen.

   B. the kinds of food ants eat.

   C. the design and purposes of an ant nest.

   D. the way ant nests differ from other nests.

   HINT What kind of information does the diagram mainly provide?

Use the Reading Guide to help you understand the passage.

Reading Guide

Read the passage carefully and look at the chart. Do you see any connections?

In the chart, notice the headings in the columns *Year Invented* and *Purpose*. Read each row for information.

Why do you think the author included this chart?

Ben Franklin: Inventor and Problem Solver

Ben Franklin was a famous inventor and problem solver. He had a lot of good ideas. One of his best was the volunteer fire company.

There was a big fire in Philadelphia, and many buildings burned down. So Franklin decided to organize a fire company. He did not have money to pay people, so he asked people to volunteer. Thirty men said that they would help. In 1736, the Union Fire Company began.

Whenever there was a fire, these men would stop what they were doing. They would get together and put out the fire.

Today, there are volunteer fire companies all over the world. They help people every day. This is just one example of Franklin's good ideas.

Benjamin Franklin's Inventions

Invention	Year Invented	Purpose
armonica	1762	a musical instrument made of glass
bifocals	1784	glasses that allow the wearer to see at a distance and up close
Franklin stove	1742	a stove that uses less fuel than a fireplace and prevents fires
lightning rod	1752	a rod that prevents lightning from hitting a house and causing a fire
odometer	1775	a device that measures how many miles a vehicle has traveled

Answer the following questions.

1. According to the chart, what was Franklin's LAST invention?

    A. armonica

    B. bifocals

    C. Franklin stove

    D. lightning rod

2. Other than the volunteer fire company, what else did Franklin think up that prevented fires?

    A. odometer and armonica

    B. lightning rod and odometer

    C. bifocals and armonica

    D. Franklin stove and lightning rod

3. Which of the following did Benjamin Franklin invent FIRST?

    A. lightning rod

    B. odometer

    C. Franklin stove

    D. armonica

4. The information in the chart shows that Benjamin Franklin

    A. had different skills and interests.

    B. worked for the fire department.

    C. was a famous musician.

    D. traveled often.

5. How does the information in the chart help you to better understand the passage?

    _____

    _____

    _____

    _____

    _____

    _____

    _____

Use the Reading Guide to help you understand the passage.

Reading Guide

What is the topic of the passage?

What is the topic of the diagram?

Identify areas of the diagram that connect to information in the text.

How does the diagram help you understand the passage?

Black Holes

The term "black hole" doesn't really describe these incredible space oddities at all. Black holes are actually invisible. And they aren't holes because they aren't empty. So how do you describe black holes? Black holes are areas in space where there is so much gravity that all of the light is pulled into them. Black holes are typically formed when a giant star "dies." Stars are made up of energy. When an enormous star uses up all its energy, the edges of the star begin to fold in, causing what is left of the star to collapse or explode. What is left is a black hole—an area that is filled with an amazing amount of gravity.

Gravity is a force that pulls things down. Because a black hole has so much gravity, it pulls in everything surrounding it, such as light. Do you see now why it is called a black hole, even though that isn't entirely accurate? All of the light is pulled in, so the area is black. All of the gravity pulls things toward the center, like a hole. Because all of the light is pulled in, black holes are invisible. If black holes aren't visible, how do we know they are there? Scientists use special telescopes to find areas in space where stars orbit, or move around, black holes. Scientists can also look for areas where stars' light is pulled into a black hole.

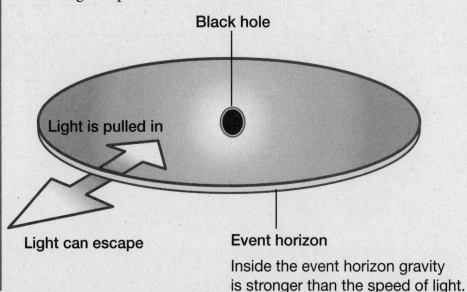

Black hole

Light is pulled in

Light can escape

Event horizon

Inside the event horizon gravity is stronger than the speed of light.

Answer the following questions.

6. Use your answer to Part A to answer Part B.

Part A

Based on the passage and the diagram, which is the BEST definition of a black hole?

A. Gravitational fields that use energy from stars

B. Enormous stars that have incredible amounts of light

C. An area in space that pulls in light due to high amounts of gravity

D. Special telescopes used to view invisible areas in space

Part B

Which detail from the article BEST supports the answer to Part A?

A. "Gravity is a force that pulls things down."

B. "Because all of the light is pulled in, black holes are invisible."

C. "The term 'black hole' doesn't really describe these incredible space oddities at all."

D. "Black holes are areas in space where there is so much gravity that all of the light is pulled into them."

---

7. Read the sentence in each choice. Then match the sentence to the description(s) on the right.

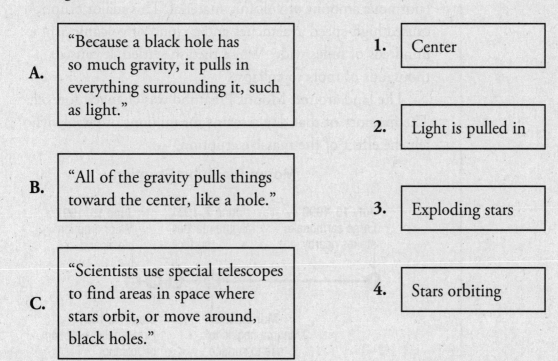

A. "Because a black hole has so much gravity, it pulls in everything surrounding it, such as light."

1. Center

2. Light is pulled in

B. "All of the gravity pulls things toward the center, like a hole."

3. Exploding stars

C. "Scientists use special telescopes to find areas in space where stars orbit, or move around, black holes."

4. Stars orbiting

Use the Reading Guide to help you understand the passage.

Reading Guide

How does the information from the passage connect to the timeline?

Underline any dates you see in the passage. Are those dates shown on the timeline?

How is the timeline organized?

Mount Pinatubo

The 1991 eruption of Mount Pinatubo in the Philippines was the one of the largest volcanic eruptions of the twentieth century, second only to the 1912 eruption of Mount Novarupta in Alaska. The destruction that it caused was devastating, and the impact of the eruption is still felt today in the area near the volcano.

Geologists believe that the events leading to the eruption actually began with an earthquake the year before. The earthquake struck about 60 miles northeast of Mount Pinatubo. This earthquake caused a landslide and an increase in steam spewing from the mountain, but the volcano remained dormant, as it had for 500 years before its last eruption.

In early 1991, though, 20 miles beneath Pinatubo, magma began to rise to the surface. This triggered thousands of small earthquakes as well as explosions of steam. By June, the magma had reached the surface.

On June 15, Mount Pinatubo finally erupted with an enormous amount of volcanic material. This major eruption caused high-speed avalanches and a cloud of volcanic ash hundreds of miles wide. When the ash settled, it caused thousands of roofs to collapse.

The land around Mount Pinatubo was changed forever. The memory of that day remains for millions of people who felt the effect of the massive eruption.

Mount Pinatubo Eruption

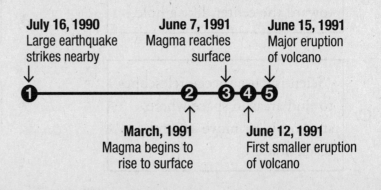

July 16, 1990
Large earthquake strikes nearby

June 7, 1991
Magma reaches surface

June 15, 1991
Major eruption of volcano

March, 1991
Magma begins to rise to surface

June 12, 1991
First smaller eruption of volcano

Answer the following questions.

8. Over what period of time did the events of the timeline take place?

   A. six months

   B. one year

   C. one week

   D. several years

9. What information is included in the passage but not the timeline?

   A. the event that started the process of the eruption

   B. how long Mount Pinatubo had been dormant

   C. when the largest eruption of the volcano occurred

   D. what Mount Pinatubo looks like now

10. Which event from the passage would fit on the timeline AFTER the second event?

    A. Magma rising causes earthquakes.

    B. Thousands of roofs collapse.

    C. Mount Novarupta erupts.

    D. High-speed avalanches occur.

11. Which event from the passage would be first on the timeline?

    A. the eruption of Mount Novarupta

    B. the cloud of volcanic ash

    C. geologists studying the causes of the eruption

    D. the previous eruption of Mount Pinatubo

12. Why does the author of this passage include a timeline?

   _____

   _____

   _____

   _____

   _____

   _____

   _____

   _____

   _____

15 Compare and Contrast Informational Texts

Getting the Idea

When you **compare** informational texts, you examine how they are alike. When you **contrast** them, you see how they are different. Comparing and contrasting texts on the same topic often give you a fuller understanding of it. One text can add to the information given by another text on the same topic.

When comparing and contrasting informational texts on the same topic, pay attention to how the texts are organized. Read these two passages.

Passage 1

The Battle of the Alamo happened because of a conflict between Texas and Mexico. At the time, Texas belonged to Mexico. Mexico was angry at Texas for taking over their military fort, the Alamo. This caused the Mexican army to attack the fort to try to take it back. The Mexican troops won the battle, but this made Texas fight even harder for its independence.

Passage 2

In February 1836, over a thousand Mexican troops arrived in San Antonio. Twelve days later, the troops attacked the Alamo. They climbed the walls of the fort. Twice, the Texas troops inside the fort pushed them back. The Mexican troops attacked for a third time. They entered the fort and defeated the Texas troops in a terrible battle.

Both passages are about the battle of the Alamo. But the first passage explains the causes and effect of the battle. The second passage tells about the events in chronological order.

You might also read about a topic in which each passage is told from a different **point of view**. You can compare and contrast those as well. Read the two passages on the next page.

Passage 1

Working as a professional diver is exciting. I get to see many different underwater fish and plants. My diving suit and equipment are fun to wear. They keep me safe and warm in the chilly deep sea.

Passage 2

Scuba diving is a method of exploring underwater. A scuba diver wears a diving mask that protects the eyes. A scuba tank is worn to provide air for breathing. Scuba divers wear wet suits to keep warm and swim fins to help move through the water.

The first passage is a personal account. The *I* refers to the diver. The diver gives the reader personal details about his experience underwater. The second passage is not personal. It states facts and gives descriptions of a diving method and diving equipment. Comparing and contrasting the information from both passages give you a fuller understanding of the topic of diving than if you had only read one of them.

Some texts look at the same topic from a different perspective. **Perspective** is the attitude or feeling of the author toward the topic. Read these two passages.

Passage 1

Dams are helpful. They provide water for farmers. They create new lakes and waterways for boaters. Many dams produce electricity for homes, businesses, and schools.

Passage 2

Cedar Creek Dam caused a lot of flooding. The floodwaters damaged nearby homes, crops, and a wildlife habitat. Now, many fishermen can no longer earn enough money to make a living.

If you had only read the first passage, you might think that dams are always helpful. But in the second passage, you learn that dams may have negative effects, too.

Thinking It Through

Read the following passage, and then answer the questions that follow.

Chess is a fun and challenging game. Children and adults throughout the world play chess. Chess players have different ranks. The best chess players are known as grand masters. Next come masters, and after that, experts. Most chess players agree that you need a lot of natural talent to become a grand master.

In 2009, 14-year-old Ray Robson became the youngest American grand master ever. He believes that studying the game hard and playing it every day is the best way for a chess player to improve.

Compare and contrast the information in paragraph 2 of the passage to the information in paragraph 1. How is it similar? How is it different?

_____

_____

_____

_____

 Look closely at the types of details given in each paragraph. What kind of information do you learn about in each paragraph?

 **DISCUSS** With a partner, discuss how the information in this passage could have been presented from a different point of view. From whose point of view could it have been presented?

Coached Example

Read the passages and answer the questions.

Being a Geologist

Being a geologist is hard work, but it is a rewarding job. Mostly, I work outdoors. I climb up and down rocks. I chip off samples. I try to learn how rock and mineral formations were created.

Sometimes I work on a team with other geologists. We might spend weeks in an area looking at the different types of rocks and minerals. We often make maps of what we see. For example, we might show where a bed of limestone meets a layer of hard shale. We trace these rock formations through hills and valleys and fields and wherever they go.

Part of my job is also trying to figure out what kinds of rocks, minerals, and other valuable resources are underground. We look for oil as well as the mineral gold.

Indoors, I work in a lab on my computer. I use computer programs to find out how the earth might have shifted to form rocks. It may look like I'm playing a video game, but this is a real-life game about our planet! Every day, I think how lucky I am to have this job.

The Scratch Test for Mineral Hardness

One way geologists identify minerals is by figuring out their hardness. The scale of hardness goes from 1 to 10. Diamond is the hardest mineral. It is rated 10 on the scale. Talc is the softest mineral. It is rated 1 on the scale. Geologists use a scratch test to rate minerals. If one mineral can scratch another mineral, it is harder than the mineral it scratches.

An easy way to get an idea of a mineral's rating is to scratch it with a material whose rating is already known. For example, your fingernail has a hardness of 2.5. A penny has a hardness of about 3.5. A steel nail or a piece of glass is about 5.5. Scratch the unknown mineral with each of the known materials and see if any leave a scratch line. If your fingernail leaves a scratch line on the mineral, you know the mineral has a hardness rating of less than 2.5. If the fingernail does not leave a scratch but the penny does, you know the mineral has a hardness rating between 2.5 and 3.5. If only the nail or glass leaves a scratch, the mineral's rating must be between 3.5 and 5.5. If none of the materials leave a scratch, the mineral has a hardness rating of above 5.5.

1. How are both passages alike?

   A. Both provide step-by-step instructions.

   B. Both contain information about minerals.

   C. Both give a personal point of view about a topic.

   D. Both organize information by cause and effect.

   HINT What types of materials do geologists study?

2. Which statement BEST describes how the two passages are different?

   A. The passages describe topics that are not related.

   B. The passages contain different types of information about related topics.

   C. The passages show different perspectives of the writers.

   D. The passages describe different ways of performing a similar activity.

   HINT Pay attention to the kinds of details and descriptions each passage presents

3. Do you think the information in the second passage gives you a better understanding of the information in the first passage? Explain your answer.

   _____

   _____

   _____

   _____

   _____

   HINT Review the information about point of view. Each passage is told from a different point of view.

Lesson Practice

Use the Reading Guides to help you understand the passages.

Reading Guide

What kind of information is contained in this passage?

How is the information in this passage organized?

Does this passage give information about all kinds of trees or just one type of tree?

excerpted and adapted from

How Trees Grow and Multiply
by Charles Lathrop Pack

The trees of the forest grow by forming new layers of wood under the bark. Trees are held upright in the soil by roots that reach to a depth of many feet where the soil is loose. These roots are the supports of the tree. They hold it stiffly in position. They also supply the tree with food. The body of the tree acts as a passageway through which the food and drink are moved to the top, or crown. The crown is the place where the food is digested and the renewal of trees occurs.

After the first year, trees grow by increasing the thickness of the older buds. Increase in height and density of crown cover comes from the development of the younger twigs. New growth on the tree is spread evenly between the wood and bark over the entire plant. Year after year, new layers of wood are formed around the first layers. This first layer finally develops into heartwood. As far as growth is concerned, heartwood is dead material. Its cells are blocked up and prevent the flow of sap. It aids in supporting the tree. The living sapwood surrounds the heartwood.

Each year, one ring of this sapwood develops. This process of growth may continue until the annual layers amount to fifty or a hundred, or more, according to the life of the tree.

The Bristlecone Pine Tree

Reading Guide

Do both passages share similar topics?

What does the first passage help you to understand about bristlecone pine trees?

Does this passage provide facts or a personal point of view?

Bristlecone pine trees are the oldest trees in North America. They are found in the western states of Nevada, New Mexico, Arizona, California, Utah, and Colorado. The oldest bristlecone pines grow in the Bristlecone Pine Forest in the White Mountains of California. While most bristlecone pines in this forest are around a thousand years old, some of the trees are more than four thousand years old!

Bristlecone pines live in windy, harsh areas. Each tree has many trunks, each of which is twisted and gnarled. Sand and ice carried by the wind has polished and smoothed the surface of the bristlecone's bark. Dead layers of the bark peel back after damage from storms and fire. This shedding helps keep the trees healthy.

Bristlecone pines grow to a height of about sixty feet. Like other pine trees, bristlecone pines have needles instead of leaves. The needles grow in bunches of five. The bristlecone has dark purple egg-shaped cones. The cones are covered with bristly or prickly scales. This is what gives the tree its name.

The wood of the bristlecone pine is very thick and heavy. Because of this, a bristlecone pine can remain standing for hundreds of years after it has died. Only when its roots have worn away will the bristlecone finally fall.

The single oldest bristlecone pine tree is known as Methuselah. At more than 4,750 years old, this ancient tree has been growing since the time the ancient pyramids of Egypt were being built!

Answer the following questions.

1. Information in the first passage could help readers better understand

   A. how bristlecone pines stand upright in the soil.

   B. why bristlecone pines grow in windy areas.

   C. how bristlecone pines got their name.

   D. why bristlecone pines grow to only sixty feet in height.

2. Which statement BEST describes how both passages are alike?

   A. Both describe past events.

   B. Both give personal points of view.

   C. Both describe a problem and how it was solved.

   D. Both provide information about related topics.

3. What kind of information does the second passage MOSTLY provide?

   A. facts and details

   B. personal account

   C. causes and effects

   D. opinions and beliefs

4. What is one difference between the passages?

   A. The first passage tells about events in chronological order; the second passage tells about causes and effects.

   B. The first passage describes all trees; the second passage describes a particular type of tree.

   C. The first passage describes forests in a positive way; the second passage describes forests in a negative way.

   D. The first passage contains facts and explanations; the second passage tells about personal feelings.

5. Explain whether the information in the first passage gives readers a better understanding of information in the second passage.

_____

_____

_____

_____

Lesson Practice

Use the Reading Guides to help you understand the passages.

Reading Guide

What is the topic of the passage?

Look for clues that tell you the point of view.

What kind of details are included in the passage?

Speeding Along

I travel to many countries for business, and I was lucky enough to get the chance to ride a bullet train in Japan. Riding a train can be exciting when the train travels up to 200 miles per hour. The Shinkansen railway network connects most of Japan with webs of tracks that are each dedicated to a single train. I was surprised to learn that trains in Japan are usually on time to the second. But when you realize that each track only carries one train, it makes sense. Trains in the United States often share tracks. U.S. trains are often late because they are waiting for the track to be clear.

The trains in Japan are shaped like bullets. They are designed to reduce wind resistance, which can slow trains down. They are long, white, and look like something you might ride into space! Bullet trains are carefully designed on the inside for peaceful, quiet rides. Train interiors look more like those in planes than those in other trains.

Though the train was full, there was plenty of room. Each car has a restroom, and there are vending machines for snacks. An attendant also brings snacks around on a cart. As we zoomed over the tracks, there was little noise. This is quite different from trains in the United States, where you can not only hear the train slide over the tracks but can also feel the train cars shaking.

It was interesting to ride the bullet train. The trip was smooth and quiet, and I arrived in Tokyo in record time. It is an experience I won't forget.

Shinkansen

Reading Guide

Is the topic of this passage similar to or different from the first passage?

Is new information presented in this second passage?

Is the narrator making personal observations or stating facts?

When it began operating in 1964, the Shinkansen was an innovative method of railway transportation in Japan. The trains covered 320 miles between the major Japanese cities of Tokyo and Osaka. The Shinkansen trains traveled up to 130 miles per hour. The train and railway system were designed by Hideo Shima. Shima helped design the trains and the tracks, which were unique because they were not shared. Only one train travels along a track. This greatly improves safety because there is no danger of accidental collisions. Introduced in time for the 1964 Olympics, the trains were soon nicknamed "bullet trains" by excited passengers. They traveled faster than a bullet, and sleek designs resembled a bullet shape.

Japan has added many more routes to the Shinkansen since 1964. Planners even added a tunnel to accommodate the tracks. Bullet trains have also increased in speed over time, traveling from 150 miles per hour and topping out at 185 miles per hour. In 2013, some Shinkansen trains can attain speeds of 200 miles per hour! The speed of these trains can pose safety risks, however. Special technolology has been added to make Shinkansen trains safe. For example, all of the trains are tracked by computers, so each train's location is always known. Another safety feature includes special parts on the brakes that ensure that the trains can stop suddenly. These measures have been taken so that passengers will arrive at their destinations quickly and safely.

Answer the following questions.

6. Use your answer to Part A to answer Part B.

   Part A

   Which sentence describes how "Speeding Along" is organized?

   A. The narrator compares traveling by train in Japan and the United States.

   B. The narrator presents the problem of train travel and a solution.

   C. The narrator includes information chronologically, or by date.

   D. The narrator provides facts about the history of the Shinkansen train.

   Part B

   Which detail from the article BEST supports the answer to Part A?

   A. "The trip was smooth and quiet, and I arrived in Tokyo in record time."

   B. "They are designed to reduce wind resistance, which can slow trains down."

   C. "Riding a train can be exciting when the train travels up to 200 miles per hour."

   D. "The Shinkansen railway network connects most of Japan with webs of tracks that are each dedicated to a single train."

   E. "This is quite different from trains in the United States, where you can not only hear the train slide over the tracks but can also feel the train cars shaking."

---

7. Read a portion of paragraph 1 from "Speeding Along."

   I travel to many countries for business, and I was lucky enough to get the chance to ride a bullet train in Japan. Riding a train can be exciting when the train travels up to 200 miles per hour. The Shinkansen railway network connects most of Japan with webs of tracks that are each dedicated to a single train. I was surprised to learn that trains in Japan are usually on time to the second.

   Underline the phrases in the paragraph that are clues that this is a personal account.

Answer the following questions.

8. Choose all of the information that is given in both passages. There is more than one correct answer choice.

    A. speed of train   **D.** description of interior

    B. shape of train   **E.** tracks that are each built for one train

    C. dates   **F.** travel to Tokyo

---

9. Write the details from the word box in the correct locations in the chart to compare and contrast each passage.

Date train introduced	Description of quiet ride
History of speeds	Factual account
Description of interior	Designer of train
Safety concerns	Comparison to U.S. trains
Original route	Personal account

Information in Passage 1	Information in Passage 2

Use the Reading Guides to help you understand the passages.

Reading Guide

Read the title. Does it help you understand the perspective of the first passage?

How does the author organize the information in this passage?

What does the last paragraph tell you about the author's opinion?

The Dangers of Camping

Many families choose to spend their vacations or weekends camping in nature. A camping trip can be very exciting, but many people do not realize the hazards that exist in the wilderness—or even at a busy campsite. Families should consider these dangers before setting out on a trip into the great outdoors.

Something as simple as the weather can lead to a rough experience. Often, storms blow in without much notice. The precipitation and wind can lead to a sudden drop in temperatures, especially at night. Excessive heat is another major weather-related issue. If shaded areas and adequate water are not available, campers, especially young children and older adults, will be at risk.

Whether on a hike or just choosing a spot to camp, you should look carefully at the plants growing nearby. Poison ivy and poison oak are two plants you should avoid. Depending on the severity of the reaction, you may need to cut your camping trip short if someone in your party touches one of these plants.

Plants are not the only living things that can ruin a camping trip. Animals, big and small, can get in the way of a fun night outdoors. Bears are common in the forests of the United States. They can often be found looking for food near campsites. Insects such as mosquitoes and ticks may not be as noticeable as bears, but they can be more dangerous. A tick bite can lead to Lyme disease, a potentially serious illness.

Regardless of how long you plan to camp out, being prepared for every situation should be the first priority. If you do not take the time to plan ahead, perhaps a camping trip is not for you.

An Outdoor Adventure

Reading Guide

Is the perspective of this passage different from the first passage?

Underline any information that this passage shares with the first passage.

How is the last paragraph different from the last paragraph of the first passage?

A great way to get friends and family together in a fun environment is to plan a trip to the great outdoors. A camping trip can be a wonderful way to experience nature while exercising and learning about the world around you.

It is important to start any camping trip by preparing before you depart. Be sure to make a list of everything you may need to make your stay outdoors safe and satisfying. Bring appropriate clothing for all weather conditions, bug spray, sunscreen, and a first-aid kit. If you plan on bringing food, be sure it is packed properly so that it does not attract bears or other animals. If you are camping at a campsite, take the time to read the rules and regulations of the site prior to arriving.

When you finally make it to your site, think about what activities you would like to do. A hike on a trail is a great way to see plants and animals. Take precautions before you hike, and never hike alone. As you walk the trail, keep your eyes open for the wonders of nature. Plants and animals will be everywhere, and you should take the time to enjoy them. Just watch out for the poison ivy!

If the weather gets rough, as long as you are prepared with the correct gear, there is no need to panic. In fact, a rainy day is an opportunity to play a card game, tell stories, or talk about the day's events.

With the right combination of preparation and spontaneity, a camping trip can be the perfect vacation. It is something that every family should try.

Answer the following questions.

10. How are both passages organized?

    A. They are both in chronological order.

    B. They both include causes followed by effects.

    C. They both give opinions supported by facts.

    D. They both share personal accounts by the author.

11. What information is included in both passages?

    A. Poison ivy is a dangerous plant.

    B. Lyme disease is a serious illness.

    C. Proper clothing is important when camping.

    D. Temperatures can drop quickly at night.

12. How would you compare the perspectives of both passages?

    A. The first passage is positive; the second passage is negative.

    B. Both passages are positive.

    C. Both passages are negative.

    D. The first passage is negative; the second passage is positive.

13. What information in the second passage could BEST help readers understand information in the first passage?

    A. Take a hike for exercise.

    B. Pack your food properly to avoid bears.

    C. Play a card game if it rains.

    D. Read the campsite rules.

14. What topic does ONLY the first passage discuss?

    A. plants at campsites

    B. why bears go to campsites

    C. the problems excessive heat might cause

    D. the importance of being prepared

15. Which passage would you use to convince your friends to go camping? Use text evidence from both passages to support your answer.

_____

_____

_____

_____

_____

_____

_____

_____

_____

_____

_____

16 Compare and Contrast Texts Across Genres

Getting the Idea

When you compare and contrast texts, you think about how they are alike and different. Comparing and contrasting texts about the same topic help you get a better understanding of the topic. There are many things to compare and contrast in informational texts. You can compare and contrast how the texts are organized; the details each author uses to support the main ideas; and the author's purpose, or reason, for writing each text.

Not all informational text is the same—it comes in different **genres**, or forms. All informational text contains facts, but how the facts are presented varies in different texts. Opinion articles are a type (or genre) of informational text where the author's purpose is to give an opinion on a subject. A science article, on the other hand, is a genre of informational text where the author's sole purpose is to give facts. Science articles sometimes use the text structure called *compare and contrast* to tell why things happen in nature. An opinion article will often use the text structure called *problem and solution* to tell about a problem or issue and a solution the author believes is correct. Reading two different genres of text on the same topic can help you better understand the topic because you understand the information in different ways. For instance, a reader who has read an objective history of an important event might more easily understand the personal experience of someone who lived through the event.

Read the two passages below about Ghost crabs. Think about how the texts are alike and different.

Passage 1

Ghost crabs are a species of crab that live on sandy beaches and dunes around the world. Their tough outer shell is usually a pale gray color that blends in with the sand. They have six legs that extend from the sides of their shell and two long, stalk-like eyes that extend from the top of their shell. Ghost crabs can travel at speeds of up to 10 miles an hour and see 360 degrees around them. During the day, the crabs build long tunnels deep in the sand for shelter. At night, ghost crabs scan the beaches for clams, lizards, insects, and other food. This is how the crabs earned their name "ghost crabs."

Passage 2

As a resident of Town Beach, I am happy that our beach has been renovated. With the new bathhouse, shops, and restaurants along the boardwalk, we have more to offer visitors after a refreshing dip in the ocean. This is great for our local businesses but not great for our ghost crabs. With more people walking the beach, the ghost crab burrows are getting damaged. I want to remind everyone that these crabs live here, too. So next time you are on the beach, please be careful of the ghost crabs' homes.

The first passage is from a science article that contains facts and details about the ghost crab. The second passage is from a letter written by someone worried about ghost crabs. It states an opinion about the topic. By reading both passages, you will understand more about ghost crabs. In the first passage, you learn why the crabs dig burrows. In the second passage, you learn that when people walk on the beach, they can damage the crabs' homes. Reading texts of different genres helps you to understand more about ghost crabs' homes.

Thinking It Through

Read the following passages, and then answer the question that follows.

Passage 1

Nestled in the middle of Indonesia lies one of Earth's truly unique features: a set of hills known as the "Chocolate Hills of Bohol." The "hills" are not actually hills but grass-covered limestone. They are the result of the buildup of limestone that was pushed up from the earth and shaped by rainwater and erosion. There are over 1,270 hills covering an area of 20 square miles. All of the hills share a similar cone shape that gives the landscape a uniform quality. In the summer, when there is less rain, the grass dries and turns brown. The hills look like the chocolate candies called "kisses."

Passage 2

When I was growing up in Bohol, Indonesia, I heard many legends about the Chocolate Hills. One story I had heard told of two angry giants who threw boulders and sand at each other for days. They eventually became exhausted and decided to become friends. When they went back home, they forgot to clean up their mess, and the boulders they left behind became the "Chocolate Hills." Another story I heard described how a giant named Arogo fell in love with a woman named Aloya. When Aloya died, Arogo cried for days. His tears dried and became the "Chocolate Hills." If anyone asked me, I would tell the second story—it's my favorite one.

Write one similarity and one difference between these texts.

_____

_____

_____

 Think about the author's purpose in each text. Why does the author write the first passage? How is the author's purpose different in the second passage?

 How do the genres of both passages help you understand the topic in a deeper way? Discuss with your partner.

Coached Example

Read the passages and answer the questions.

Butterfly Anatomy

The body of a butterfly is divided into three major sections: head, thorax, and abdomen. Each major section contains other parts that play important roles in a butterfly's survival.

On its head, a butterfly has eyes, antennae, and a proboscis, or nose. A butterfly's eyes are made up of thousands of tiny structures. The antennae are long and thin and stretch above the butterfly's head. The antennae give the butterfly a sense of smell. The proboscis is a long, straw-like structure used to suck nectar from flowers.

The thorax is the middle part of the butterfly's body. The wings and legs are attached to the thorax. A butterfly has four wings. Its forewings are the large wings that grow up from the thorax, and its hind wings are the smaller wings that extend below the thorax. Tiny muscles attach the wings to the thorax and control their movements. Finally, below the thorax is the butterfly's cone-shaped abdomen.

A Butterfly Display

Entomologists (scientists who study insects) preserve insects to learn about their anatomy. It is important not to destroy the important identifying characteristics of an insect's body when you prepare it for display. Follow the steps below:

1. Prepare a display box with a plastic foam base to use for pinning and mounting your butterfly.
2. Lay the butterfly faceup on the plastic foam. Gently relax the wings open. Make sure they are pressed flat against the foam.
3. Place a pin through the thorax, or center body part, of the butterfly and into the plastic foam to hold it securely in place.
4. Next, place the butterfly in the freezer for several days until it is completely dry.
5. Place a pin between each of the bases of the forewings.
6. Finally, label your butterfly. Create labels for its antennae, head, wings, thorax, and abdomen. Then secure the display box. Your butterfly display is complete!

1. What topic do both passages discuss?

   A. how butterfly wings function

   B. the body structure of butterflies

   C. preserving butterflies

   D. why butterflies have antennae

 The answer will apply to both passages.

2. What is the main difference between the passages?

   A. One is a science text, and the other is a how-to text.

   B. One is a science text, and the other is an opinion article.

   C. One is a news article, and the other is a science text.

   D. One gives only facts, while the other contains opinions.

HINT Think about how the author presents the information in each text.

3. Tell how each passage helps you understand more about butterflies.

_____

_____

_____

_____

HINT How are the facts and details different in each passage?

Lesson Practice

Use the Reading Guides to help you understand the passages.

Reading Guide

What is the main topic of the passage?

What is the author's purpose?

How is the text structured?

Owls of North America

The burrowing owl is found in central and western North America. These owls have brown and white feathers and large yellow eyes. They have no ear tufts, and their heads and bodies are round and stubby. Burrowing owls are seen quite frequently because they live in low, open areas. These ground-dwelling owls are usually found on prairies and grasslands where there are few trees. As their name suggests, burrowing owls dig holes in the ground where they nest.

Burrowing owls make different calls. The call of the male owl sounds like a deep "cu-cuhooh." The female owl's call is like the male's song, but the pitch is slightly higher. If their nests are bothered, they make a hissing sound to protect their babies. They feed on insects, reptiles, and small mammals such as mice, rats, and squirrels.

The barn owl is also found in North America. The barn owl looks different from most owls because of its heart-shaped face and characteristic white color. Barn owls have long, lanky bodies and a wide wingspan, which helps them fly gracefully. Their heads are round without ear tufts, and their eyes are dark. Barn owls are found in marshes, grasslands, and agricultural fields. They can be found nesting and roosting in large, dark covered areas, such as barns and abandoned buildings. The barn owl's call can sound like a low, steady hiss, and a short, high-pitched screech. They eat small mammals like mice and rats. Rarely, they eat reptiles.

Most owls, like the barn owl, are nocturnal. This means they hunt during the night and sleep during the day. Burrowing owls, however, hunt during the early morning and at dusk.

Owl Sighting

May 5, 2015

Yesterday I drove out to the Grant Park Nature Reserve again to try to take a video of the greater prairie chicken that I had seen last week. Armed with my binoculars and my camera phone, I was hoping to catch one of the males doing its unique dance. Now that I had seen the dance once, I could recognize the sound if I heard it. The males drum their feet and make a noise that can be heard from more than a mile away!

I wasn't able to get out to the reserve as early as I would have liked. It was dusk by the time I arrived, but there was still about forty-five minutes of daylight left. It was nice being in the grasslands at that hour. It was cool, and the grasses swayed in the breeze as I walked quietly along the trail.

After about twenty minutes, I hadn't heard any sounds of the prairie chickens, but I did catch sight of something interesting. I saw what appeared to be a short, fat bird in the distance, searching the ground. It looked like an owl, but I couldn't be sure. It was brown and had white spots.

When I got closer, I heard a hissing sound. It was an owl! I must have stepped near its nest. I took a quick picture and then hustled away, leaving it alone. From the distance, with the little daylight I had left, I took more pictures. I am excited to show them to my friends at the Birdwatcher's Society tomorrow.

Answer the following questions.

1. What text structure BEST describes "Owl Sighting"?

   A. compare and contrast

   B. chronological

   C. cause and effect

   D. problem and solution

2. Which of the following is true of the burrowing owl?

   A. It is nocturnal like most owls.

   B. It has a white, heart-shaped face.

   C. It hunts during dawn and at dusk.

   D. It lives in barns.

3. What is the genre of "Owls of North America"?

   A. science article

   B. opinion article

   C. e-mail

   D. letter

4. What main event does the author describe in "Owl Sighting"?

   A. seeing a prairie chicken dance

   B. unexpectedly coming upon an owl

   C. using a camera phone to take videos of birds

   D. being a member of the Birdwatcher's Society

5. Based on the information in both passages, what kind of owl did the author of "Owl Sighting" most likely see? Explain why.

   _____

   _____

   _____

Use the Reading Guides to help you understand the passages.

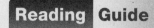

Reading Guide

Pay attention to the facts provided in the passage.

What clues do you have that help you identify the genre of this passage?

How do organisms use bioluminescence?

Bioluminescence

Bioluminescence is light that is released by an organism. This glow is caused by a chemical reaction that occurs inside a living organism. Bioluminescence is sometimes referred to as "cold light." Unlike other chemical reactions, bioluminescence does not create heat.

Bioluminescence occurs in a variety of organisms, including bacteria, fungi, insects, and marine life. Inside the organism, chemical energy is converted into radiant energy, which gives the organism a glow. Organisms "bioluminesce" for protection and mating. In lower organisms such as bacteria, scientists believe bioluminescence may be related to an organisms' metabolism, or digestion.

Bioluminescence can help protect an organism from predators and other threats. Squids, for example, secrete bioluminescent clouds when predators draw near. The clouds confuse predators, and the squids are able to swim away. Some fish use bioluminescence to attract prey to their glowing light or as a disguise. Other fish simply use bioluminescence to light their way in the darkness of the deep ocean.

Some organisms use their bioluminescence to signal other organisms during mating. The male North American firefly, for example, flashes a bioluminescent light while flying to signal females below. When a female sees the flash, she responds with her own specific light pattern.

The color of bioluminescence can vary depending on the environment in which it occurs. In the ocean, for instance, bioluminescence appears a blue-green color. These happen to be the colors that are most visible in the deep ocean. They are also the only colors that most marine organisms are sensitive to. On land, bioluminescence can appear blue, but it is more often seen as yellow, like fireflies.

Night Diving Adventure

Reading Guide

Which passage best helps you understand bioluminescence?

Which passage contains more descriptive language?

Which passage contains more facts?

Come experience the best night dive in Hawaii! Our night water dive eco-adventure is like no other. Diving isn't just for daytime. During our night dives, the ocean comes alive with shimmering and shining creatures!

Journey with us over two miles off the Kona coast of Hawaii to see this ocean "light show" that occurs every night! After a leisurely drive to this magical spot, you will dive from our boat to depths of nearly forty feet. Our experienced guides will make sure you are safely tied to the boat before you descend into the warm ocean waters. From there, you will have a front row seat for the action!

Incredible sea creatures will swim, slide, and shimmer their way through the ocean water. Jellyfish, fish, and bacteria are just some of the incredible bioluminescent creatures you will see. Their eerie "glow" will mesmerize you. Touch the mysterious manta rays—they will greet you with their undulating wingspans before quickly gliding away. Watch the jellyfish swell and inflate like tiny marine blimps. Let yourself drift with the ocean currents as you witness spectacular beauty!

Once you come back up on the boat, our knowledgeable guides will explain the science behind these fantastic wonders. They'll describe how bioluminescent creatures use their "glow" to hunt for prey, defend themselves against predators, and signal potential mates in the deep ocean.

Back at the dock, a 30-minute video from a marine biologist is available for those who are interested in learning more about these fabulous creatures and their bioluminescence! Come with us—you won't want to miss Hawaii's most fantastic wonder!

Answer the following questions.

6.   Read this paragraph and answer the questions that follow.

>   Bioluminescence can help protect an organism from predators and other threats. Squids, for example, secrete bioluminescent clouds when predators draw near. The clouds confuse predators, and the squids are able to swim away. Some fish use bioluminescence to attract prey to their glowing light or as a disguise. Other fish simply use bioluminescence to light their way in the darkness of the deep ocean.

Part A

What problem does bioluminescence solve?

A.   It makes predators go away.

B.   It creates light.

C.   It protects animals.

D.   It attracts prey.

Part B

What detail from the paragraph BEST supports your answer in Part A?

A.   "Bioluminescence can help protect an organism from predators and other threats."

B.   "Squids, for example, secrete bioluminescent clouds when predators draw near."

C.   "Other fish simply use bioluminescence to light their way in the darkness of the deep ocean."

D.   "Some fish use bioluminescence to attract prey to their glowing light or as a disguise."

7. Below are three statements that could be made about the passages.

Statements	entertaining to read
	describes the occurrence of bioluminescence
	contains no opinions

Part A

Circle the statement that can be made about BOTH of the passages.

Part B

Circle details in both passages that support the statement you circled in Part A.

8. Write the words from the word box in the correct locations on the Venn diagram to compare and contrast the characteristics of each passage.

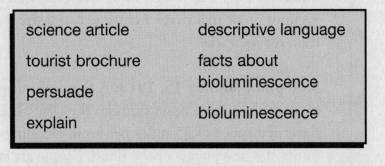

science article   descriptive language

tourist brochure   facts about
                         bioluminescence
persuade

explain   bioluminescence

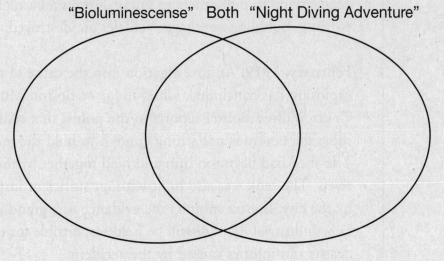

"Bioluminescense"   Both   "Night Diving Adventure"

Use the Reading Guides to help you understand the passages.

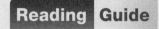

How does the text structure help you understand the passage?

What details help you understand why the explosion occurred?

Look for clues that tell you the author's purpose.

The Great Molasses Flood of 1919: A Chronology

9:00 a.m., January 15, 1919: Boston residents awaken to an unusually warm winter day. It is 45 degrees Fahrenheit outside. A 50 ft. tall metal tank stands in the North End district of Boston. Pressure from 2,300,000 gallons of molasses inside the tank is about to reach a critical point. The owners of the tank, U.S. Industrial Alcohol, had been warned months before that the tank was leaking.

12:30 ap.m., January 15, 1919: Workers begin to hear a rumbling sound and then the sound of screeching metal. The half-inch thick metal rivets holding the tank together blow apart. Flying metal tears through the air. Nearby buildings topple to the ground. The explosion causes a vacuum of air that drags a truck across a street and pulls a train off its tracks.

3:00 p.m., January 15, 1919: A flood of molasses 15 ft. high in places now flows through the city. The molasses flows at a speed of 35 miles per hour. Buildings are flattened under the heavy mass of the flood. People are stuck, waist-deep, trying to pull others to safety. Horses are caught in the swirling, bubbling wreckage. Vehicles are destroyed.

February, 1919: An investigation into the cause of the explosion has concluded. Chief Judge of Boston Municipal Court Wilfred Bolster reports to the public that results show the tank was not strong enough to hold the molasses. The shell had been too thin and held together by too few rivets. The tank was also built without sufficient inspection by the city. Bolster submits the evidence to a grand jury. U.S. Industrial Alcohol will be held responsible for the deaths and injuries caused by the accident.

Reading Guide

What does this passage add to what you already know about the explosion in the first passage?

How is the information in this passage organized?

Tank of Molasses Explodes in Boston

Boston, Jan. 15, 1919 - An explosion of a huge tank of molasses occurred earlier today on Commercial Street near the waterfront in the North End of Boston. The tank was owned by U.S. Industrial Alcohol Company.

Witnesses reported hearing a dull, muffled roar before the tank exploded. Then they heard a sharp, screeching sound. They described the top of the tank being blown off first, followed by the circular wall of the tank. They reported that the wall was broken into two large segments that were pulled apart in opposite directions by the force of the molasses.

Over two million gallons of molasses flowed into the streets. Some estimated the molasses flowed at a rate of thirty-five miles per hour. The explosion smashed several buildings in the vicinity. One city building where workers were eating their lunch was completely demolished. One section of the tank's metal walls fell on the roof of a firehouse, crushing the firehouse to the ground.

A number of wagons, carts, and motor vehicles were crushed and overturned. Debris and molasses choked the nearby streets and stopped traffic. A group of children on their way home from the Michelangelo School were picked up by the wave of molasses and carried several yards before tumbling to safety. Officials have not yet determined when the molasses will be cleaned up.

First responders included a squad under the direction of Lieutenant Commander H. J. Copeland, which were stationed on the school ship Nantucket, anchored at the playground pier nearby. They offered first aid and other assistance to victims and patrolled the district. Police reserves as well as a military company from an army station arrived shortly after, along with Red Cross volunteers.

Answer the following questions.

9. What is the genre of "Tank of Molasses Explodes in Boston"?

   A. memoir

   B. informational article

   C. newspaper article

   D. historical account

10. What is the main difference between the passages?

   A. facts and opinions

   B. text structure and genre

   C. use of persuasive language

   D. dates of the events

11. Which statement about the passages is correct?

   A. Both passages tell the order of events.

   B. Both passages have the same details.

   C. Both passages have the same topic.

   D. Both passages describe the first responders.

12. What is the author's purpose in "The Great Molasses Flood of 1919: A Chronology"?

   A. to provide a timeline of the events

   B. to explain how the disaster happened

   C. to give a personal account of the day

   D. to tell about the people involved in the disaster

13. Read this sentence from "Tank of Molasses Explodes in Boston."

   Then they heard a sharp, screeching sound.

   Based on information from "The Great Molasses Flood of 1919: A Chronology," this was most likely

   A. the sound of a street car being pulled off its tracks.

   B. the sound of the molasses beginning to pour out of the tank.

   C. the sound of the rivets holding the tank together tearing apart.

   D. the sound of a building's roof collapsing.

14. Explain how the information in both passages helps you understand the cause and effect of the molasses tank explosion. Use evidence from each passage to support your answer.

_____

_____

_____

_____

_____

_____

_____

_____

_____

_____

_____

2 Cumulative Assessment

Read the passage and answer the questions that follow.

John James Audubon

Many people have painted the birds of America, but John James Audubon is said to be the greatest artist ever to have done so. His famous book, *The Birds of America*, is a collection of 435 paintings. These detailed paintings are considered to be the best. For that reason, people judge other wildlife artists by comparing them to Audubon.

Audubon was born on April 26, 1785, in Les Cayes, Santo Domingo (now Haiti). He was the son of a French sea captain and a servant. His mother died when he was still a baby. In 1789, he was taken to France, where he was raised by his father and stepmother. The young Audubon had a happy childhood. He studied math and geography, but he took a greater interest in nature. He loved birds. He spent hours collecting and drawing birds' nests and eggs.

In 1803, at the age of eighteen, Audubon was sent to America. He managed Mill Grove, his family's farm near Philadelphia. He studied and drew birds there. He also met his future wife, Lucy Bakewell. The couple married in 1808. During that time, Audubon performed one of the earliest experiments with banding birds in North America. He tied strings around the legs of one species of migrating bird. By doing this, he learned that the birds returned to the same places to nest every year.

Audubon spent more than ten years at Mill Grove. Then, he traveled down the Ohio River to Henderson, Kentucky, where he opened a store. Still, he continued to draw birds as a hobby. In 1820, Audubon decided to publish a book of bird illustrations. He began collecting and drawing with that goal in mind. Audubon set off on his quest to draw all of America's birds. He traveled first to the South, bringing along his art supplies and an assistant. He had been working mainly with pastels, but around this time, he began to use more watercolors.

In 1826, Audubon sailed to England in hopes of finding a way to publish his book. He successfully showed his work at the Royal Institution in Liverpool. He soon began his project of creating life-size, dramatic portraits of American birds. These portraits showed the birds as they appeared in real life, eating or flying. Audubon traveled back and forth between England and the United States many times over the next few years.

His work, *The Birds of America*, contained 435 hand-colored pictures. It showed a portrait of every bird then known in the United States. Most people were used to seeing birds shown simply, against a blank background. Some people objected to Audubon's use of dramatic poses and settings. Yet his attempt to show birds as they actually looked in the wild was very important. Today, Audubon's colorful paintings are widely admired. Art lovers appreciate their liveliness and realistic qualities.

Audubon had spent eighteen years searching for and observing the birds, creating his book, and selling it to subscribers. After that huge effort, he traveled across the United States a few more times in search of birds. Some say that he saw more of the North American continent than anyone else had before. During his lifetime, he discovered twenty-five new species of birds. He also produced a version of *The Birds of America* that was made up of illustrations that were reduced in size. This book was quite successful. It allowed the artist to retire in comfort. Now famous, Audubon spent his last years in New York City. He died there on January 27, 1851, at the age of sixty-five.

John James Audubon had no relationship with the Audubon Society, an organization that bears his name today. But the name *Audubon* is still connected with birds and nature conservation all over the world.

Some Birds Painted by Audubon

Bird	Appearance	Where It Lives in North America	Interesting Fact
Ivory-billed woodpecker	black and white streaks, red crown, long white bill	southeastern and south central American states	It is the largest woodpecker in North America.
Bald eagle	dark brown body, white head and tail	most of North America	Its name comes from *piebald*, meaning "spotted" or "patchy," which is how bald eagles look when young.
California condor	triangular patches of white on undersides of wings	Southern California, Arizona	It is one of the largest birds in the world.
Brown pelican	brown body, white head, large bill and pouch	southern and Gulf coasts	It is known for its seven-foot wingspan and can live over forty years.
Barn owl	round face, stubby body, long wingspan	everywhere, except polar and desert areas	It is known for its beautiful plumage and graceful flight.

1. According to the passage, what happened LAST?

   A. Audubon was sent to America.

   B. Audubon moved to New York City.

   C. Audubon was taken to France.

   D. Audubon moved to Kentucky.

2. What is the main idea of this passage?

   A. John James Audubon had no relationship with the Audubon Society.

   B. John James Audubon was America's leading wildlife artist for fifty years.

   C. John James Audubon saw more of the North American continent than anyone else had before.

   D. John James Audubon learned that some birds return to the same nesting sites each year.

3. Both the chart and the passage provide evidence that

   A. Audubon only painted extinct or endangered species of birds.

   B. Audubon won many awards in his lifetime.

   C. Audubon traveled widely to paint different birds.

   D. Audubon was a difficult, unpleasant person.

4. What is the MAIN text structure the writer uses in this passage?

   A. cause and effect

   B. comparison

   C. problem and solution

   D. chronology

Read the passage and answer the questions that follow.

"American White Pelican"
excerpted and adapted from
The Birds of America
by John James Audubon

I feel great pleasure, good reader, in telling you something. Until now, our white pelican has been seen as the same bird as the one found in Europe. But it is quite different. As a result of this discovery, I have honored it with the name of my country. May this splendid bird wander free over its mighty streams.

I first moved to Kentucky more than thirty years ago. At that time, I often saw these birds on the banks of the Ohio River. A few years later, I moved to the town of Henderson. There were so many white pelicans there that I often saw dozens at a time. I found them on a sandbar that protects Canoe Creek Island. During those pleasant days of my youth, how often did I watch them with delight! I think those days have returned to me now. This has allowed me once more to read the scattered notes contained in my treasured journals. Here is one such page:

A hundred large pelicans stand near the sides of the sandbar. They are in small groups. Gorgeous fall colors enrich the leaves of every tree. Their reflections are like fragments of the rainbow. They seem to fill the very depths of the calm and almost sleeping waters of the Ohio River. The red beams of the sun assure me that the Indian summer has started. This happy season is lovely and still. It is also a symbol of the later years of life. To every nature lover, it must be the purest and calmest period of his career.

The full pelicans are patient. They wait for the return of hunger. Should someone chance to watch, one after the other they open their long and broad bills and yawn lazily. Now, the whole length of their largest quills is passed through the bill. At last their feathers are beautifully trimmed. But look! The red beams of the setting sun color the tops of the forest trees. The birds feel the cravings of hunger. To satisfy themselves, they must now work. They rise clumsily on their long legs and waddle heavily to the water. But now, how changed they seem! How lightly they float! They patrol themselves and extend their line. Now, like paddles, their broad feet push them onward.

In another spot, the young birds are dancing in the quiet water. Perhaps in their own way they are bidding farewell to the sun. Or maybe they are seeking something for their supper. There are thousands of them, and they are all happy. The very manner of their joy causes the waters to sparkle. It invites the small fish to come closer, to swim in shallow water. Now the pelicans are aware of their fishy prey. At once, they spread out their broad wings. They press forward with powerful strokes of their feet. They drive the little fishes toward the shore. Then, with the huge pouches under their bills wide open, the pelicans scoop the fishes out and eat them by the thousands.

American white pelican, from *The Birds of America*, by John James Audubon

5. Which is the BEST summary of the passage?

   A. The author remembers a time when he watched a group of pelicans.

   B. The author tells how he discovered a new kind of bird.

   C. The author describes how pelicans eat fish.

   D. The author tells about life in Kentucky.

6. Reading through his journals and notebooks, the writer MOST LIKELY feels

   A. sad and lonely.

   B. eager to fight for animal rights.

   C. happy and content.

   D. bored and dissatisfied.

7. Which of the following is a fact from the passage?

   A. "A few years later, I moved to the town of Henderson."

   B. "I feel great pleasure, good reader, in telling you something."

   C. "Gorgeous fall colors enrich the leaves of every tree."

   D. "There are thousands of them, and they are all happy."

8. What does the word <u>quills</u> mean?

   A. beams

   B. feathers

   C. legs

   D. birds

Use "John James Audubon" and "American White Pelican" to answer questions 9–10.

9. Compare the two passages. How does information in the first passage give readers a better understanding of information in the second passage?

_____

_____

_____

_____

_____

_____

_____

10. Which passage could be used as a source for the other passage? Explain.

_____

_____

_____

_____

_____

_____

_____

CHAPTER

3 Writing

Chapter 3: Diagnostic Assessment

Chapter 3: Cumulative Assessment

3 Diagnostic Assessment

This passage contains mistakes. Read the passage and answer the questions that follow.

Snowed In

(1) Although the curtains were still closed, Misha could tell it was a bright, sunny day outside. (2) He also knew that it must be very cold. (3) He could hear the sounds of children shouting and laughing. (4) He heard the swishing of their sleds as they zipped down the hill. (5) Misha's dog was named Scout.

(6) Misha looked at his mother. (7) She was standing beside his bed holding a thermometer in her hand. (8) "Did it snow a lot last night?" he asked.

(9) "Yes, more than two feet—which is a new record," she said. (10) "Now open up so I can take your temperature."

(11) The bulb of the thermometer felt icy and slightly bitter under Misha's tongue. (12) Although Misha was sick, the last thing he felt like doing was staying in bed. (13) Now he was getting antsy. (14) His friends was having so much fun! (15) He <u>desperatly</u> wanted to go out and play in the snow, too. (16) He'd been in bed for two whole days.

(17) "Am I still running a fever?" he asked his mother.

(18) "Yes, Misha," his mother said. (19) "I'm sorry to tell you this, but you still have a fever. (20) That means you'll have to stay in bed until you get better."

(21) Misha felt his heart sink. (22) There was nothing in the world more exciting than playing with his friends, but he knew it was out of the question. (23) He pulled the blankets back up over him. (24) He sunk down into his pillows. (25) This was hard.

(26) That evening, Misha ate dinner. (27) He watched a little TV. (28) Then he read a book and fell asleep. (29) Misha awoke the next morning and feels much better. (30) His mother took his temperature just as she had the day before. (31) His curtains were closed. (32) Yet he could hear the children out on the hill, laughing and having fun.

(33) "You don't have a temperature any more," his mother said. (34) "How do you feel?"

(35) "I feel great!" Misha said. (36) "Can I go out and play now?"

(37) "Yes," his mother replied, smiling. (38) "Go out and have fun!"

1. Which sentence does NOT belong in paragraph 1?

    A. "He also knew that it must be very cold."

    B. "He could hear the sounds of children shouting and laughing."

    C. "He heard the swishing of their sleds as they zipped down the hill."

    D. "Misha's dog was named Scout."

2. Which sentence is the BEST revision of sentence 29?

    A. When Misha awoke the next morning, he felt much better.

    B. Misha awakes in the morning and feels much better.

    C. Misha was awake in the morning and felt much better.

    D. If Misha awoke the next morning, he felt much better.

3. Which sentence has incorrect subject-verb agreement?

   A. Then he read a book and fell asleep.

   B. His friends was having so much fun!

   C. Misha felt his heart sink.

   D. His mother took his temperature just as she had the day before.

4. What is the correct spelling of the underlined word in sentence 15?

   A. desperately

   B. despertly

   C. desperatelee

   D. desperatelly

5. Which is the BEST way to reorder paragraph 4?

   A. Move sentence 15 before sentence 14.

   B. Move sentence 12 before sentence 11.

   C. Move sentence 16 before sentence 13.

   D. Move sentence 15 before sentence 12.

6. Which of the following is the BEST way to paraphrase sentence 11?

   A. The thermometer felt weird.

   B. The cold bulb of the thermometer tasted bitter.

   C. Misha hates being sick and feels cold.

   D. The thermometer felt cold and tasted bitter in Misha's mouth.

Narrative Prompt

Write a story about a boy (or a girl) who wakes up one day and discovers he or she has superpowers. Be sure to include characters, a setting, and events in your story. Include description and dialogue to make your story interesting.

Use the checklist below to help you do your best writing.

Does your story

❏ have a situation and characters?
❏ use dialogue and description to develop the story?
❏ have a clear plot?
❏ use good word choice?
❏ have a satisfying ending?
❏ have good spelling, capitalization, and punctuation?
❏ follow the rules for good grammar?

Write your response on the page provided. You may use your own paper if you need more space.

17 Writing Opinions

Getting the Idea

We write to express our ideas, thoughts, and feelings. An **opinion** is a statement about how you feel about something. Here are some examples of opinions: *Our school needs a new gymnasium. Science is the best subject. Everyone should eat cereal for breakfast.* Each of these statements is a personal belief. They cannot be proven, and other people may disagree with them.

An **argument** is piece of writing that states and defends an opinion. The purpose of an argument is to persuade, or convince, your audience to agree with your opinion.

An effective argument takes a clear position on a topic. You begin by stating your opinion or view in a **position statement**. Suppose you are writing an argument to persuade your school principal to buy new uniforms for the baseball team. Here are two examples of possible position statements for that argument:

Strong Position Statement	Weak Position Statement
Our baseball team's uniforms need to be replaced because they are worn-out and out of style.	I think our baseball team's uniforms sometimes look bad, so the team probably needs new uniforms.

The strong position statement takes a definite stand on the issue. The writing is specific and clear. The weak position statement uses words like *sometimes* and *probably*. The writer does not seem so sure of his opinion.

After writing your position statement, you need to back up it up with reasons that are supported by facts and details. Finally, provide a **concluding statement** to sum up your argument.

Use a graphic organizer to help you plan your essay. An **outline** is a "skeleton" of your essay in list form. In the outline below, the position statement and concluding statement are numbered I and II. You can include as many reasons and details as you want.

I. Our baseball team's uniforms need to be replaced because they are worn-out and out of style.

   A. Uniforms are worn-out.

      1. Some have holes in them.

      2. Some do not fit properly because they are stretched out or shrunken.

   B. Uniforms are out of style.

      1. They do not look like most other teams' baseball uniforms.

      2. The colors of the uniforms do not match the school's colors.

II. If we want to support our baseball team and give them confidence, then they need great new uniforms!

Think about the style of your writing, too. There is a time for an **informal style** of writing, which is more relaxed, familiar, and casual. Most people text and e-mail with friends in an informal style. A **formal style** of writing is more proper, impersonal, and polite. You are trying to convince your audience to agree with your opinion, so remember to write in a formal and respectful tone.

Formal	Informal
Please consider getting us new uniforms this year.	You need to get us cool new duds.

Use **transitions** to achieve a smooth flow of ideas. Use transitional phrases such as *in addition* and *for example* to introduce your reasons and details. Use words such as *first, then, next, however,* and *finally* to connect sentences and paragraphs. That way, your audience will be able to follow your argument more easily.

Finally, carefully proofread your writing. Check for any errors in grammar, spelling, and punctuation, and be sure to correct them.

Coached Example

Read the position statements below. Then rewrite each one so that the positions are clearer to the reader.

> **1.** I think we should get a hamster for a pet, or maybe a bird. I have always wanted a dog, too.

_____

_____

_____

_____

 The writer mentions too many pets. Which pet does the writer really want, and why?

> **2.** I love salad. The cafeteria better give us salad more often.

_____

_____

_____

_____

 This writer does not use a formal style. The audience is probably the principal of the school. How should you write for this kind of audience?

Lesson Practice

Use the Writing Guide to help you understand the passage.

Writing Guide

The writer's position is clearly stated right away.

Notice the formal language the writer uses. Words such as *please* and *consider* are appropriate for this audience.

Notice how transitional words like *first* and *in addition* connect parts of the writing.

Each paragraph has a strong opening sentence followed by details that support the main idea.

Sports for All!

Every student should be required to play a sport. While kids should be allowed to choose the sport they prefer, everyone should play something for at least one season. Some people may think that students who don't like sports should not be required to play, but I think that kids should choose a sport that they like. Please consider making all students join a team. There are so many benefits to sports!

First, playing a sport is a great way to exercise regularly. Exercise is an important part of a healthy lifestyle. Some kids just play video games on the weekends. Sports would help them be more active. Rather than just staying in all day, kids could run around outside and enjoy the fresh air!

In addition, being on a sports team helps build a strong school community. It can be nice to get to know your fellow classmates outside of the classroom. People could make new friends through sports. Usually, students just hang out with the same people every day. Playing a sport forces you to interact with new people.

Write a concluding statement for this argument.

_____

_____

_____

_____

HINT What examples does the writer use to support his position? A strong concluding statement should sum up those reasons.

Plan Your Writing

Read the writing prompt, and then plan your response below.

> Think about all the things you like to do in your spare time. Some people play sports. Others play a musical instrument. And some may prefer writing or creating art. Imagine your school is looking for a new after-school activity. Write a letter to your principal in which you propose a new after-school activity. Include reasons, facts, and details that convince the principal to agree with your opinion.

I. Position statement: _____

_____

A. Reason: _____

_____

    1. Detail: _____

_____

    2. Detail: _____

_____

B. Reason: _____

_____

    1. Detail: _____

_____

    2. Detail: _____

_____

II. Concluding statement: _____

_____

Write Your Response

Write your response on the pages provided.

Opinion Writing Checklist

Use the checklist below to help you do your best writing.

Does your letter

❏ have a clear topic?

❏ show a point of view about that topic?

❏ have a logical structure?

❏ support reasons with details?

❏ connect reasons and details with the right words or phrases?

❏ use transition phrases properly?

❏ use a style and vocabulary that are correct for the audience and purpose?

❏ have a solid concluding statement?

❏ have good spelling, capitalization, and punctuation?

❏ follow the rules for good grammar?

Use the Writing Guide to help you understand the passage.

Writing Guide

What is the writer's position on energy drinks?

Does the writer use formal or informal language? Give examples that support your answer.

Identify transition words from the passage.

How does the conclusion restate the author's position?

The Case Against Energy Drinks

Energy drinks are advertised as an alternative to coffee. They promise plenty of natural energy to accomplish tasks. Some people love a quick energy boost, but I think these drinks are more harmful than healthful.

Most energy drinks don't contain harmful ingredients. For example, when consumed in small amounts, caffeine is safe. It interacts with our nervous system to make us more alert and sharpen our senses. The danger in energy drinks lies in the *amounts* of the ingredients. Most adults can safely consume up to 400 milligrams of caffeine per day. The levels of caffeine in popular energy drinks can be more than 200 milligrams per serving. Now consider that some bottles of energy drinks have more than one serving. One bottle packs a huge caffeine punch! Too much caffeine won't simply keep you awake. In addition to making you jumpy, it can increase your heart rate and raise your blood pressure.

The truth is that most energy drinks provide energy through caffeine and sugar! Sugar might provide a short burst of energy, but too much sugar leads to weight gain. Consuming too much sugar can also cause diabetes, which is becoming a big problem in the United States.

Studies have shown that the best way for a person to maintain a good energy level is through diet and exercise. A balanced, nutritious diet has great benefits, and the energy it provides is not just a "boost." Likewise, a steady program of exercise helps you feel better all day and sleep better at night. If we can maintain great energy levels naturally, we certainly don't need energy drinks.

Plan Your Writing

Read the information and the writing prompt, and then plan your response on the next page.

Some reasons to discontinue publishing the yearbook include:

- Students post pictures on social media, so a yearbook is not necessary.
- Digital photos can be collected and stored on the school's Web site for everyone to access.
- The school newspaper publishes an end-of-year issue that is similar to the yearbook.
- Discontinuing the yearbook will save money for the school and the students.

Some reasons to continue publishing the yearbook include:

- Students participate in various activities. A yearbook shows them all in one publication.
- A yearbook includes interviews with teachers and notable students, as well as stories about clubs, dances, fundraisers, and special achievements.
- Reading the yearbook allows students to learn more about their school and their peers.
- Friends and teachers can sign a yearbook, and an actual book can last forever.

Using the information provided above, write a letter to your principal arguing to continue or to discontinue publishing the yearbook. Include facts, reasons, and details to support your opinion.

I.   Position statement: _____

_____

A.   Reason: _____

_____

    1.   Detail: _____

_____

    2.   Detail: _____

_____

B.   Reason: _____

_____

    1.   Detail: _____

_____

    2.   Detail: _____

_____

II.   Concluding statement: _____

_____

Write Your Response

Write your response on the pages provided.

Opinion Writing Checklist

Use the checklist below to help you do your best writing.

Does your letter

❏ have a clear topic?

❏ show a point of view about that topic?

❏ have a logical structure?

❏ support reasons with details?

❏ connect reasons and details with the right words or phrases?

❏ use transition phrases properly?

❏ use a style and vocabulary that are correct for the audience and purpose?

❏ have a solid concluding statement?

❏ have good spelling, capitalization, and punctuation?

❏ follow the rules for good grammar?

18 Writing Informational Texts

Getting the Idea

The purpose of an **informational text** is to provide the reader with facts and details about a topic. You read informational texts every day. When you read from your science or social studies textbooks, you are reading informational texts. Newspapers are filled with informational text. You probably also write informational texts in the form of reports for school.

When writing an informational piece, you should begin with a clear statement of your topic, provide facts and details to support that topic, and close with a **concluding statement** about the information you just explained.

One kind of graphic organizer you can use to help you plan your informational writing is a **web**. For example, suppose you were planning to write an informative paragraph about the country of Brazil. Your completed web might look like this:

The main topic is shown in the center circle. The subtopics are categories of information about Brazil—its cities, climate, special events, and landscape. They are connected to the main circle. The outer circles contain details about each subtopic.

Once you have organized your text, it is time to write. You will probably want to add small details as you put your information into sentences. Your **topic sentence** should clearly state what your paragraph is about. For example, if you write "Brazil is an interesting country in South America," details should include the specific kinds of weather and the names of the cities.

In longer informational articles, the text is often divided into sections with bold **headings** that say what the section is about. Each paragraph should have a topic sentence that tells what that paragraph is mainly about. Each sentence that follows should provide information that supports the topic sentence. For example, you can use any of the following:

- Fact: a true statement about something that can be proved
- Detail: descriptive information about a topic
- Quotation: specific words said by someone. The speaker's words are put in quotation marks. For example: President Franklin D. Roosevelt said, "The only thing we have to fear is fear itself."
- Example: something that represents the point you are trying to make. If you were writing about good citizenship, you could include voting as an example.

Connect your facts, details, quotations, and examples with linking words, as shown in the chart below.

If you want to show...	use transitions like...
comparison	similarly, also, like
difference, or contrast	on the other hand, but, however
examples	for example, for instance
more examples	in addition to, as well, further

Try to use the vocabulary, or words, that fit the subject area you are writing about. For example, in science, some words might include *data* or *experiments*. *Data* is information. *Experiments* are tests or trials to prove something. In social studies, some terms might include: *population* (how many people live in a location), *government* (the people running a country or state), *culture*, or *transportation*.

Watch for any mistakes in grammar, spelling, and punctuation. To pass on correct information to your readers, it is best to write it in the clearest way possible.

Coached Example

Read the paragraphs and answer the questions.

> Alligators have long bodies and short legs. Their feet are webbed, which helps them swim. Alligators are fierce hunters who eat only meat.

1. **Write a topic sentence for this paragraph.**

_____

_____

_____

_____

 A topic sentence tells what the whole paragraph is about.

> A food chain shows how living things get and use energy. Simple food chains exist in our own backyards. The grass uses the sun's energy to make food. A bird eats grass from the lawn. Then your neighbor's cat eats the bird. Most cats eat fish. That's a food chain!

2. **Which sentence does NOT support the topic sentence of the paragraph?**

_____

_____

_____

_____

 Think about what the main idea of the paragraph is. Find the sentence that does not relate to that idea.

Lesson Practice

Use the Writing Guide to help you understand the passage.

Owning a Pet

Many families own pets and enjoy caring for them. The responsibilities of owning a pet are often shared by children and parents. There are some things to keep in mind when you open up your heart and home to a new pet.

First, decide what kind of pet to get. If you live in a small apartment, a large dog that needs room to run around is not the best choice. Dogs need to go on walks. If this is a job that you cannot commit to, then a pet that does not need walking would be better for your lifestyle. For example, a cat, a hamster, or fish are possibilities.

In order for a pet to stay healthy, it needs to get enough exercise. Pets also need the right kind and right amount of food. An animal's diet is usually also based on how large, how active, and how old it is. The wrong diet can make a pet overweight, lazy, or sick.

Most people agree that owning a pet involves a lot of work. But if you ask any pet owners, they will say it is well worth it!

What is the main idea of this informational text?

_____

_____

_____

_____

_____

HINT Look for the topic sentence at the beginning of the passage.

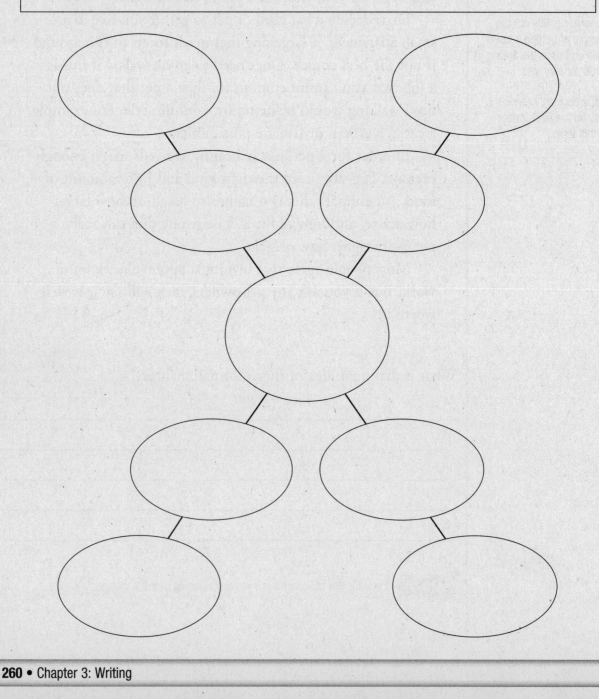

Plan Your Writing

Read the writing prompt, and then plan your response below.

Choose a place that you like to visit. For example, it could be a relative's house, a park, or someplace farther away that you have been to with your family. Write an informative piece about this place. Tell where it is, what it looks like, and what you do there. Include details about the place to support your writing.

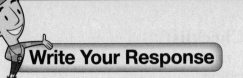

Write Your Response

Write your response on the pages provided.

_____

_____

_____

_____

_____

_____

_____

_____

_____

_____

_____

_____

_____

_____

_____

_____

_____

_____

_____

_____

_____

_____

_____

_____

Informational Text Writing Checklist

Use the checklist below to help you do your best writing.

Does your informational essay

❏ have a clear and focused subject?

❏ have a strong topic sentence?

❏ have a logical structure?

❏ present information clearly?

❏ use linking words and phrases to join ideas?

❏ use a style and vocabulary that are correct for the audience and purpose?

❏ have a solid conclusion?

❏ have good spelling, capitalization, and punctuation?

❏ follow the rules for good grammar?

Use the Writing Guide to help you understand the passage.

Writing Guide

What is the passage about?

Identify one example of how to keep a social networking account safe.

Find an example of linking words in the passage. What do these linking words show?

Social Networking Tips

Social networking is a popular method for connecting with family and friends. You can make sure that the experience is a positive one by taking a few simple steps.

Safety All sites include safety features, such as passwords. Too many people use passwords that are simple to figure out, such as their birthday, pet's name, or address. The strongest passwords use a combination of characters: numbers, letters, and punctuation marks. Once you have a strong password, don't share it. Be sure to sign out of each site when you are finished.

Privacy Remember that the automatic setting for many sites is public—what you share online can be viewed by anyone. Most sites have privacy settings that you can change. The safest settings are those that allow only people you approve to view your posts. If you have trouble understanding the privacy settings, read the FAQ ("Frequently Asked Questions") section or contact a representative of the site to help you.

Verify Before you accept someone into your social networking circle, be sure that he or she is someone you know and trust. Many sites encourage users to build networks with many connections, but it isn't always safe to let everyone in. In addition, double-check any files, photos, or videos before you download them. Some can damage your computer or can access your personal files.

Social networking sites keep people connected. They are an inexpensive, easy way to share details of your life with people you care about. But taking precautions to keep your account(s) safe, private, and protected are worth the time.

Plan Your Writing

Read the writing prompt, and then plan your response below.

> Why is it important to follow safety procedures when using a social network? What can happen if you are not careful and thoughtful when social networking? Use what you already know about social networking and the information provided in the article "Social Networking Tips" to write an informational essay about responsible social networking. Give your essay an original title. Be sure to include a strong topic sentence and concluding statement. Use headings if they help you to organize your ideas.

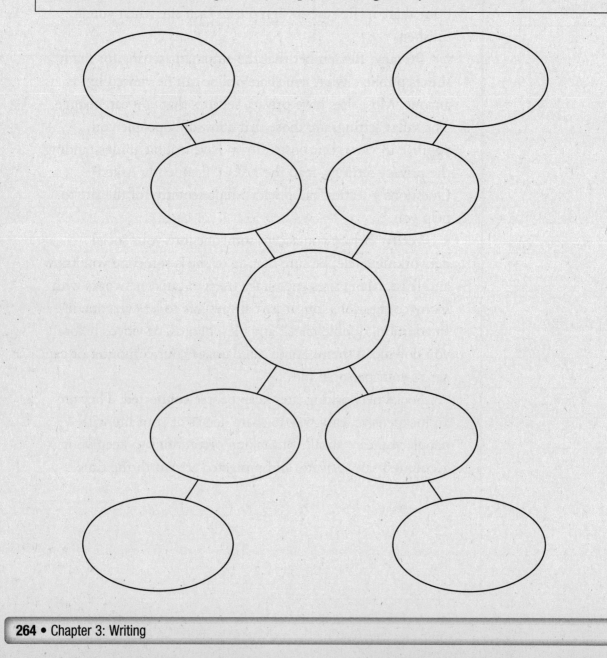

Write Your Response

Write your response on the pages provided.

_____

_____

_____

_____

_____

_____

_____

_____

_____

_____

_____

_____

_____

_____

_____

_____

_____

_____

_____

_____

_____

_____

_____

_____

_____

_____

_____

Informational Text Writing Checklist

Use the checklist below to help you do your best writing.

Does your informational essay

❏ have a clear and focused subject?

❏ have a strong topic sentence?

❏ have a logical structure?

❏ present information clearly?

❏ use linking words and phrases to join ideas?

❏ use a style and vocabulary that are correct for the audience and purpose?

❏ have a solid conclusion?

❏ have good spelling, capitalization, and punctuation?

❏ follow the rules for good grammar?

19 Writing Narratives

Getting the Idea

The purpose of **narrative text** is to entertain the reader with a story. Every novel or story you have ever read is an example of narrative text.

When you write a narrative, you use characters, setting, and plot. The **characters** are the people in your story. The **setting** is where and when your story takes place. The **plot** is the series of events that take place in the story.

A plot includes three main parts: the beginning, where you meet the characters and learn the main problem, or conflict; the middle, where the characters try to solve the problem; and the conclusion, the part where the story ends and you see how the characters did or did not solve the problem.

One way to make your story more interesting is to use **descriptions** of the people and places you are writing about. Vivid descriptions appeal to the reader's five senses: touch, taste, smell, sight, and hearing. Here are some examples:

Sense	Description
sight	the lake glittering like a shiny mirror
smell	the sweet aroma of warm apple pie
taste	the salty crunch of a pickle
touch	a sweater as soft as a kitten's fur
hearing	music hammering inside my head

When planning a narrative, remember that a plot usually follows a particular order, or **sequence**. Each event comes after the one before. A helpful graphic organizer for this kind of writing is a flowchart. A **flowchart** shows the order of events in a story from start to finish. A flowchart can be horizontal (left to right) or vertical (top to bottom). Read this flowchart.

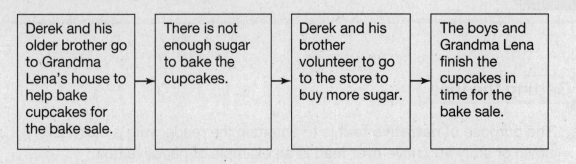

Notice what is written in each box of the flowchart. You can see what happens in each event, or part, of the story. Planning your story on a flowchart first will help you to write it in paragraphs later.

The arrows on the flowchart represent the links from one event to the next. Of course, when you write, you use words instead of arrows to move your narrative along. The chart below shows some sequence words you can use.

Sequence Words	Examples
first, once	Derek and his older brother first went to Grandma Lena's house to help her get ready for the bake sale.
then, next	Then, they realized there wasn't enough sugar for the cupcakes.
finally, at last	Finally, the boys went to the store to buy more sugar.

You can add to your narrative by using dialogue. **Dialogue** is the words that the characters say to each other. Dialogue makes the characters come alive on the page. Notice the use of commas, quotation marks, and capital letters in the following dialogue:

"Would you like a piece of pie?" Grandma asked.

"Yes, please," Derek replied. "Thank you."

Be sure your narrative has a conclusion. This is also called the resolution, where mysteries and problems are solved and all loose ends are tied up.

Coached Example

Read the paragraphs and answer the questions.

> The house was old. It was on a hill. All the kids in the neighborhood were afraid to go into that house. It always looked like no one was home there.

1. **Rewrite this story's setting using vivid description.**

   _____

   _____

   _____

   _____

   _____

   HINT Your description should relate to one or more of the five senses: touch, taste, smell, sight, and hearing.

> On Saturday, Sara saw Minh at the park. The girls looked at each other for a long time.
> "I can't believe I haven't seen you all summer!" Minh exclaimed.
> "I know," replied Sara. "What have you been doing these past few months?"

2. **Add dialogue to continue the conversation between the characters.**

   _____

   _____

   _____

   _____

   _____

   HINT Put quotation marks around the words each character says. End punctuation should be inside the quotation marks.

Lesson Practice

Use the Writing Guide to help you understand the passage.

Writing Guide

The setting of the story is Keiko's neighborhood. What words help you to know the setting?

What is Keiko's main problem in the story? How does she solve it?

Notice the quotation marks around the characters' spoken words.

Looks Aren't Everything

Keiko looked around nervously. She hadn't seen the big gray dog yet, but it always seemed to show up at some point on her walk home from school.

Everything felt new to her lately. Keiko and her family had recently moved to California from Japan. The kids at school seemed to be from another planet. As she came to her block, Keiko saw her neighbor, Mrs. Landis, wave to her.

"How is school going?" Mrs. Landis asked with a smile.

"Not bad," Keiko began. Then she heard a bark. Her head jerked up, and she saw the big gray dog running toward them. Suddenly, the dog stopped right in front of Mrs. Landis.

"Do you know this dog?" asked Keiko, backing away.

"Oh, yes. Ben's a good dog," said Mrs. Landis. "He wouldn't hurt a fly."

"But he's so big," said Keiko, still staring at the dog.

Mrs. Landis smiled again. "Looks aren't everything, you know. It's what's underneath that really counts. And Ben has a heart of gold. Right, boy?"

Keiko smiled. She hadn't given Ben a fair chance—just like the kids at school. Slowly, she reached out to pet Ben's back. "Hello, Ben. I'm Keiko. It's nice to meet you."

What lesson does Keiko learn at the conclusion of this story?

_____

_____

_____

_____

HINT Keiko's main problem in the story is her fear of the big gray dog. This problem gets solved in the conclusion.

Plan Your Writing

Read the writing prompt, and then plan your response below.

> Write a story about a boy or girl who wins a contest. Tell what kind of contest it is. Describe the main character. Tell how the character wins the contest. Finally, tell what happens after the contest is over. What prize does the winner receive? Plan the events in your narrative. Be sure to include description and dialogue to make your story interesting.

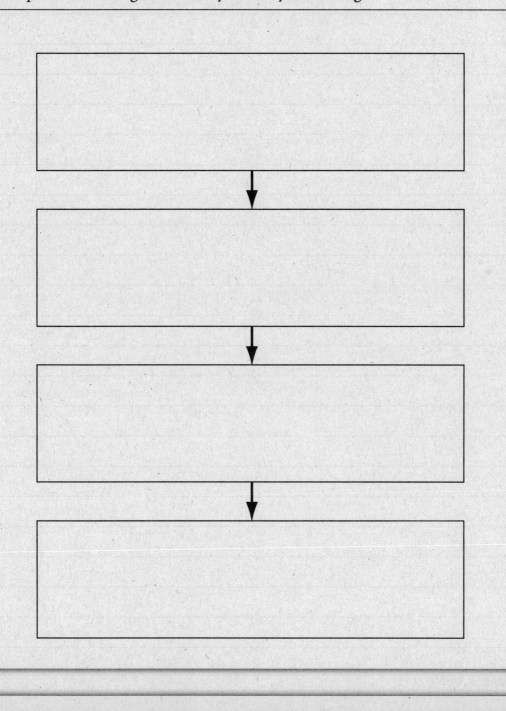

Write Your Response

Write your response on the pages provided.

_____

_____

_____

_____

_____

_____

_____

_____

_____

_____

_____

_____

_____

_____

_____

_____

_____

_____

_____

_____

_____

_____

_____

_____

_____

_____

_____

_____

_____

Narrative Writing Checklist

Use the checklist below to help you do your best writing.

Does your story

❏ have a situation and characters?

❏ have a clear sense of setting?

❏ use dialogue and description to develop the story?

❏ have a clear plot?

❏ use good word choice?

❏ have a satisfying ending?

❏ have good spelling, capitalization, and punctuation?

❏ follow the rules for good grammar?

Use the Writing Guide to help you understand the passage.

Think about how the author organizes events in the story.

Where does the story take place? What details describe the setting of the story?

Which sentence best explains the conflict, or problem, of the story? Is the problem resolved?

The New Coworker

The automatic doors opened, and Gus felt a blast of air conditioning as he entered the enormous grocery store. It was his first day at his first part-time summer job, stocking shelves at the store where his mother worked. Gus finally felt grown-up.

He reported to the Customer Service station to check in with the store manager. "Gus, is that what you're wearing to work?" he heard his mother call out from behind the checkout counter. *So much for feeling like an adult*, Gus thought, but soon he was happily filling shelves from loaded shopping carts.

"Gus, did you take your vitamins this morning?" Mom asked, suddenly behind him.

"You scared me!" he whispered, "and yes, I took them."

"When is your break? I brought carrots and hummus!" Mom said, grinning.

Gus felt his cheeks burn as he heard another stocker laugh.

"Come find me when you are ready," she said as she smoothed his hair with her hand. His coworker laughed even louder.

After Gus returned his empty cart, he met Mom for their break, but he barely touched the snacks. "What's wrong? Don't you like your new job?" Mom asked.

How could Gus get her to understand that he couldn't be seen eating carrots and hummus with his mother? "Well, I just wonder if you could not be so . . . *mothering* when we are here."

She looked confused for a moment, but then she smiled and said, "I'll try to do better tomorrow. After all, it is my first day as your coworker."

Gus grinned, taking a carrot and some hummus.

Plan Your Writing

Read the passage and the writing prompt, and then plan your response below.

> Emily had been playing soccer for the past five years. She loved the smell of the grassy field, the *whack* of the ball as she kicked it, and the fun she had with her teammates. But Emily wanted to learn a new sport, and she worried that she wouldn't have time for two sports. Every time she thought about quitting soccer, she remembered that Coach Jennings had called her his star player.
>
> "What would we do without you?" Coach had said to Emily.
>
> Emily lost the courage to quit, but one day she heard there was a spot open on the track team. She really wanted it.

Think about the character Emily and the conflict she faces. Will she try out for the track team? Will she have to quit soccer? Write an original story that continues where the passage ends. In your story, keep the setting in mind, use descriptions and dialogue, and organize events in a sequence that makes sense.

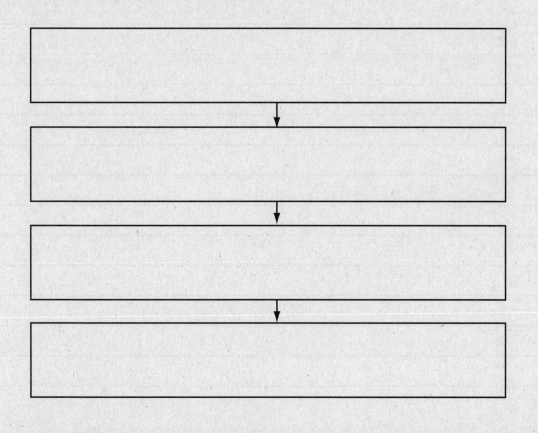

Write your response on the pages provided.

Narrative Writing Checklist

Use the checklist below to help you do your best writing.

Does your story

❑ have a situation and characters?

❑ have a clear sense of setting?

❑ use dialogue and description to develop the story?

❑ have a clear plot?

❑ use good word choice?

❑ have a satisfying ending?

❑ have good spelling, capitalization, and punctuation?

❑ follow the rules for good grammar?

20 Responding to Literature

Getting the Idea

Responding to literature is something you do frequently in school. You write your opinions, ideas, and feelings about a poem, story, or novel. There are different ways to respond to literature. Book club members discuss what they think about a book, book critics write articles that share their opinions about the plot or characters, and people tell friends whether they should read a book, based on their own response to the story.

When responding to literature in writing, you should keep the passage in mind. For example, you might be asked to write about characters, setting, and plot. You might be asked to write about how a character reacts to an event, or how the setting affects the plot. You could also be asked to compare the figurative language in two poems or the characters in two stories. In your response, you should use details from the text as evidence to describe characters, setting, or events in greater detail. Here are some examples:

Feature of Literature	Details
character	thoughts, dialogue, actions, reasons for actions, traits, appearance
setting	location, weather, mood, geography, culture
plot	events, reasons events happen, results of events

Readers' opinions on literature are personal, and there usually isn't a right or wrong response. However, your response needs to be supported with evidence from the text.

A response to literature is often an essay assignment. Frequently, you are given a writing prompt that includes a question about the story. State your response to the question first. In the middle paragraphs, provide two or three of your ideas or opinions on the topic. Support your ideas with text evidence—details and examples from the story. Finally, include a conclusion that summarizes your response. Be sure to keep the tone formal.

When planning your response, one graphic organizer you can use to help you is a **web**. A web can help you organize your ideas and opinions and the text evidence. Suppose you read a story about a family that had to move out of state, and you are asked to write about the main character's reaction to the news. Your completed web might look like this:

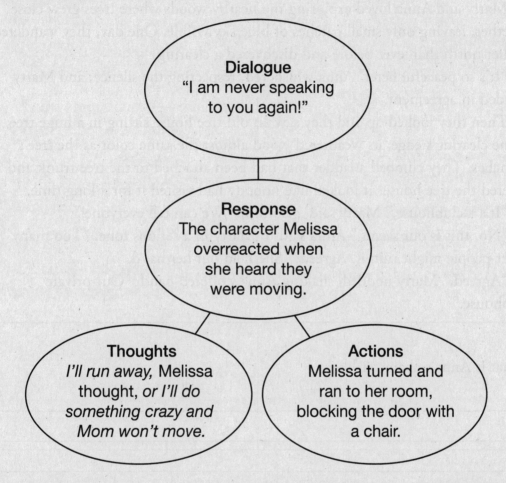

The main idea of your response is in the center circle. The text evidence that supports your response is in the outer circles. You may have more circles, depending on how much evidence you can find in the text.

A response to literature combines your ideas and opinions with detailed text evidence. The chart below shows words and phrases that help keep the two separate.

Reader's Response	Text Evidence
I think	The text states that
I feel	I read in the story
In my opinion	On page 23,
I believe	In paragraph 3,
In my view	The following sentence

Coached Example

Read the paragraphs and answer the questions.

> Marty and Anna loved exploring the nearby woods where trees grew close together, leaving only small patches of blue sky visible. One day, they wandered farther north than ever before and discovered a clearing.
>
> "It's so peaceful here!" Anna whispered, respecting the silence, and Marty nodded in agreement.
>
> Then they looked up and they saw an old tree house sitting in a huge tree at the clearing's edge, its weathered wood almost the same color as the tree's branches. They climbed a ladder that had been attached to the tree trunk and entered the tree house. It looked like nobody had visited it for a long time.
>
> "It's a clubhouse," Marty said, grinning. "We can tell everyone!"
>
> "No, this is our secret," Anna said to Marty in a serious tone. "Too many other people might ruin it. Agreed?" She held out her hand.
>
> "Agreed," Marty nodded, shaking Anna's offered hand. "Our private clubhouse."

1. What is Anna's character like?

_____

_____

_____

HINT Remember that your response is your idea or opinion about what you read. Think about Anna. What words in the story best describe her?

2. Write the evidence from the text that supports your opinion of Anna.

_____

_____

_____

HINT Cite details from the text about Anna's thoughts, actions, or words.

Lesson Practice

Use the Writing Guide to help you understand the passage.

Writing Guide

Identify the features in the story. Who are the characters? What is the setting? What is happening?

What details can you locate in the text that describe the characters, setting, and plot?

Seeking adventure, Wendy and her brothers, John and Michael, follow Peter Pan to Neverland. They are kidnapped by Peter's enemy, Captain Hook. Hook holds them prisoner on his ship.

The Prisoner's Choice
adapted from Peter and Wendy, *by J. M. Barrie*

The wretched prisoners were dragged from the ship's hold, all except Wendy, and arranged in line in front of Captain Hook.

"Now then, bullies," Hook said briskly, "six of you will walk the plank tonight, but I have room for two cabin boys. Which of you is it to be?"

"You, boy," Hook said, addressing John, "you look as if you had a little pluck in you. Did you never want to be a pirate, my hearty?"

Now John had sometimes experienced this hankering during school, and he was struck by Hook's picking him.

"I once thought of calling myself Red-handed Jack," he said hesitantly.

"And a good name too. We'll call you that if you join."

"What do you think, Michael?" asked John.

"What would you call me if I join?" Michael demanded.

"Blackbeard Joe."

Michael was impressed. "What do you think, John?"

"Shall we still be subjects of the King?" John inquired.

Through Hook's teeth came the answer, "You would have to swear, 'Down with the King.' "

Perhaps John had not behaved very well so far, but he shone out now.

"Then I refuse!" he cried.

"And I refuse!" cried Michael.

Hook roared out, "That seals your doom! Get the plank ready."

Plan Your Writing

Read the writing prompt, and then plan your response below.

> How would you describe John's character in "The Prisoner's Choice"?
> What things are important to him? Write a response that includes your
> thoughts, ideas, and opinions. Be sure to provide evidence from the text
> for support.

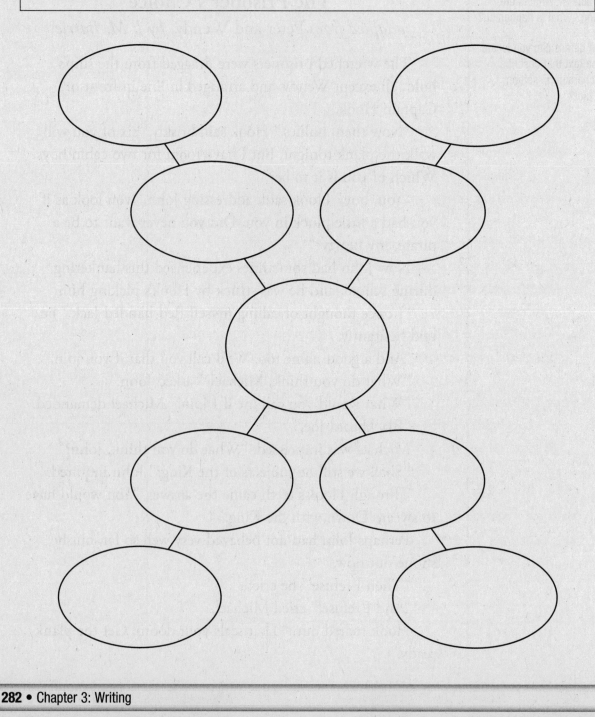

Write Your Response

Write your response on the pages provided.

_____

_____

_____

_____

_____

_____

_____

_____

_____

_____

_____

_____

_____

_____

_____

_____

_____

_____

_____

_____

_____

_____

_____

_____

Response to Literature Checklist

Use the checklist below to help you do your best writing.

Does your response

❏ state your ideas, thoughts, and opinions?

❏ include text evidence that supports your response?

❏ include details about characters, setting, or plot related to your response?

❏ have a concluding statement that sums up your response?

❏ use a formal and respectful tone?

❏ have good spelling, capitalization, and punctuation?

❏ follow the rules for good grammar?

Use the Writing Guides to help you understand the passages.

The Archaeologist

Writing Guide

How would you describe
Samuel's character? How
does he behave?

What details in the text
describe Samuel?

What does Samuel learn?

Sitting on his bed, Samuel thought about the documentary he had watched the night before with his father. Cameras followed archeology expeditions in faraway locations where archaeologists uncovered secrets of past civilizations. The walls of Samuel's bedroom disappeared, replaced by golden deserts that held treasures.

Samuel jumped off of his bed, bumping into his dog, Boomer, who yelped. "Sorry, Boomer," Samuel called, "but I have an idea!" Samuel watched archaeologists dig in heavily populated areas, unearthing incredible objects—tools, pottery, even bones! Different civilizations must have lived in Samuel's neighborhood years ago, and though Samuel didn't want to find human bones, he hoped he could find ancient tools in his own backyard.

"Speaking of tools," Samuel muttered, walking to the garage, "I'll need a shovel." Samuel already felt like an archaeologist as he dug about the cluttered garage, finally finding a square shovel and heading to the yard.

Instead of neighbors having cookouts, Samuel imagined Native Americans carrying pots and baskets in the backyards next to his. Boomer began barking when Samuel pushed the shovel into the ground. Then he heard his father's voice call out, "What are you doing?"

He replied breathlessly, "I'm an archaeologist looking for artifacts."

"All you'll find under here is rock and clay," Dad said. "Archaeologists study the area first, learning about its history. Don't you remember that part of the program?"

"I guess I got a bit excited about finding treasure," Samuel admitted.

"Archaeology is a precise science," Dad said. "Let's read about discoveries at the library instead of digging up the yard."

"Okay," Samuel agreed. "Let me change. Archaeology is sweaty work!"

How does the setting affect the passage?

What is the conflict, or problem, that Bea faces?

How would you describe Bea's character?

Baking Bea

Early on Saturday, Bea was ready to begin. It wasn't quite dawn, and the kitchen was dim as she pulled all the ingredients she needed from the refrigerator and pantry. She propped Papa's cookbook on the counter, turning the page to the recipe for his favorite dessert. Bea knew that it was a complicated recipe, but she also knew that he would be so proud to end his birthday dinner with a homemade cake made by his favorite fifteen-year-old granddaughter. Bea quickly scanned the recipe, confident that she had what she needed.

When she began mixing ingredients together, she realized that she didn't have enough eggs. So she decided to add more milk instead. She remembered that she should have preheated the oven, so she stopped mixing and turned the oven on. When she returned to the bowl, Bea had a hard time getting the wet ingredients to combine with the dry ingredients. The batter looked a bit stiff, but she forced it into the pan and put it into the oven, then started to make the filling. Once she finished the strawberry filling, she mixed up the frosting.

The timer went off and she grabbed oven mitts to pull the cake out. But the oven was cold—she had forgotten to hit the start button! Bea was starting to cry when Papa shuffled into the kitchen in his bathrobe. "Papa, everything has gone so wrong!"

Papa smiled kindly, patted her hand, and said, "Baking takes patience and planning. Let me get dressed and we will go to the store. I'd love nothing more than baking with you today."

Plan Your Writing

Read the writing prompt, and then plan your response below.

Think about the characters Samuel in "The Archaeologist" and Bea in "Baking Bea." Based on the texts, would you describe Samuel and Bea as having similar or different personalities? Are they practical and logical or passionate and impulsive? Use the web below to organize a response that includes your thoughts, ideas, and opinions. Be sure to cite evidence from the text for support.

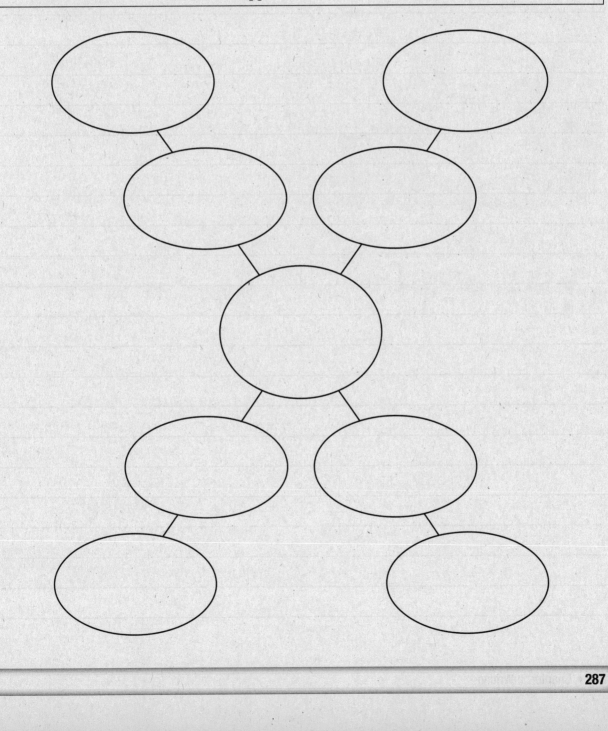

Write Your Response

Write your response on the pages provided.

_____

_____

_____

_____

_____

_____

_____

_____

_____

_____

_____

_____

_____

_____

_____

_____

_____

_____

_____

_____

_____

_____

_____

_____

_____

_____

Response to Literature Checklist

Use the checklist below to help you do your best writing.

Does your response

❏ state your ideas, thoughts, and opinions?

❏ include text evidence that supports your response?

❏ include details about characters, setting, or plot related to your response?

❏ have a concluding statement that sums up your response?

❏ use a formal and respectful tone?

❏ have good spelling, capitalization, and punctuation?

❏ follow the rules for good grammar?

21 Responding to Informational Text

Getting the Idea

We read informational texts to learn something new, to learn more about a subject we enjoy, or to gather information for research. A reader's **response to informational text** is often based on his or her purpose for reading. For example, if you read to learn something new, your response to the text might be about whether you think the information is accurate or interesting. If you read to research a topic, your response might be to decide if the information is important or appropriate enough to include in your research. While informational text is based on facts, writers and readers still have thoughts and opinions about the information.

An opinion is a statement about what you think or how you feel about something. Opinions cannot be proven; however, they can be supported by facts. For example, *Eggs make the best breakfast* is an opinion. Other people may disagree, but you can use facts to support the opinion:

- Most doctors advise people to eat more protein at breakfast.
- Eggs are an excellent source of protein.

So while *Eggs make the best breakfast* is still an opinion, it can be supported by using evidence and facts.

Informational texts include facts that help the writer support his or her ideas or opinions. Find and evaluate reasons and evidence the writer uses to support his or her ideas. A **reason** tells why the writer thinks a certain way. **Evidence** is factual information from other sources.

Reasons	Evidence
detailed explanation	facts from reliable sources
presenting pros and cons	opinions or ideas from experts on a topic
presenting an opposing view and explaining why it is incorrect	quotations from other texts

Once you have identified the writer's reasons and evidence, you can form a response. In some cases, the reasoning will make sense and there will be enough good evidence. However, if the reasons don't make sense or if there isn't any evidence, it is likely that the writer's thoughts and ideas are not supported by facts.

When planning your response, one graphic organizer you can use to help you is a **chart**. A chart can help you focus on the writer's idea or opinion and then organize reasons and evidence. Your completed chart might look like this:

Writer's Idea or Opinion: Most people are unprepared for flash floods.	
Reason: Flash floods are unexpected, so people are unable to take steps to prepare for them.	**Evidence:** Summer thunderstorms or melting snow result in flash floods. It is difficult for experts to predict the amount of rainfall or snowmelt.
Your Response: I agree that it can be difficult to prepare for a flash flood.	

The writer's idea or opinion is recorded in the first row. Underneath, reasons and evidence that the author includes are recorded. You may have several rows for reasons and evidence. Finally, write your response.

In a response to informational text, you are analyzing the writer's reasons and evidence to see if they support his or her ideas and opinions. In a way, you are sharing your ideas and opinions about what the writer thinks, using the text. Some phrases that may be useful:

Reader's Response	Writer's Ideas or Opinions	Text Evidence
I think I feel In my opinion I believe In my view	The writer states The writer believes The writer feels In the writer's view The writer wants readers to understand that	The text states that An expert on the topic On page 23, In paragraph 3, One reason provided

A response to informational text is often an essay assignment, so be sure to keep the tone formal. Frequently, you are given a writing prompt that includes a question about the text. Sometimes you will be asked to combine information from more than one text on the same subject. Also be sure to include a conclusion that summarizes your response, restating your ideas, thoughts, and/or opinions.

Coached Example

Read the paragraph and answer the questions.

Owning a pet can be a rewarding experience. Many people choose to buy pets from breeders, but adopting a pet from a rescue organization is a safer option. According to the National Humane Society, it can be difficult to find a responsible breeder who follows guidelines for breeding healthy animals. Many breeders keep many animals, forcing them to produce multiple litters. Called "mills," these places usually are unsafe and unhealthy. The Humane Society notes that at many of these mills, the breeders don't know about typical health issues of the breed. Sometimes they don't make sure the breed is pure. Rescue organizations can help you find the right animal for you. They even let you foster animals. When you foster, you take the pet home for a trial period to make sure you and the animal are a good match.

1. **Write the author's opinion on breeders and rescue organizations.**

   _____

HINT The author's opinion is often the main idea of an informational text and the author's purpose for writing.

2. **Write reasons and evidence the author includes that support his or her opinion.**

   _____

HINT Reasons can tell why the author thinks or believes something. Evidence includes facts and information.

3. **Write a response to the informational text. Is the author's opinion well supported?**

   _____

   _____

HINT A valid opinion is supported by reasons and evidence.

Lesson Practice

Use the Writing Guide to help you understand the passage.

Writing Guide

What is the main idea of the passage?

What does the author think about the topic?

What evidence does the author provide to support his or her opinion?

Is the author's opinion valid? How do you know?

Walking Wonders

Walking is one of the simplest and best forms of exercise. All you need are a good pair of walking shoes. Many city planners are organizing neighborhoods and city centers around walking to encourage people to exercise more. But health is not the only benefit. Walkable neighborhoods also help the environment and our finances. Walking to and from places that you go to every day, such as work, school, and the store, adds up to an amazing combination of benefits.

According to Walk Score, a company that analyzes neighborhoods for how "walkable" they are, walking reduces pollution. Burning fossil fuels, such as using gas while driving, creates 82 percent of the carbon dioxide in the air. The environment is better off when you put on your walking shoes.

Walking can also save us money. One obvious way is buying less gas for your car. But you will also likely spend less on repairing and maintaining your car. Some people commute using public transportation. Walking saves people money because they don't have to pay for trains or buses. Walking to a store can also help you save money. If you know you have to carry your purchases home, you are probably only going to buy what you need.

America Walks educates people on the benefits of walkable cities. The group notes that people who live in walking neighborhoods get to know each other. America Walks states in its newsletter that knowing your neighbors can reduce crime. "In areas where people get out and know one another, the chances are much greater that a stranger will be noticed and reported."

If city planners can help make it easier for people to walk, there is a good chance we will all be healthier, save money, and be happier and safer in our neighborhoods.

Plan Your Writing

Read the writing prompt, and then plan your response below.

After reading "Walking Wonders," think about people's reliance on cars as their main form of transportation. Do you think that more cities should be planned around walking? Why or why not? Is the writer's opinion convincing? Write a response that includes your thoughts, ideas, and opinions, the writer's ideas and opinions, and evidence from the text.

Writer's Ideas or Opinion:	
Reasons:	**Evidence:**
Your Response:	

Write Your Response

Write your response on the pages provided.

_____

_____

_____

_____

_____

_____

_____

_____

_____

_____

_____

_____

_____

_____

_____

_____

_____

_____

_____

_____

_____

_____

_____

_____

_____

_____

_____

Response to Informational Text Checklist

Use the checklist below to help you do your best writing.

Does your response

- ❏ state the writer's ideas or opinions?
- ❏ include text evidence that supports the writer's ideas or opinions?
- ❏ state your ideas, thoughts, or opinions?
- ❏ include text evidence that supports your response?
- ❏ have a concluding statement that sums up your response?
- ❏ use a formal and respectful tone?
- ❏ have good spelling, capitalization, and punctuation?
- ❏ follow the rules for good grammar?

Use the Writing Guides to help you understand the passages.

Predicting Tornadoes

Writing **Guide**

What is the topic of the passage?

What is the writer's main point?

What reasons and evidence does the writer provide to support his or her opinion?

When a serious storm is coming, it is very important for weather experts and professionals to warn people so that they can take precautions to keep themselves safe. The timing of these storms is often difficult to predict, even with the best weather technology. Some scientists have tried to improve warnings by taking equipment to the storms. Called storm chasers, these scientists research tornadoes up close. There are safer ways to learn more about tornadoes. In 2012, meteorologists, scientists who study weather, made important discoveries that will improve warnings.

Scientists have used Doppler radars to study weather patterns. Beginning in 2012, the systems have been used to measure wind movement around and *inside* tornadoes. This helps researchers learn more about how tornadoes move. Scientists can better predict the direction of a tornado by analyzing the wind speed and movement within the storm. If scientists know which direction a tornado will move toward, they can warn people nearby. This information can help storm chasers follow a tornado. Storm chasers provide video of tornadoes that can be studied later.

Scientists have learned more about how tornadoes form. Doppler radar systems scan storms to look for information that indicates a tornado will form. These storms are called parent storms because they produce tornadoes. The radars help scientists predict which storms will produce tornadoes. The radars give information about the area around the storm. Based on the data, scientists know which storms to track.

Although scientists understand tornadoes better, it is still difficult to predict where they will appear. Using Doppler radar systems and other equipment, meteorologists can predict storms only within an hour or two before they arrive. An hour isn't much time to keep people safe. A better understanding of how tornadoes work is needed to improve that timeframe.

What is the topic of the passage?

What details does the writer provide to describe storm chasers?

Did the writer provide enough evidence to prove his or her main point?

Storm Chasers

You've probably heard of storm chasers. You might think of them as adventure seekers racing around in pickup trucks. But many storm chasers are scientists with backgrounds in weather. Their motivations for chasing storms are in the name of science. They learn more about how tornadoes act on the ground. These scientists are heroes to many because they save lives.

Storm chasers have a respect for tornadoes' power. While technology improves every day, storm chasers know that people need more time to get to safety. Measuring the area surrounding a tornado and the area inside a tornado can lead to valuable data. So storm chasers take existing technology and figure out how it can be used closer to tornadoes. For example, in 1979, researchers created the Totable Tornado Observatory. It was a machine that was placed in the path of tornadoes. Sensors recorded data about how the tornado moved. Placing equipment in the path of a tornado is risky. However, the information helps scientists make more accurate predictions.

By getting close to storms, scientists can also record close-up views. The videos of storms can be played on television news reports, which make people more likely to take shelter. Television and radio warnings and sirens alone sometimes can't convince people to seek shelter; a video of a twister three miles from your house is pretty convincing.

Storm chasing can be deadly and unpredictable. In 2013, three well-known scientists were killed while chasing a deadly outbreak of tornadoes in Oklahoma. But many jobs, such as firefighting and even professional sports, pose risks. The risk may be worth it as long as lives are saved. Storm chasers know that learning more about these storms is the best method for more accurate predictions, keeping more people safe.

Plan Your Writing

Read the writing prompt, and then plan your response below.

> After reading "Predicting Tornadoes" and "Storm Chasers," think about whether storm chasers are necessary to keep people safe. What does the author of each informational text think? Write a response that includes the authors' opinions on storm prediction and storm chasers. Be sure to cite evidence from both texts that supports both authors' opinions and your own response.

Writer's Ideas or Opinion for "Predicting Tornadoes":

Reasons:	Evidence:

Your Response:

Writer's Ideas or Opinion for "Storm Chasers":

Reasons:	Evidence:

Your Response:

Write Your Response

Write your response on the pages provided.

_____

_____

_____

_____

_____

_____

_____

_____

_____

_____

_____

_____

_____

_____

_____

_____

_____

_____

_____

_____

_____

_____

_____

_____

_____

Response to Informational Text Checklist

Use the checklist below to help you do your best writing.

Does your response

❏ state the writers' ideas or opinions?

❏ include text evidence that supports the writers' ideas or opinions?

❏ state your ideas, thoughts, or opinions?

❏ include text evidence that supports your response?

❏ have a concluding statement that sums up your response?

❏ use a formal and respectful tone?

❏ have good spelling, capitalization, and punctuation?

❏ follow the rules for good grammar?

22 Revising, Editing, and Publishing

Getting the Idea

No matter what you write, you should always review your work. Revising and editing your writing can make it better. **Revising** means correcting and organizing your writing to make it as clear, effective, and engaging as it can be. Parents, teachers, older siblings, and even other classmates can often make helpful suggestions. Read this paragraph.

> The weather is cold outside, and I plant seeds in small containers. I make sure they have enough sunlight. They sit in the sun. The seeds sprout and the weather is warm enough. I put the plants in the ground. We have fresh vegetables to eat! Peas are my favorite vegetable. Then I watch them grow.

There are some problems with this paragraph. First, it needs a topic sentence. Some sentences are out of order and repetitive. The paragraph needs transitions to help the reader move from one idea to the next. One sentence does not belong in the paragraph. It also needs a concluding sentence at the end. Read this revised paragraph.

> I grow vegetables in my backyard. While the weather is still cold outside, I plant seeds in small containers. I make sure they have enough sunlight. When the seeds sprout and the weather is warm enough, I put the plants in the ground. Then I watch them grow. By the end of summer, we have fresh vegetables to eat!

The **topic sentence** tells you what the paragraph is about. The sentence *They sit in the sun* has been deleted because it repeats an earlier sentence. Notice the words *while, when, then,* and *by the end.* They connect ideas and help the writing to flow. The last two sentences have been reordered, so the ideas make more sense. The sentence about the peas has been deleted because it does not relate to the main idea. The concluding sentence sums up the ideas in the paragraph. All of these revisions greatly improve the writing.

When you **edit**, you look for and correct mistakes such as words that are not spelled correctly, missing or incorrect punctuation, or errors in grammar.

Spelling can be tricky. Pay attention to plurals. Many nouns form their plurals by adding -s (friend—friends). When pluralizing nouns ending in -s, -z, -x, -sh, or -ch, add -es (gas—gases, fox—foxes, branch—branches). For nouns ending in -y, drop the -y and add -ies (memory—memories). Here are some more words and their plurals: tomato—tomatoes, foot—feet, deer—deer.

When you learn a new word, learn how it is spelled, too. For example, see how these words are spelled: *celebrate, organize, fraction, ingredient, university.* Keep a dictionary nearby when you read or write, so you can look up the correct spelling of unfamiliar words.

Check your punctuation. Sentences should end with a period, a question mark, or an exclamation point. Use quotation marks around a speaker's words.

> "Our team won by two points," said Levon.

Subject-verb agreement is an important part of grammar. The **subject** is the person or thing doing the action in a sentence. The **verb** is the action word. If the subject is singular, the verb must be singular. If the subject is plural, the verb must be plural.

> *Singular:* <u>Brad</u> happily <u>hugs</u> his brother.
> *Plural:* <u>Brad and Joe</u> happily <u>hug</u> their brother.

The **tense** of a verb tells you the time in which the action takes place—past, present, or future. Regular past-tense verbs end in -ed. Some past-tense verbs are irregular. They do not end in -ed. Future-tense verbs are paired with the helping verb *will*.

To **publish** means to produce your writing for others to read. You could write an editorial to be published in the school newspaper. A description of your science project and its findings could be published on the school's Web site. When you publish electronically, you can add links in your writing to related sites and to the sources of your research.

Thinking It Through

Read the following passage, and then answer the question that follows.

One unusual pizza topping is macaroni and cheese. It is a favorite in Wisconsin. Another type is mashed potatoes. This topping is often eaten in Brazil. Perhaps the weirdest topping is found in Japan. It is squid. (A squid is a sea animal.) The next time you get bored with pepperoni, think about trying one of these unique varieties.

Write a topic sentence for this paragraph.

_____

_____

_____

 What is the main idea of this paragraph? What sentence could sum up that idea?

DISCUSS Discuss your answer with a partner.

Coached Example

Read the passage and answer the questions.

(1) Visiting Abuela, my grandma, in New York City is so much fun! (2) The <u>nieghborhood</u> she lives in has so many things to see and do. (3) For example, local artists have painted beautiful murals on some of the buildings. (4) We also like to visit different bodegas to find the most unusual one. (5) A bodega is a grocery store. (6) We like to look at the murals together. (7) As fun as all those activities are, my favorite one is playing street ball with the neighborhood kids while Abuela cheers me on. (8) I love visiting Abuela. (9) There is never a dull moment when I stay with her.

---

1. Read this sentence from the passage.

   The <u>nieghborhood</u> she lives in has so many things to see and do.

   What is the correct spelling of the underlined word in the sentence?

   A. nieghburhood

   B. neighborhood

   C. neighborhod

   D. neiborhood

   HINT Words with a long *e* (rhymes with *me*) are spelled *ie*, and words that have a sound other than a long *e* generally are spelled *ei*. What sound do you hear in the first syllable of the underlined word?

2. What is the BEST way to reorder the passage?

   A. Move sentence 3 before sentence 2.

   B. Move sentence 9 before sentence 8.

   C. Move sentence 6 before sentence 4.

   D. Move sentence 4 before sentence 3.

   HINT Reread the part about the murals. Which sentence seems out of place?

This passage contains mistakes. Use the Reading Guide to help you find the mistakes.

Reading Guide

When does this story take place: the past, present, or future? Look at the action words in the sentences to help you figure it out. Now look at sentence 12. Is the tense of the verbs correct?

Suppose Jeremiah had been given more than one puppy in sentence 4. What is the plural of *puppy*? How do you spell it?

Look at sentences 8 and 9. The dad is speaking in both sentences. How would you correct the punctuation?

Look at sentence 19. The subject is Jeremiah. Does it agree with the verb that follows it?

Reread the last paragraph. Is there a sentence that does not seem to belong with the rest of the story?

A Dream Come True

(1) Jeremiah begged his dad for a pet again and again. (2) He was an only child, so he wanted a playmate. (3) A week ago, Jeremiah's wish was finally granted. (4) His dad came home with the cutest puppy Jeremiah ever saw. (5) Jeremiah could hardly believe it! (6) He named the puppy Linus.

(7) "Thanks, Dad!" Jeremiah exclaimed.

(8) It was my pleasure, buddy, his dad replied. (9) "But remember, you promised to take care of him all by yourself."

(10) Jeremiah nodded. (11) Minutes later, he raced outside to teach Linus how to fetch. (12) They run around in the yard together for what seems like forever. (13) Jeremiah couldn't remember the last time he was so happy.

(14) The next week was a blur for Jeremiah as he got used to his new <u>responsibilitys</u>. (15) These included playing, walking, and feeding. (16) He never realized owning a dog was so much work. (17) He had to take care of Linus every day.

(18) Linus was a great friend, though. (19) Jeremiah love to watch him run and play. (20) The best part was that Linus seemed to enjoy keeping Jeremiah company, no matter what he did. (21) Jeremiah had a lot of homework. (22) Linus was Jeremiah's dream come true. (23) He had a terrific new friend!

Answer the following questions.

1. Read this sentence from the passage.

    The next week was a blur for Jeremiah as he got used to his new responsibilitys.

    What is the correct spelling of the underlined word?

    A. responsibilities

    B. responsibilitees

    C. responsabilities

    D. responsabilitys

2. Read this sentence from the passage.

    It was my pleasure, buddy, his dad replied.

    What is the correct way to write this sentence?

    A. "It was my pleasure, buddy, his dad replied."

    B. "It was my pleasure, buddy," his dad replied.

    C. "It was my pleasure," buddy, his dad replied.

    D. "It was my pleasure, buddy." his dad replied.

3. Which sentence has incorrect subject-verb agreement?

    A. He was an only child, so he wanted a playmate.

    B. Minutes later, he raced outside to teach Linus how to fetch.

    C. Jeremiah love to watch him run and play.

    D. Linus was Jeremiah's dream come true.

4. Which sentence does NOT belong in the last paragraph?

    A. He had a terrific new friend!

    B. The best part was that Linus seemed to enjoy keeping Jeremiah company, no matter what he did.

    C. Jeremiah had a lot of homework.

    D. Linus was Jeremiah's dream come true.

5. How does the writer use transitions in the passage to connect ideas? Give examples from the passage.

    _____

    _____

    _____

The following questions do not relate to a passage.

6.   Choose all the words that are the correct spelling of plural nouns. There is more than one correct choice listed below.

    A. buddies

    B. fairyes

    C. hunches

    D. boxes

    E. dishs

    F. puppyes

---

7.   A student is writing a story about her cousin. Read this paragraph from the story and the directions that follow.

> Today the weather was beautiful, and Samara had hoped to see the city during her visit with cousin Tia. "Tia, do you think maybe we could go for a walk?" Samara asked. "You can show me your favorite spots in the neighborhood," she said. Yesterday, all Tia had wanted to do was to show Samara how to play her favorite video games. Samara has fun; but after a while, it were boring just to watched Tia play video games.

The student needs to revise the last sentence by using correct grammar. Which sentence shows the BEST revision of the last sentence?

    A. Samara had fun; but after a while, it was boring just to watches Tia play video games.

    B. Samara is fun; but after a while, it is boring just to watch Tia play video games.

    C. Samara was fun; but after a while, it got boring just to watchs Tia play video games.

    D. Samara was having fun; but after a while, it was boring just to watch Tia play video games.

8. For language arts class, Mark has written a paragraph about a special memory. Read the following paragraph and the directions that follow.

> **One of my favorite memorys is watching movies at the drive-in theater with my family. We would all pile into my grandfather's truck? At the theater, we parked next to a speeker with the truck bed facing the huge movie screen. We spreaded blankets out on the truck bed and settled in, passing out bages of snackes. Usually they showed double features—two diferent movies playing in one night. I often fall asleep halfway through the second movie!**

Revise the paragraph to correct errors in spelling, grammar, and punctuation. The revised paragraph should be well organized and should include sentences that are clear and complete.

Write your answer on the lines below.

_____

_____

_____

_____

_____

_____

_____

_____

_____

_____

_____

_____

_____

_____

23 Research and Resources

Getting the Idea

Suppose you have to write a report for your social studies class. You know you want to learn more about Uganda, a country in Africa. So, where do you start? First, you need to narrow your topic. What specifically about Uganda do you want to know?

Let's say you decide to research what school is like in Uganda. When you do **research**, you gather information about a topic. You can organize your research by looking at your topic from different angles. For example, you might ask questions such as: How are schools in Uganda similar to schools in the United States? How are schools in Uganda different from schools in the United States?

Now that you know *what* you want to find out, *where* are you going to find the information? There are several print and online **resources** to look at, such as the ones listed in the chart below.

Resources	
almanac	an online or print collection of information for a given year
atlas	an online or print collection of maps and geographical information
encyclopedia	an online or print collection of short articles about many topics, organized in alphabetical order by topic
newspaper	an online or print collection of articles about current events, usually published daily
Web site	an online page of information that can be published by almost anyone

Be sure that the information you find is reliable and accurate. One way to do this is to use more than one resource. Then, you can see if the information in your main resource is backed up by information in another. If it is not, check a third resource. When doing research on a computer, remember that not all Web sites are trustworthy. The most reliable Web sites have addresses that end in *.gov*, *.edu*, or *.org*.

Once you have located your resources, it is time to take notes. As you read, organize and label your notes based on the information they provide. For a report about schools in Uganda, for example, you might organize and label your notes into two categories: similarities and differences.

An important rule of research is never to copy what you read. Instead, **paraphrase**, or restate the information in your own words. Look at the examples below.

Original Source	Paraphrased Statement
The typical school day starts at 7:30 a.m. and does not end until 5:30 p.m.	Most students begin school at 7:30 in the morning and return home at 5:30 in the afternoon.
Sports are a popular after-school pastime.	Students like to play sports when the school day is done.

Though you are paraphrasing the author's original words, it is still important that you give credit to the authors whose information you used to write your report. As you work, keep a list of every resource you use. A **bibliography** is an organized list of resources on a topic. Each entry in a bibliography should include the book's title, author, and place and date of publication. A bibliography is alphabetized by the authors' last names.

The following is a partial bibliography that a student used when researching schools in Uganda. Notice that titles of articles are put in quotation marks. Titles of books are underlined.

Martin, Roger. <u>Education Around the Globe</u>. Chicago: World Press, 2009.

Smith, Leena. "Studying in Uganda." <u>Schools Throughout the World</u>. New York City: Smart Publishing, 2008.

Thinking It Through

Read the following paragraph, and then answer the question that follows.

People use many different kinds of transportation, or ways to get around. Cars, buses, and trucks are the most popular kinds of road transportation. Other ways to travel include jet planes and helicopters, railroad trains, and subways that run underground. In some cities, people ride in pedicabs, which are tricycles with passenger seats attached.

Paraphrase the information in the paragraph.

_____

_____

_____

_____

_____

 Remember to use your own words to paraphrase a source.

DISCUSS In which resource might you find this type of information—an almanac, atlas, or encyclopedia? Discuss it with a partner.

Coached Example

Read the passage and answer the questions.

The mantis is an insect. It gets the nickname "praying mantis" from the way it holds its front legs. They are bent up and pressed together, as if the insect were praying. Actually, the mantis uses these front legs to grab and hold its prey.

It takes a sharp eye to spot a mantis. This is because these insects look a lot like twigs, leaves, or blades of grass. Their thin brown or green bodies blend in with their environment. Their camouflage serves two purposes. It helps them hide from predators. It also helps them stay hidden until their prey gets close enough to grab and eat.

Like ladybugs, mantises are "good" garden insects. They do not eat plants. Instead, they eat the insects that would eat the plants. In this way, they can naturally help control pests in the garden.

---

1. Which of the following is the BEST way to paraphrase paragraph 3?

   A. Mantises can naturally help control pests in the garden.

   B. Like ladybugs, mantises are "good" garden insects.

   C. Mantises are good to have around because they eat other insects.

   D. Mantises are good in the garden because they eat insects that eat plants.

    HINT A paraphrase should include all the important information from the original text. Be sure it is in your own words.

2. Where would you look for more information about the mantis?

   A. almanac

   B. atlas

   C. encyclopedia

   D. newspaper

   HINT Choose a resource that contains short articles about a lot of different topics.

Use the Reading Guide to help you understand the passage.

Earth's Bright Neighbor

by Janice Wheeler

Venus is the only planet with a female's name. It gets its name from Venus, the Roman goddess of love and beauty. The other planets, except for Earth, get their names from Greek or Roman gods. Venus is special in other ways, too.

Venus is worthy of a name meaning "beauty." For us on Earth, Venus is the brightest object in the night sky besides the moon. Venus shines brightest just before sunrise and just after sunset. For this reason, it has been called "the morning star" and "the evening star."

Why is Venus so bright? There are two main reasons. One is the blanket of clouds that surrounds the planet. These clouds reflect sunlight back out into space. Another reason is its closeness to Earth. Venus is the second planet from the sun, and Earth is third. Venus's brightness is close enough to dazzle us.

Until the mid-1900s, details of Venus's surface were a mystery. The cloud blanket blocked any view of the planet's surface. People wondered if Venus was suitable for human life, or if it had any life of its own. The possibilities were fascinating.

In 1962, the United States sent a robotic space probe to Venus. The *Mariner 2* measured the surface temperature of Venus. It was 797 degrees Fahrenheit! In contrast, Earth's surface temperature is just under 60 degrees Fahrenheit. We won't be living on Venus anytime soon.

Answer the following questions.

1. Which of the following is NOT related to the topic of the passage?

   A. the planets in the solar system

   B. Greek and Roman god names

   C. living conditions on planets

   D. ways to time travel

2. If you wanted to see a map of where the United States is on Earth, which resource would you use?

   A. almanac

   B. atlas

   C. encyclopedia

   D. newspaper

3. Which is the BEST way to label notes from paragraph 3?

   A. why Venus is so bright

   B. how Venus got its name

   C. what the surface of Venus is like

   D. why humans cannot live on Venus

4. Which is the correct bibliography entry for this passage?

   A. "Earth's Bright Neighbor" by Janis Wheeler, 2009.

   B. Janis Wheeler. "Earth's Bright Neighbor." <u>Our Solar System</u>.

   C. "Earth's Bright Neighbor." Wheeler, Janis. Boston" Science Times, 2009.

   D. Wheeler, Janis. "Earth's Bright Neighbor." <u>Our Solar System</u>. Boston: Science Times, 2009.

5. Paraphrase paragraph 1 of the passage on the lines below.

   _____

   _____

   _____

   _____

   _____

   _____

The following questions do not relate to a passage.

6. Suppose that you need to write a report for social studies that describes the state of Alaska, including its geographical location, climate, main industries, and population. Choose all the sources that you could use to find facts for your report. There is more than one correct choice listed below.

   A. nonfiction book

   B. current atlas

   C. Web site ending *.com*

   D. fiction book

   E. encyclopedia entry

   F. Web site ending *.edu*

---

7. Read the bibliographies below and the directions that follow.

Jaros, Phillip. <u>Computer Technology Today</u>. New York: Ideal Publishing, 2011.
Sarah Hart. Learning Apps Quickly. <u>Smartphones in a Smart World</u>. New York City: 2010.
Mueller, B.J. <u>Adding Technology to Everyday Life</u>. San Francisco: Golden Gate Press, 2013.

   Part A

   Circle the entry that is incorrect.

   Part B

   State the reasons that the bibliographic entry is incorrect. Write your responses on the lines below.

   _____

   _____

   _____

8. Read the title in each choice. Then match the title to one type of resource on the right.

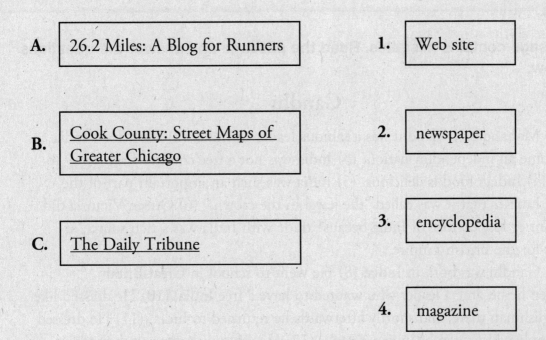

A. 26.2 Miles: A Blog for Runners

B. Cook County: Street Maps of Greater Chicago

C. The Daily Tribune

1. Web site

2. newspaper

3. encyclopedia

4. magazine

5. atlas

Cumulative Assessment

This passage contains mistakes. Read the passage and answer the questions that follow.

Gandhi

(1) Mohandas K. Gandhi was a famous leader in India. (2) He helped India to become an <u>independint</u> nation. (3) India was not a free country from 1869 to 1948. (4) Indian food is delicious. (5) India was such an important part of the British Empire that it was called "the jewel in the crown." (6) Queen Victoria did not want to lose control of India because trade with India was a rich source of money for the British Empire.

(7) Gandhi was born in India. (8) He went to school in Great Britain. (9) Then he became a leader who wanted to have a free India. (10) He dressed like an Englishman there, and shortly afterwards he returned to India. (11) He dressed in a simple white wrap of Indian cotton. (12) He refused to wear cloth made in Britain.

(13) Gandhi believed that India should not try to become free by fighting. (14) He will want Great Britain to free India. (15) Gandhi felt certain that India could persuade the British peacefully. (16) Soon, he led his people on a 200-mile-long walk to protest the British tax on salt. (17) He led people all the way to the coast. (18) They reached the ocean and made salt from the seawater. (19) They showed the British that Indians did not need to use British salt.

(20) Gandhi planned and led many protests. (21) He was arrested many times for participating in these activities. (22) Sadly, he died before Great Britain freed India. (23) Most people gives Gandhi credit for India becoming free.

1. Which sentence does NOT belong in paragraph 1?

   A. Indian food is delicious.

   B. India was such an important part of the British Empire that it was called "the jewel in the crown."

   C. India was not a free country from 1869 to 1948.

   D. Mohandas K. Gandhi was a famous leader in India.

2. Which sentence is the BEST revision of sentence 16?

   A. Later, he led his people on a 200-mile-long walk to protest the British tax on salt.

   B. Once, he led his people on a 200-mile-long walk to protest the British tax on salt.

   C. Next, he led his people on a 200-mile-long walk to protest the British tax on salt.

   D. Finally, he led his people on a 200-mile-long walk to protest the British tax on salt.

3. Which sentence has incorrect subject-verb agreement?

   A. He dressed like an Englishman there, and shortly after, he returned to India.

   B. Then he became a leader who wanted to have a free India.

   C. He dressed in a simple white wrap of Indian cotton.

   D. Most people gives Gandhi credit for India becoming free.

4. Which is the correct spelling of the underlined word in sentence 2?

   A. indapendent

   B. independence

   C. indupendent

   D. independent

5. Which is the BEST way to reorder paragraph 2?

   A. Move sentence 8 before sentence 7.

   B. Move sentence 12 before sentence 10.

   C. Move sentence 10 before sentence 9.

   D. Move sentence 11 before sentence 10.

6. Which is the BEST way to paraphrase sentence 6?

   A. The British Empire made money from trading with India, so Queen Victoria wanted to keep India under her control.

   B. Queen Victoria wanted to keep India because the British Empire saw it as a rich source of money.

   C. The British Empire knew India was a rich source of money, so Queen Victoria did not want to lose control of the country.

   D. Losing control of India would be bad for Queen Victoria because the British Empire would lose a lot of money.

Informational Prompt

Write an informational piece about your favorite holiday. Tell what the holiday is, at what time in the year it falls, how you celebrate it, and why it is your favorite. Be sure to include facts and details about the holiday to support your writing. Use the checklist below to help you do your best writing.

Does your essay

❑ have a clear and focused subject?

❑ have a strong topic sentence?

❑ have a logical structure?

❑ present information clearly?

❑ use linking words and phrases to join ideas?

❑ use a style and vocabulary that are correct for the audience and purpose?

❑ have a solid conclusion?

❑ have good spelling, capitalization, and punctuation?

❑ follow the rules for good grammar?

Write your response on the page provided. You may use your own paper if you need more space.

CHAPTER

4 Language

4 Diagnostic Assessment

This passage contains mistakes. Read the passage and answer the questions that follow.

How to Pack for a Trip

(1) Have you ever gone on a trip somewhere? (2) It's so exciting to get ready for a trip away from home! (3) Whether it is a short weekend at a relative's house or an extended stay in a foreign <u>location</u>, traveling can be a great way to relax. (4) But what should you bring with you on your trip? (5) There are so many things to think about. (6) What will you <u>where</u>? (7) What kinds of personal items do you need? (8) Are there other things to bring along, too?

(9) The first thing to consider when planning what to pack is your Destination. (10) Are you going somewhere tropical and warm like Aruba, or someplace cooler like Alaska? (11) Be sure to pack clothing that is appropriate for the weather. (12) Even if you are going somewhere warm, bring at least one long-sleeved shirt in case the temperature drops at night. (13) Likewise, when traveling somewhere cold, bring a cotton, comfortable T-shirt in case the weather warms up. (14) Shoes are also an important part of your wardrobe. (15) Bring sandals for warm weather. (16) Heavy boots for the cold.

(17) Don't forget the following personal items soap, toothbrush, toothpaste, and shampoo. (18) You may also want to bring a book to keep you entertained. (19) Music may help you as well. (20) Some travelers bring a journal who they use to record all the details of their trip. (21) Keep your journal under your backpack. (22) If this is your first trip, you may want to think about writing down your experiences each day. (23) That way, you can remember your trip after you've come home. (24) You can also share your experiences with friends and family. (25) Try to bring a camera to snap some pictures of special things you see. (26) It's a wonderful way to remember your trip.

(27) Whatever corner of the world you're off to, happy travels! (28) Remember, the best part of traveling is whom you meet. (29) Especially when you were visiting a new place, people can be so helpful! (30) Have a great time on all your adventures!

1. Which word from paragraph 2 is NOT capitalized correctly?

   A. Alaska

   B. Aruba

   C. Destination

   D. Likewise

2. Which of the following is the correct revision of sentence 17?

   A. Don't forget the following personal items, soap, toothbrush, toothpaste, and shampoo.

   B. Don't forget the following personal items: soap, toothbrush, toothpaste, and shampoo.

   C. Don't forget the following personal items; soap, toothbrush, toothpaste, and shampoo.

   D. Don't forget the following personal items "soap, toothbrush, toothpaste, and shampoo."

3. The correct spelling of the underlined word in sentence 6 is

   A. ware.

   B. were.

   C. we're.

   D. wear.

4. Which of the following is NOT a complete sentence?

   A. What will you wear?

   B. Heavy boots for the cold.

   C. Music may help you as well.

   D. Have a great time on all your adventures!

5. What is the correct way to write the verb in sentence 29?

   A. are visiting

   B. should visit

   C. will visit

   D. was visiting

6. What is the correct way to write sentence 13?

A. Likewise, when traveling somewhere cold, bring T-shirt of cotton and comfortable in case the weather warms up.

B. Likewise, when traveling somewhere cold, bring a T-shirt of more comfortable cotton in case the weather warms up.

C. Likewise, when traveling somewhere cold, bring a comfortable and cotton T-shirt in case the weather warms up.

D. Likewise, when traveling somewhere cold, bring a comfortable cotton T-shirt in case the weather warms up.

7. How could sentence 20 be corrected?

A. Change *who* to *whom*.

B. Change *who* to *which*.

C. Change *they* to *we*

D. Change *their* to *our*.

8. What is the BEST way to rewrite sentence 21?

A. Keep your journal in your backpack.

B. Keep your journal above your backpack.

C. Keep your journal on your backpack.

D. Keep your journal next to your backpack.

9. What is the suffix in the word <u>location</u>? What does the word <u>location</u> MOST LIKELY mean?

_____

_____

_____

_____

Read the passage and answer the questions that follow.

Matthew's Sunday

Matthew was not having a good day. It was Sunday morning and he was supposed to be going to the mall. But he couldn't find his running shoes anywhere, and his favorite jeans were dirty. Outside, clouds were gathering. But the biggest problem was that Matthew didn't want to go to the mall. He had a new puppy, Jasper, which his family had adopted from the animal rescue. Jasper's fur was as white as snow. Matthew already taught Jasper how to sit on command.

"Woof!" Jasper barked, at the foot of Matthew's bed. The puppy shivered with excitement, as if he knew that Matthew was thinking about him. Jasper bounced around Matthew's legs like a jumping bean. The thought of having to leave his pup to go to the mall was putting Matthew in a cranky mood. Just then, Sam, Matthew's older brother, popped his head in the doorway. He seemed as happy as could be.

"Ready, Jubilee?" Jubilee was Matthew's nickname.

"No," Matthew said, frowning, "I'm not."

Then Matthew hatched a plan. He clutched his stomach and stretched his mouth into a fairly fearsome-looking frown. "I don't feel very good. My stomach hurts," Matthew groaned. He got on his bed, stomach first. He stayed there, hoping Sam would go away. But Sam just stood there.

"Mom!" Sam hollered. "Matthew is being difficult."

Matthew heard his mother's footsteps as she walked down the hall toward his room.

"What's the deal, Matthew Timothy Jones?"

Matthew felt nervous. The only time his mother called him by his full name was when he was about to get into trouble. Matthew eyed his mother from the safety of his bed. She did not look pleased. Jasper was now in his dog bed, with his head between his paws. He looked as unhappy and <u>forlorn</u> as Matthew.

"Why are you in your pajamas?" his mother asked. "I told you last night at dinner that we were going shopping today."

"I don't think I should go to the mall," Matthew whined, rubbing his belly. "I don't feel well."

Matthew's mother walked over and put her hand to his forehead.

"You don't feel like you have a fever, Jubilee," his mother said.

"It's my stomach," Matthew complained, sitting up. "It's burbling inside. My stomach is like a battlefield. I'm afraid it will get worse if I don't rest."

Jasper jumped up beside Matthew, nudging his hand with his cold, wet nose. Matthew nearly laughed, but let out a burst of air that sounded like a half-cough, half-snort instead.

"See?" Matthew pointed to his throat. "It's getting worse already."

Matthew's mother eyed Sam, who was standing in the doorway, shaking his head.

"All right," she said. "Sam, let's go to the mall. Your brother should stay at home with Dad, as it seems that he needs to rest."

Before shutting the door, Matthew's mother turned back to look at him. He was now under the covers, and Jasper was underneath them, too, walking beside Matthew's legs like a lumpy ghost. Seconds after the door closed, Matthew whipped off the blankets.

"Hurray!" he whisper-shouted to Jasper, who was sniffing one of Matthew's pillows. "We did it! We get to spend the afternoon together!"

Jasper was just as excited as Matthew was, and jumped on the floor to do his jumping-bean dance again. Matthew danced in the middle of his room, hopping from one foot to another, trying to imitate Jasper. Right then, Matthew's door opened. Matthew's mother stood there, with Sam right behind her. She had her hands on her hips and looked <u>furious</u>. Without another word, Matthew walked to his dresser. He pulled out a pair of jeans and a shirt, and then he went to his closet and grabbed a pair of socks and shoes.

"Matthew, grow up. Meet us in the car in five minutes, please," his mother said, before turning to walk down the hallway.

"Yes, ma'am," Matthew answered. Then Matthew looked at Jasper and said, "Well, you win some, you lose some." And with those words, Matthew's Sunday was decided.

10. Read this sentence from the passage.

> **Jasper bounced around Matthew's legs like a jumping bean.**

What does the simile in the sentence mean?

  A. Jasper looked like a bean.

  B. Matthew's legs were shaking.

  C. Jasper ran in circles around Matthew's legs.

  D. Jasper bounced energetically and quickly.

11. What is the BEST way to paraphrase the adage <u>you win some, you lose some</u>?

  A. Sometimes things don't go your way.

  B. The most important thing is winning.

  C. Play the best game you can.

  D. Listen to the advice of others.

12. What is a synonym for the word underline{furious}?

   A. worried

   B. waiting

   C. angry

   D. patient

13. Read this sentence from the passage.

   He got on his bed, stomach first.

Which word would make the underlined word more precise?

   A. was

   B. flopped

   C. stayed

   D. sat

14. Read this sentence from the passage.

He looked as unhappy and <u>forlorn</u> as Matthew.

What does the word <u>forlorn</u> mean? What context clue helped you figure out the meaning of the word?

_____

_____

_____

24 Grammar and Usage

Getting the Idea

A **verb** is a word that shows action or a state of being. A **modal auxiliary verb** relates a possibility or necessity of an action. The words *can*, *may*, *must*, *should*, and *will* are modal verbs. A modal verb can express a level of certainty or a suggestion. (*You should have more salad.*) A modal verb can also show permission or a requirement. (*You may have more salad.*)

Verb tense is the time in which a sentence takes place, in the past, present, or future.

> **Progressive tense:** expresses an ongoing action without a specific end time. (*Dina was jogging in the park when it started to rain.*)

> **Past progressive tense:** tells about an ongoing action that already happened. (*I was talking to Mom when the phone rang.*)

> **Present progressive tense:** tells about an ongoing action that is happening now. (*Joel is reading a book about Albert Einstein.*)

> **Future progressive tense:** tells about an ongoing action that has not happened yet. (*Mark will be waiting for you on the front porch.*)

An **adjective** tells more about a noun. Up to three adjectives can be used with the same noun. The adjectives should appear in the following order, from left to right: opinion, size, age, shape, color, origin (where something comes from), and material. (*The big blue rubber ball bounced into the street.* size, color, material)

An **adverb** tells more about a verb, adjective, or another adverb. The **relative adverbs** *when*, *where*, and *why* are used at the beginning of a **relative clause,** a group of words that tells more about a noun. In this sentence, the relative clause is underlined, and the relative adverb is in *italic* print: Jason never told us the reason *why* he left.

Thinking It Through 1

Read the following sentences. Write them correctly on the lines provided.

1. You should brush your teeth twice a day.

_____

HINT This is a suggestion. Use *may*, *must*, or *can*.

2. Glen should eat more fruit.

_____

3. Tomorrow we were going to the movies.

_____

4. I going to the store now.

_____

5. My grandmother gave me this silver, lovely necklace.

_____

6. Mr. Lopez spends all day rocking on his wooden old porch.

_____

7. I don't remember a time where we had more fun.

_____

8. That girl, which swims like a fish, stayed in the pool all afternoon.

_____

A **pronoun** is a word that takes the place of a noun. The **relative pronouns** *who*, *whom*, *that*, *which*, and *whose* are used in relative clauses. The relative clause in this sentence is underlined, and the relative pronoun is in italic print: The runner *who* finished last was hurt. The relative pronoun stands for the noun that comes before it.

Prepositions are words that are used to name a point in time, a direction, or to show where something is. (*Wash your hands before dinner.*)

A **prepositional phrase** is a group of words that begins with a preposition and includes its object (a noun or pronoun). (*We hiked up the path.*) A prepositional phrase can act as an adjective or an adverb. (Adjective: *The birds in that tree sing every morning.* Adverb: *Their mother woke before dawn.*)

A **complete sentence** expresses a complete thought with a subject, a verb, and proper punctuation. A **fragment** is an incomplete sentence, missing a subject or a verb. You can fix a fragment by adding the missing subject or verb. (Fragment: *Going to the beach.* Corrected sentence: *Tyrone is going to the beach.*) A **run-on sentence** combines at least two sentences. Here are ways to fix a run-on sentence: split it into two separate sentences, separate the two parts of the sentence with a semicolon, or separate the two parts of the sentence with a comma and a conjunction. (Incorrect: *I love surfing I also love skateboarding.* Correct: *I love surfing, and I also love skateboarding.*)

Homophones are words that sound the same, but have different spellings and meanings.

to = in the direction of	there = in a certain location
too = also	they're = they are
two = the number 2	their = something belonging to them
Lucy will go to the store later. Ann will go, too.	*They're headed to school with their backpacks.*

When writing, choose **precise**, or specific, words to express your ideas. (General: *The purse is big.* Precise: *The purse is gigantic.*) Precise nouns, verbs, adjectives, and adverbs will help you express your ideas. Two of the most common styles of writing are **formal** and **informal**. A formal style uses language that is proper and serious. (*In 1776, the American colonists declared their independence.*) An informal style is more personal, casual, and conversational. (*In 1776, the Americans decided to run things themselves.*) Choose a style that suits the **purpose**, or reason, for your writing. If you are writing a history report, use a formal tone. If you are writing a fictional story, an informal tone may be a good idea.

Thinking It Through 2

Read the following sentences. Write them correctly on the lines provided.

1. You may see fish from the boat under the water's surface.

   _____

   HINT Is it likely that the boat is underwater? Where are the fish?

2. On the table, Dave put the books back.

   _____

3. My family and I love to go sledding in the winter

   _____

4. Will watch the shuttle launch on TV.

   _____

5. Marissa is going on vacation with her family they are going to New York.

   _____

6. My sister wants to go to the movies two.

   _____

7. Victor, Leo, and I.

   _____

8. Please give that book. Its mine.

   _____

This passage contains mistakes. Use the Reading Guide to help you find the mistakes.

Reading Guide
Remember, perfect tenses show action already completed.

The Audition

(1) Last month, I decided I am going too try out for the school play. (2) It seems that the same kids always get the parts. (3) I felt it was time for a new face on the stage. (4) I was hoping that the teachers would feel the same way.

(5) The play the teachers chose this year was Oliver Twist. (6) I knew it was about a poor boy in England, but that was about it. (7) On the day of try-outs, my hands started sweating. (8) I am regretting my decision to show up for the audition.

(9) One by one the students were called onto the stage. (10) Suddenly I heard my name called. (11) I felt tiny metal ugly butterflies in my stomach. (12) My friend Patrick was sitting next to me. (13) He told me I should not worry, and that I would do fine.

(14) I stood on stage and looked at the script. (15) I was thinking about how the play takes place in England. (16) I guess that was why a strange voice came out of my mouth when I started to speak. (17) I sounded like those people in a British TV show, not a kid from America. (18) I could not stop myself. (19) Instead, I kept reading my lines.

(20) When I finished, everyone clapped! (21) Some people whistled and cheered. (22) "Well," one teacher joked, "Guess what be playing the part of Oliver?"

Answer the following questions.

1. What is the BEST way to rewrite sentence 1?

   A. Last month, I decided I were going to try out for the school play.

   B. Last month, I decided I will be going too try out for the school play.

   C. Last month, I decided I was going two try out for the school play.

   D. Last month, I decided I was going to try out for the school play.

2. What is the correct way to write the verb in sentence 8?

   A. was regretting

   B. will be regretting

   C. should regret

   D. will regret

3. What is the best way to correct sentence 11?

   A. I felt metal tiny ugly butterflies in my stomach.

   B. I felt ugly tiny metal butterflies in my stomach.

   C. I felt ugly metal tiny butterflies in my stomach.

   D. I felt tiny metal butterflies in my stomach.

4. What is the BEST way to replace sentence 13 with a modal verb?

   A. He told me I might not worry, and that I would do fine.

   B. He told me I should not worry, and that I might do fine.

   C. He told me I must not worry, and that I would do fine.

   D. He told me I cannot worry, and that I would do fine.

5. Read sentence 22. Write it correctly on the line below.

   _____

   _____

   _____

   _____

   _____

The following questions do not relate to the passage.

6. Read the phrases and the directions that follow.

   Sue needs school shoes.

   The mall opens at 10:00.

   It will take her an hour to find shoes.

   She plans to get lunch next.

   Which sentence below BEST combines the sentences above using prepositions?

   A. Sue shops at the mall from 10:00 until 11:00 to buy school shoes before lunch.

   B. Sue first goes to the mall to buy school shoes and then goes to lunch.

   C. Sue goes at 10:00 for an hour to the mall to get shoes before she has lunch.

   D. Sue will be at the mall near 10:00 at a shoe store to buy shoes and eat.

   _____

7. Read the paragraph and then the directions.

   Every August. A festival takes place in our town. The festival includes rides, games, music, and food the food is my favorite part! Although they are not very nutritious. festival foods such as hot dogs, funnel cakes, and snow cones are always delicious. It is OK to eat foods like that once in a while!

   Revise the paragraph to correct sentence errors. The revised paragraph should be well organized and should include sentences that are clear and complete.

   Write your answer on the lines below.

   _____

   _____

   _____

   _____

   _____

   _____

   _____

8. A student is writing an essay describing her favorite room. Read this paragraph from the essay and then read the directions that follow.

    > **My room is next to the kitchen. The bedspread has <u>colors</u>. I put <u>a lot of</u> pictures of <u>people</u> on the walls.**

    The student needs to revise her essay to use precise words. Which words BEST replace the underlined words?

    A. blue colors; many; faces

    B. many colors; tons of; everyone

    C. multiple colors; several; people I know

    D. bright, happy colors; dozens of; family and friends

---

9. Choose all the options that would be best suited for a formal writing style and tone. There is more than one correct choice listed below.

    A. e-mail to a friend

    B. science experiment

    C. essay about the Civil War

    D. letter to a cousin

    E. letter to a store manager

    F. history report

    G. note to a family member

25 Capitalization and Spelling

Getting the Idea

Following the rules of capitalization and spelling is important because it will help you write clearly. **Capitalization** is using capital (or uppercase) letters where necessary. The chart below lists rules for when to capitalize a word.

Capitalize	Examples
the first letter of the first word in a sentence	Everyone should read a mystery novel.
proper names	Heidi, James, Central Elementary School, Iowa, Los Angeles
titles that come before someone's name	Mrs. Chung, Dr. Jeffries, Principal Graziano
the main words in a title	*Charlie and the Chocolate Factory*
days, months, and holidays	Friday, June, Memorial Day
the greeting in a letter	Dear Jose,
the first word in a letter's closing	Sincerely yours,
the pronoun "I"	I love playing soccer.

Here are some common mistakes in capitalization to avoid.

Incorrect: My family visited my uncle in a nearby Town.
Correct: My family visited my uncle in a nearby town.
Why: Since the town is not a proper name, it does not need to be capitalized.

Incorrect: Julie went camping in Yosemite National park.
Correct: Julie went camping in Yosemite National Park.
Why: Yosemite National Park is the complete name, so all three words should be capitalized.

Incorrect: This year, independence day is on a sunday.
Correct: This year, Independence Day is on a Sunday.
Why: Always capitalize days, months of the year, and names of holidays.

Thinking It Through 1

Read the following sentences. Write them correctly on the lines provided. If the sentence is correct, write "correct as is."

1. the trees outside swayed in the breeze.

_____

> **HINT** The first word of a sentence should be capitalized.

2. I asked maria for help with my homework.

_____

> **HINT** Proper names should be capitalized.

3. Nathan brought the package to mrs. Boyce.

_____

4. Have you seen the movie *The Incredibles*?

_____

5. My mom and i love going to flea markets.

_____

6. Every year, we have a block party on memorial day.

_____

7. Mrs. Freeman took the class on a trip.

_____

8. We got ice cream last night at an ice cream parlor called scoop's.

_____

Here are some general rules that can help you know how to spell a word.

Spelling Rule	Examples
Put *i* before *e*, except after *c*, or when sounding like "ay" as in *neighbor* and *weigh*.	believe, field, receive, ceiling (*weird* is a word that breaks this rule)
Drop the silent *e* when adding a suffix that starts with a vowel.	bike—biking, wave—wavy
Don't drop the silent *e* when adding a suffix that starts with a consonant.	use—useless, state—statement
If a word ends with a consonant + *y*, change the *y* to *i* when adding a suffix (unless the suffix begins with *i*).	plenty—plentiful, happy—happiness
If a word ends with a vowel + *y*, just add the suffix.	play—playful, stray—strayed
If a one-syllable word ends in one vowel + one consonant, double the consonant before you add a suffix that begins with a vowel.	swim—swimming, bat—batter
If a word has more than one syllable where the accent is on the final syllable, double the final consonant.	control—controlled, prefer—preferred

Most nouns have plurals that follow regular rules. These nouns can be made plural by adding the suffix *-s* or *-es* (*star—stars, box—boxes*). Some nouns are irregular. They do not follow these rules. Here are some examples: *life—lives, wolf—wolves, tooth—teeth, mouse—mice, child—children, sheep—sheep*. If you are unsure of a noun's plural form, look it up in a dictionary.

Thinking It Through 2

Read the following sentences. Write them correctly on the lines provided. If the sentence is correct, write "correct as is."

1. The gooses ran around in the park.

_____

HINT The word *goose* forms a plural irregularly. It's similar to the word *foot* and its plural, *feet*.

2. She was decieved by her best friend.

_____

HINT Always remember to put *i* before *e* except after *c*.

3. I was very grateful for the help Julius gave me.

_____

4. The fury dog was soft to hold.

_____

5. The climbers hikked up the mountain.

_____

6. May I please have a piece of cake?

_____

7. The dentist told Ken that his two front tooths would grow back soon.

_____

8. Aaron beleives he can finish the race.

_____

This passage contains mistakes. Use the Reading Guide to help you find the mistakes.

Reading Guide

In sentence 1, *America* is a proper noun. Proper nouns, including the names of places and holidays, are always capitalized.

Is the word *countrys* correct in sentence 2? Apply the rule: If a word ends in *y*, change the *y* to *i* and add *-es*.

In sentence 12, the word *people* is an irregular plural of the word *person*.

Find the word that is incorrectly capitalized in sentence 16.

In sentence 18, the word *stepped* was formed in the following way: The word *step* is a one-syllable word ending in a vowel, *e*, and a consonant, *p*. Doubling the consonant before adding a suffix that begins with a vowel, *-ed*, gives you *stepped*.

A New Land

(1) In one hundred years, between 1824 and 1924, close to thirty-five million people came to America. (2) They left the countrys where they were born to find a new life. (3) It took courage to leave everything that was familiar.

(4) Until 1924, there were no strict laws about who could come into the United States. (5) New, stricter laws were passed in 1924. (6) The new laws made getting into our country more difficult.

(7) Many of the people who came here from Europe between 1824 and 1924 came on a ship, in steerage. (8) Steerage was in the bottom of a ship. (9) The people were jamed together. (10) They had a very uncomfortable voyage. (11) Many were seasick.

(12) Most of these people coming to America from Europe could only speak their own Language. (13) They would have to learn English as soon as they arrived.

(14) When the ships got to new york, the people in Steerage had to be examined at Ellis island. (15) Doctors looked at them to see if they had any diseases. (16) People from steerage had to answer questions about how they could take care of their Families. (17) They would have to be able to work and earn money.

(18) It is safe to say that when people first stepped into their new country, they were a little frightened. (19) They were also very hopful.

Answer the following questions.

1. The correct way to spell <u>jamed</u> in sentence 9 is

   A. jameed.

   B. jammed.

   C. jamd.

   D. jammd.

2. Which word in sentence 12 should NOT be capitalized?

   A. Most

   B. Europe

   C. Language

   D. America

3. Read this sentence from the passage.

   When the ships got to new york, the people in Steerage had to be examined at Ellis island.

   What is the correct way to rewrite this sentence?

   A. When the ships got to New York, the people in steerage had to be examined at Ellis Island.

   B. When the ships got to new York, the people in Steerage had to be examined at ellis island.

   C. When the ships got to New York, the people in steerage had to be examined at Ellis island.

   D. When the ships got to New york, the people in Steerage had to be examined at Ellis island.

4. The correct way to spell <u>hopful</u> in sentence 19 is

   A. hoppeful.

   B. hopiful.

   C. hopefull.

   D. hopeful.

The following questions do not relate to a passage.

5. A student is writing a report about China. Read these sentences from the report and then read the directions that follow.

> **Over one billion people live in china, working at factorys in large cities like beijing. People live in large apartment buildings and bike or walk to work.**

The student needs to correct the first sentence using correct capitalization and spelling. Which words BEST correct the first sentence?

A. Billion, living, Beijing

B. over, China, citys

C. People, Factories, Cities

D. China, factories, Beijing

---

6. Use your answer to Part A to answer Part B.

Part A

Which sentence below has correct capitalization?

A. On july 20, 1969, U.S. astronaut Neil Armstrong walked on the moon.

B. On July 20, 1969, U.S. astronaut neil armstrong walked on the moon.

C. On July 20, 1969, U.S. astronaut Neil Armstrong walked on the moon.

D. On July 20, 1969, u.s. astronaut Neil Armstrong walked on the moon.

Part B

Which sentence below best supports the answer to Part A?

A. Capitalize proper names.

B. Capitalize the greeting of a letter.

C. Capitalize the main words a title of a book.

D. Capitalize the names of holidays.

E. Capitalize the first word in a sentence.

7. The following paragraph is from a student's research paper about Abraham Lincoln. Read the paragraph. Then rewrite it, revising it to correct errors.

> **Abraham lincoln was the sixteenth president of the United States. he served as president during the civil War, when the North and South fighted over slavery. lincoln did not believe in war but did not agree with slavery. He eventually abolished slavery as the war ended. He began work to reunite the country, hopeing to bring the citys together into one nation. Unfortunately, he didn't have time. lincoln was assassinated by John Wilkes Booth, an actor, on april 14, 1864, at a play in Washington, D.C.**

_____

_____

_____

_____

_____

_____

_____

_____

_____

_____

_____

_____

_____

_____

_____

_____

_____

_____

_____

_____

26 Punctuation

Getting the Idea

Punctuation is the symbols that are used to organize sentences. Using the correct punctuation helps make your writing clear.

End marks show what kind of sentence you are writing. A **period** (.) is used to make a statement. Use a **question mark** (?) when you are asking a question. An **exclamation point** (!) is used to show excitement, surprise, or strong emotion.

> What are you doing for vacation this summer?
> I'm visiting my cousin in San Francisco.
> Wow, that sounds exciting!

A **comma** (,) is used to show a pause in a sentence or to connect ideas.

When to Use a Comma	Example
to separate items in a list	I need to buy milk, eggs, and bread.
to set off words people speak	My mom said, "Don't stay up too late."
after an introductory phrase	When I was your age, I didn't like spicy foods.
before a conjunction (*and, but*) in a compound sentence	I like most fruits, but my favorite is watermelon.
between the names of cities and states	My grandparents were married in Boston, Massachusetts.
between the day and year in a date	Renee's birthday is August 24, 2000.

Use **quotation marks** (" ") around dialogue, or the words that people say.

> "Where are you going?" Dad asked.
> "I need to get a book from the library," Tim replied.
> "On your way there," Dad said, "please mail this letter."

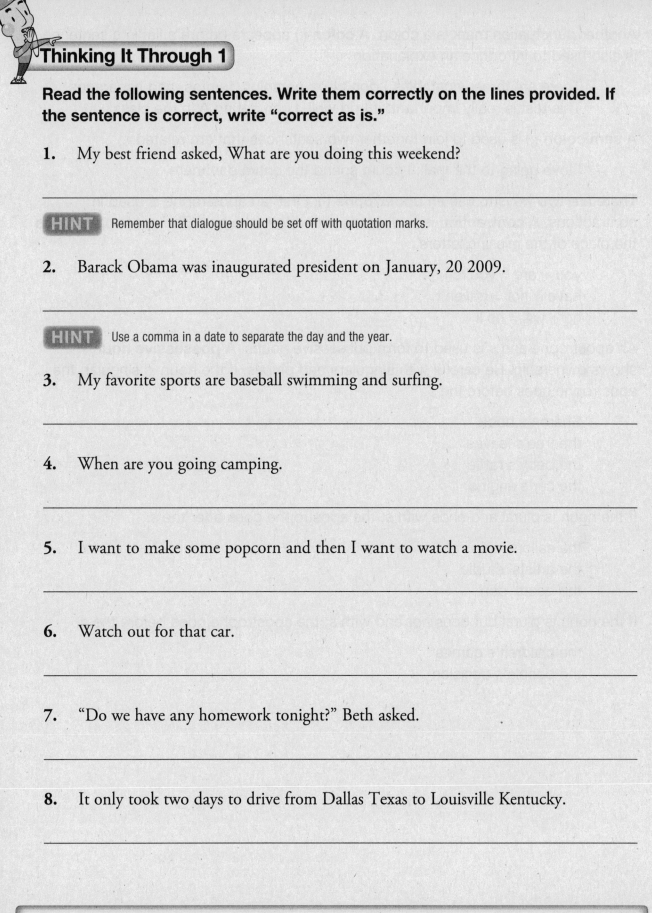

Thinking It Through 1

Read the following sentences. Write them correctly on the lines provided. If the sentence is correct, write "correct as is."

1. My best friend asked, What are you doing this weekend?

_____

HINT Remember that dialogue should be set off with quotation marks.

2. Barack Obama was inaugurated president on January, 20 2009.

_____

HINT Use a comma in a date to separate the day and the year.

3. My favorite sports are baseball swimming and surfing.

_____

4. When are you going camping.

_____

5. I want to make some popcorn and then I want to watch a movie.

_____

6. Watch out for that car.

_____

7. "Do we have any homework tonight?" Beth asked.

_____

8. It only took two days to drive from Dallas Texas to Louisville Kentucky.

_____

Another punctuation mark is a colon. A **colon** (:) appears before a list in a sentence. It is also used to introduce an explanation.

> There are three vegetables I don't like: parsnips, turnips, and asparagus.
> This test is really important: if I do well, I can get an A in the class.

A **semicolon** (;) is used to join together two sentences that are related.

> I love going to the mall; I could spend the entire day there.

There are two ways to use an **apostrophe** ('). First, an apostrophe is used in contractions. A **contraction** is two words joined to make one. The apostrophe takes the place of the missing letters.

> you + are = you're
> have + not = haven't
> he + will = he'll

An apostrophe and *s* is used to form possessive nouns. A **possessive noun** shows ownership. Be careful with singulars and plurals. If the noun is singular, the apostrophe goes before the *s*.

> Sharon's book
> the tree's leaves
> the baby's rattle
> the car's engine

If the noun is plural and ends with *s*, the apostrophe goes after the *s*.

> the sailors' ship
> the artists' studio
> the bears' den

If the noun is plural but does *not* end with *s*, the apostrophe goes before the *s*.

> the children's games
> the people's decision

Thinking It Through 2

Read the following sentences. Write them correctly on the lines provided. If the sentence is correct, write "correct as is."

1. Lee put three things in her bag a sweater, a magazine, and an apple.

_____

HINT   Use a colon before a list in a sentence.

2. I can't wait for the weekend I'm going with my friends to see a movie.

_____

HINT   Use a semicolon to join two complete sentences that relate to the same idea.

3. I asked to borrow Bens pencil because mine broke.

_____

4. Dont you just love that new dance competition show?

_____

5. I need to get some school supplies a notebook, three folders, and a box of markers.

_____

6. The babies' toys were scattered all over the room.

_____

7. I need to practice the clarinet tonight I have a concert tomorrow.

_____

8. I won't be able to go to your house after school today.

_____

This passage contains mistakes. Use the Reading Guide to help you find the mistakes.

Reading Guide

Notice the commas in sentence 1. A comma is used after the introductory phrase. A comma is also used before the word *but*.

Read sentence 2 aloud. Does it sound right to pause after the word *someone*? If not, then a comma is not necessary.

Look at the dialogue in sentence 7. Notice how the quotation marks go on either side of the speaker's words, and the end punctuation falls inside the closing quotation marks.

What punctuation marks belong around the speaker's words in sentence 8? Where should they be placed?

Planning the Perfect Party

(1) When my dad called a family meeting, I didn't know what to expect, but I feared the worst. (2) Family meetings usually meant someone, did something wrong.

(3) Hey, he said, "do you have any ideas of what we can do for your moms fortieth birthday."

(4) We considered a fancy dinner, but we'd already eaten in every nice restaurant in our town. (5) Toledo Ohio does have plenty of wonderful restaurants, but none of them would be really new or exciting for Mom. (6) I thought we should do something more original, since this was a big birthday for her.

(7) "What if we created a scavenger hunt around town that would lead her back here for a surprise party?" I asked.

(8) That's a great idea! my sister agreed.

(9) I explained that we would need to buy some party supplies balloons streamers candles and a cake. (10) My dad thought that was reasonable it shouldn't cost too much money.

(11) The next day, my dad, sister, and I began planning the perfect party for my mom.

Answer the following questions.

1. Which of the following is the correct revision of sentence 3?

    A. "Hey", he said, "do you have any ideas of what we can do for your moms fortieth birthday."

    B. "Hey," he said, "do you have any ideas of what we can do for your moms' fortieth birthday?"

    C. "Hey," he said, "do you have any ideas of what we can do for your mom's fortieth birthday?"

    D. "Hey", he said, "do you have any ideas of what we can do for your moms fortieth birthday!"

2. Why does sentence 5 need a comma added to it?

    A. to set off an introductory phrase

    B. to separate one place name from another

    C. to separate items in a list

    D. to go before a conjunction in a compound sentence

3. Which of the following is the correct revision of sentence 10?

    A. My dad thought that was reasonable. it shouldn't cost too much money.

    B. My dad thought that was reasonable and it shouldn't cost too much money.

    C. My dad thought that was reasonable, it shouldn't cost too much money.

    D. My dad thought that was reasonable; it shouldn't cost too much money.

4. Which of the following is the correct revision of sentence 9?

    A. I explained that we would need to buy: some party supplies balloons, streamers and candles, and a cake.

    B. I explained that we would need to buy some party supplies; balloons streamers and candles and a cake.

    C. I explained that we would need to buy some party supplies: balloons, streamers, candles, and a cake.

    D. I explained that we would need to buy some party supplies, balloons, streamers, and candles and a cake.

The following questions do not relate to a passage.

5. Use your answer to Part A to answer Part B.

Part A

Which sentence below has correct punctuation?

A. To research my essay, I'll read magazines, encyclopedias, and newspapers at the library in Springfield, Illinois.

B. To research my essay Ill read magazines encyclopedias and newspapers at the library in Springfield Illinois.

C. To research my essay I'll read magazines, encyclopedias, and newspapers at the library in Springfield Illinois.

D. To research my essay, Ill read magazines, encyclopedias, and newspapers at the library in Springfield Illinois.

Part B

Which sentence below best supports the answer to Part A?

A. Commas are used before a conjunction, between the names of cities and states, and after the names of states.

B. Commas are used after an introductory phrase, to separate items in a list, and between the names of cities and states.

C. Commas are used between the day and year in a date, after items in a list, and to set off words people speak.

D. Commas are used before an introductory phrase, before items in a list, and before the names of cities and states.

E. Commas are used after an introductory phrase, between the names of states, and between the day and year in a date.

6. A student is writing a narrative. Read these sentences from the narrative and then read the directions that follow.

> **Fly fishing is my favorite way to spend time. My father and grandfather take me often. We go to a nearby lake very early in the morning. The most important things to remember when fishing practice, patience, and persistence.**

The student needs to correct the last sentence using correct punctuation. Which sentence BEST revises the sentence?

A. The most important things to remember when fishing' practice, patience, and persistence.

B. The most important things to remember when fishing; practice, patience, and persistence.

C. The most important things to remember when fishing: practice, patience, and persistence.

D. "The most important things to remember when fishing," practice, patience, and persistence.

7. The following paragraphs are from the first draft of a student's story about a family reunion. Rewrite the paragraphs, revising to correct errors in punctuation.

> **The family reunion was in two days and Matthew still didn't know what everyone was going to eat for dinner.**
> **Do you think everyone likes chicken." he asked his cousin.**
> **"Not everyone eats meat?" Wanda warned.**
> **"I don't know what I am going to serve to all these people" Matthew cried!**
> **"Pasta." Wanda shouted.**
> **"Pasta." Matthew repeated Then he grinned and said "Yes! Pasta? Thanks, Wanda."**

_____

_____

_____

_____

_____

_____

27 Determining Word Meanings

Getting the Idea

Sometimes, you may come across an unfamiliar word as you read. One way to figure out the meaning of the word is by using context clues. **Context clues** are the words, phrases, and sentences around an unfamiliar word that help you understand its meaning.

There are different kinds of context clues. Some context clues *define*, or give the meaning of, an unfamiliar word right in the same (or nearby) sentence. Read the sentence below.

> One way to <u>conserve</u>, or save, water is to take shorter showers.

The word *conserve* is defined in the sentence. It means "to save." Definition context clues are often set off with commas.

Another kind of clue is an *example* clue. This means the writer provides examples of something to help you understand what it is. Read the sentence below.

> The wolves were released into the <u>wilderness</u> in places such as Denali and Yellowstone national parks.

If you do not know what the word *wilderness* means, use the clues to figure it out. The sentence gives you two examples of wilderness environments—Denali and Yellowstone national parks. Since you know what national parks are like, you have a pretty good understanding of what the word *wilderness* means.

Some context clues *restate*, or sum up, information that tells you what a word means. Read the sentences below.

> The farmers began to cut the hay and put it up for the winter, and ripe vegetables would soon be picked and stored away. The <u>harvest</u> had begun.

In the first sentence, the information about the farmers' work helps you to understand the meaning of the word *harvest*.

A context clue can also include a word's opposite, or **antonym**. If you are familiar with the antonym, you should be able to figure out the meaning of the new word.

      While Milt is tall, Louise is quite <u>petite</u>.

The word *while* signals that a difference between Milt and Louise is being described. If Milt is tall, what does that tell you about the meaning of the word *petite*?

A word's position in a sentence can also be a clue to the word's meaning. Ask yourself, what part of speech is this word—a noun, a verb, or an adjective? This strategy is especially useful for homonyms—words that look the same but have different meanings.

      How much weight can that bridge <u>bear</u>?

You know that a bear is an animal. An animal is a noun. But in this sentence, *bear* is used as a verb. It's an action word. Here, the word *bear* means "to support or hold up." That definition fits with what is being described: a bridge needs to be strong enough to support the cars and trucks that travel on it.

Besides using context clues, always remember to look up new words in either a printed or online dictionary. Dictionary entries include the word and its definition, part of speech, and pronunciation. Here is a typical dictionary entry:

---

fu•ture /ˈfyü chər/ *noun* events that come at a later time

A thesaurus is another useful tool. Look up an unfamiliar word in a thesaurus to find its synonyms and antonyms.

Thinking It Through

Read the following passage, and then answer the questions that follow.

At the beginning of spring, Andy had trouble riding his new bike very far. He got tired quickly, and he had to walk the bike up hills. Then he began taking rides with his friend Evan. They took longer rides every weekend. By summer, Andy's <u>endurance</u> was much improved. He could ride for hours on end, and hills were no problem.

What is the meaning of the word <u>endurance</u>? How do you know?

_____

_____

_____

_____

_____

HINT At first, Andy had trouble riding. But he worked at getting better. Soon, he was able to ride for longer.

Coached Example

Read the passage and answer the questions.

Yorkshire pudding is a popular English dish. Actually, Yorkshire pudding is not really a pudding at all. It is a light, puffy roll. Hundreds of years ago, roasted meat was a favorite dish in England. However, meat was very <u>expensive</u>. It cost so much that most people could only afford to eat it on special occasions.

When roasting meat, long tin pans were placed under the roast. These tins collected the meat drippings. Cooks made batter from eggs and flour, and they poured the batter into the tins with the drippings. The batter became a fluffy, delicious bread pudding. Cooks served these <u>savory</u> puddings as a first course. The puddings were cheap and flavorful. At times when there was not enough meat to go around, children would get Yorkshire pudding with gravy as their main meal.

---

1. What is the meaning of <u>expensive</u>?

   A. large

   B. hearty

   C. costly

   D. popular

   HINT Look for a context clue in the last sentence of paragraph 1.

2. Read these sentences from the passage.

   The batter became a fluffy, delicious bread pudding. Cooks served these <u>savory</u> puddings as a first course.

   The word <u>savory</u> means

   A. moist.

   B. tasty.

   C. nutty.

   D. sweet.

   HINT Read the two sentences carefully. *Savory* in the second sentence is a restatement of information in the previous sentence.

Use the Reading Guide to help you understand the passage.

Reading Guide

In paragraph 1, which words help you know what *liberty* means?

In paragraph 2, the word *colonists* is followed by its definition.

Look closely at paragraph 3. Use the first three sentences in the paragraph to help you figure out what *opposed* means.

The Path to Independence

In America, all people have the right to liberty. One person we can thank for this right to freedom is Patrick Henry.

Patrick Henry was a young man when the United States was made up of thirteen colonies. The king of England ruled the colonies. Many colonists, or people who had left England and settled in America, felt it was unfair for the king to make laws for them and impose harsh taxes. Many colonists felt they should be able to rule themselves. These people were called Patriots. Colonists who did not want to break away from England were known as Loyalists because they were loyal to the king of England. They still wanted to serve him.

In the spring of 1775, many of the Patriots got together to talk about what should be done. Some felt they should beg the king for permission to be free. Others were opposed to this idea because they had already asked the king and he refused. They wanted war. Patrick Henry stood up and interrupted the others, demanding to speak. "Give me liberty, or give me death!" he said. The men cheered and voted to be free.

Shortly afterward, the American Revolution began. The Patriots eventually won the war and created their own government. While England was a kingdom, the new country was not ruled by a king. In time, the United States became a nation where all people have the right to freedom and liberty.

Answer the following questions.

1. In the passage, the word <u>liberty</u> means

    A. rights.

    B. library.

    C. freedom.

    D. patriot.

2. Read this sentence from the passage.

    > **Others were <u>opposed</u> to this idea because they had already asked the king and he refused.**

    The word <u>opposed</u> means

    A. against.

    B. excited.

    C. angry.

    D. tired.

3. What does the word <u>loyal</u> mean?

    A. frustrated

    B. helpful

    C. interested

    D. faithful

4. The word <u>interrupt</u> means to

    A. stand up straight and tall.

    B. stop a conversation suddenly.

    C. talk a lot to other people.

    D. bring freedom to new places.

5. Read this sentence from the passage.

    > **While England was a <u>kingdom</u>, the new country was not ruled by a king.**

    What does the word <u>kingdom</u> mean? Which words help you understand what <u>kingdom</u> means?

    _____

    _____

    _____

    _____

The following questions do not relate to a passage.

6. Use your answer to Part A to answer Part B.

Part A

Read the sentence and then answer the question that follows.

> **Earthworms have the ability to regrow lost <u>segments</u> of their bodies, depending on the damage done to the body part.**

What is the meaning of <u>segment</u>?

A. a growing body

B. an earthworm

C. a part of something

D. an insect in earth

Part B

Which detail from the sentence BEST supports the answer to Part A?

A. "depending on"

B. "damage done"

C. "regrow"

D. "body part"

E. "ability"

---

7. Read the dictionary definition of *vital* and then follow the directions below.

> **vi•tal** /vī təl/ *adjective.* extremely important and necessary; full of life and energy

Choose all the words and phrases that can be used as context clues to help a reader understand the meaning of *vital*. There is more than one correct choice listed below.

A. energetic   D. absolutely needed

B. unimportant   E. lacking energy

C. very important   F. must be included

8. Read this paragraph and the directions that follow.

> Sharks are mesmerizing creatures; their features and behavior are fascinating. Many think they are <u>vicious</u> killers, but they are not dangerous or violent to humans. There are more than 350 <u>species</u> of sharks, and only 20 kinds of sharks are known to attack humans. Most sharks like to hunt <u>solo</u>, preferring to find prey on their own. Sharks swim hundreds of miles in one day. They can see underwater because they have a thin <u>membrane</u> over their eyes. This thin sheet allows an increased amount of light to enter the eye. One way that sharks find <u>prey</u> is by listening for a sound that an injured fish makes. They know where they will find their next meal.

Write the meanings of the underlined words and the context clues you used to determine the meanings. Then use a dictionary to confirm meaning.

_____

_____

_____

_____

_____

_____

_____

_____

_____

_____

_____

_____

_____

_____

_____

_____

28 Root Words and Affixes

Getting the Idea

Many common words in English came from other languages, such as Greek and Latin. For this reason, learning Greek and Latin roots can help you understand many words in English. A **root** is the base, or main part, of a word. A root needs to be joined with other word parts to make a complete word.

> geo + graphy = geography

The root *geo*, meaning "Earth," is not a word. It cannot stand alone. Add *-graphy* to get the word *geography*, which means "the study of Earth's landforms, resources, and climate." The same root can appear in many different words. The following chart lists some common Greek and Latin roots.

Root	Meaning	Examples
astr	star	astronaut, astronomy
auto	same, self	automobile, automatic
bene	good	benefit
bio	life	biography, biology
eco	environment	ecology
graph	something written	autograph, paragraph
photo	light	photograph
port	to carry	export, import
scope	a tool for seeing	microscope
tele	far away	telephone, telegraph

Read the sentence below.

> Computers designed to be <u>portable</u> in the 1980s look big and heavy now.

You can figure out the meaning of *portable* by looking at its root. The root of *portable* is *port*, which means "to carry." Something that is portable can be easily carried.

An **affix** is a word part added to the beginning or end of a word or root to change its meaning. An affix cannot stand alone as a word.

An affix added to the beginning of a base word is called a **prefix**. An affix added to the end of a base word is called a **suffix**. Read the charts below.

Prefix	Meaning	Examples
bi-	two	bicycle
co-	together, with	coworker
dis-	not, opposite	disagree, dishonest
ex-	out, away from	expand
extra-	outside, beyond	extravagant
in-	in, into	inside, infield
pre-	before	preview, prehistoric
re-	again	rewrite, resell
trans-	across, over	transmit
uni-	one	unicycle

Suffix	Function or Meaning	Examples
-able, -ible	forms adjectives, means "able to"	likable, reversible
-ation	forms nouns from verbs	imagination
-fy	forms verbs that mean "to make or become"	terrify, magnify
-logue	speech, to speak	dialogue
-ogy	science or study of	biology
-meter, -metry	a tool for measuring, a measure	kilometer, geometry
-ment	forms nouns from verbs	statement
-ty, -ity	forms nouns from adjectives	loyalty, purity

Read the following sentences. Figure out the meaning of the underlined word, based on the meaning of its affix.

> We stared at Ms. Hull in <u>amazement</u>. Did our teacher really just do cartwheels across the playground?

The affix in *amazement* is the suffix *-ment*. This suffix forms a noun from the verb *amaze*. To amaze is to surprise or astonish. *Amazement* means "surprise."

Thinking It Through

Read the following passage, and then answer the questions that follow.

Once upon a time, our cat was the most <u>adorable</u> kitten! He was skinny and fluffy and had big green eyes. His meow was so small and high that we named him Squeaky.

Now little Squeaky is a big cat. He roams around the neighborhood chasing birds, squirrels, and mice. He would be the most <u>extraordinary</u> hunter, if we did not put bells on his collar. The birds, squirrels, and mice hear Squeaky coming: *jingle, jingle, jingle*. They scatter as quickly as they can!

1. **What is the suffix in <u>adorable</u>? What does <u>adorable</u> MOST LIKELY mean?**

_____

_____

_____

HINT   Find the suffix on the chart. Use its meaning, plus the meaning of the base word, to find the meaning of *adorable*.

2. **What is the prefix in <u>extraordinary</u>? What does <u>extraordinary</u> MOST LIKELY mean?**

_____

_____

_____

HINT   What does *extra* mean? What does *ordinary* mean? What might these word parts mean together?

DISCUSS   In a small group, brainstorm words that have the *-able* suffix. Then share your words with the class.

Coached Example

Read the passage and answer the questions.

In the early 1600s, the scientist Galileo Galilei used a telescope to study the white streak across the night sky called the Milky Way. He discovered that it is actually a large collection of stars. Our sun is just one of these stars.

For hundreds of years, people thought the Milky Way was the only galaxy in the universe. In 1923 and 1924, an astronomer named Edwin Hubble studied photographs of stars in the Andromeda Nebula. He found that the stars got brighter in a regular pattern. Because of this pattern, Hubble could measure their distance from Earth. To the <u>disbelief</u> of many, he found that these stars were so far away that they could not be in our galaxy. We now know that our galaxy is only one of many.

---

1. Read this sentence from the passage.

   To the <u>disbelief</u> of many, he found that these stars were so far away that they could not be in our galaxy.

   Based on the meaning of its prefix, the word <u>disbelief</u> probably means

   A. not true.

   B. the opposite of belief.

   C. the opposite of wish.

   D. not understood.

   HINT What is the meaning of the base word? How does the prefix *dis-* affect the meaning of the base word?

2. Which of these words has roots that together mean "a tool for seeing far away"?

   A. universe

   B. astronomer

   C. photographs

   D. telescope

   HINT Look back at the roots chart. Find the roots that mean "a tool for seeing" and "far away."

Use the Reading Guide to help you understand the passage.

Reading Guide

What prefix do you see in the word *cooperate*?

Based on its use in paragraph 2, what does *enjoyment* probably mean?

What are the roots of the words *ecology* and *transport*?

Community Supported Agriculture

The supermarket is only one place where you can buy fruits and vegetables. You can also go to a stand at a farm. If you live in a city, far from a farm, you might buy produce at a farmer's market. Now there is another way for people who live in cities to get fresh fruit and vegetables: through Community Supported Agriculture, or a CSA.

Members of a CSA <u>cooperate</u> with a farmer. In the spring, CSA members <u>prepay</u> the farmer for the food they will receive that year. This way, the farmer has money to get the farm ready. Then, each week from June until as late as November, each CSA member receives a share of food from the farm. The farmer brings the food right to the neighborhood where the CSA members live. To the <u>enjoyment</u> of CSA members, the shares often include surprises: vegetables they may never have heard of before, like purslane or callaloo.

There are many benefits to Community Supported Agriculture. One benefit is the delicious, nutritious food itself. The farm benefits, too. It can count on the support of the CSA members. Also, Community Supported Agriculture is good for the environment. Small farms that grow many different plants have a healthy <u>ecology</u>. Also, small farmers are less likely to use large amounts of harmful fertilizer and pesticides. Finally, trucks <u>transport</u> the food a short distance from the farm to the community, so less pollution is created.

Answer the following questions.

1. Read this sentence from the passage.

   Members of a CSA <u>cooperate</u> with a farmer.

   Based on the meaning of its prefix, the word <u>cooperate</u> MOST LIKELY means

   A. to operate together.

   B. to practice under.

   C. to go opposite from.

   D. to come to.

2. Read this sentence from the passage.

   In the spring, CSA members <u>prepay</u> the farmer for the food they will receive that year.

   The word <u>prepay</u> means

   A. to pay too much.

   B. to pay after making a budget.

   C. to pay ahead of time.

   D. to pay in ways other than with money.

3. Which of the following BEST describes the meaning of <u>ecology</u>?

   A. study of logic

   B. study of sound

   C. study of the environment

   D. study of school

4. Which of the following BEST describes the meaning of <u>transport</u>?

   A. to drive a car

   B. to take the train

   C. to love sports

   D. to carry across

5. What is the suffix in the word <u>enjoyment</u>? What does this word MOST LIKELY mean?

   _____

   _____

   _____

The following questions do not relate to a passage.

6.　Read the word in each answer choice. Then use the underlined root to match the word to its meaning on the right.

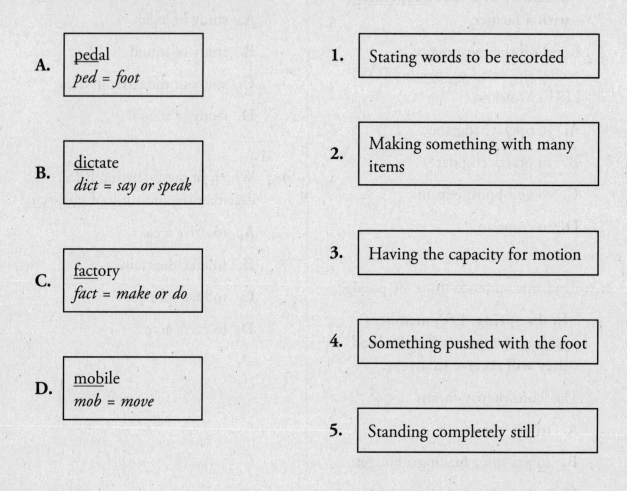

A.　pedal
　　ped = foot

B.　dictate
　　dict = say or speak

C.　factory
　　fact = make or do

D.　mobile
　　mob = move

1.　Stating words to be recorded

2.　Making something with many items

3.　Having the capacity for motion

4.　Something pushed with the foot

5.　Standing completely still

6.　Place where something is made

7. Choose all words that include an affix. There is more than one correct choice listed below.

   A. replenish

   B. edible

   C. bring

   D. preconceived

   E. transatlantic

   F. penny

   G. firefly

   H. insensitive

   I. amusement

   J. epilogue

8. A student is writing a report about plants. Read this paragraph from the report and the directions that follow.

   > **Many people confuse the sciences of space. Astrology is the study of the positions of the moon, sun, and other planets and how they affect human behavior or feelings. The scientific study of the universe, such as the motion, position, and sizes of objects in space, is called ___onomy.**

   The student needs to complete the last sentence using roots. Which root BEST completes the last sentence?

   A. uni

   B. bio

   C. astr

   D. scope

29 Synonyms and Antonyms

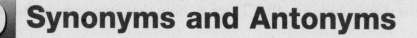

Getting the Idea

Synonyms are words that have similar meanings. The following chart lists some common synonyms.

Word	Synonyms
bad	evil, wicked
beautiful	lovely, pretty
brave	bold, courageous, fearless
happy	cheerful, glad, joyful
little	small, tiny
difficult	tough, hard
dangerous	risky, hazardous
repair	fix, mend
shout	yell, scream
quickly	fast, speedily

Notice that the meanings of synonyms are similar, but they are not exactly the same. For example, read the sentence below.

I was a bad pianist until I learned to practice.

If you were to replace the word *bad* with *evil*, the sentence would not make sense.

I was an evil pianist until I learned to practice.

The word you choose depends on the idea you are trying to express.

Recognizing synonyms can help you understand the meanings of new words. Read these sentences.

We enjoyed the carnival. We especially <u>fancied</u> the jugglers.

You may not be familiar with the use of *fancy* as a verb. The word *especially* in the second sentence gives a clue that *enjoyed* and *fancied* have similar meanings. From this clue, you can draw the conclusion that the verb *fancy* means "to like" or "to enjoy."

Antonyms are words that have opposite meanings. The following chart lists some common pairs of antonyms.

Word	Antonym
bad	good
beautiful	ugly
brave	cowardly
happy	sad
little	big
difficult	easy
dangerous	safe
repair	break
shout	whisper
quickly	slowly

As with synonyms, recognizing antonyms can help you understand the meanings of new words. Read this passage.

> Cats come in all sizes. On the one hand, there are the great cats: the lions and tigers of Africa and India. On the other hand, there are our small housecats. Most housecats weigh 12 pounds or less.

You may not be familiar with the meaning of *great* as it is used in the second sentence. The phrases *On the one hand* and *On the other hand* give you a clue that *great* and *small* have opposite meanings. From this clue, you can draw the conclusion that *great* means "big."

Thinking It Through

Read the following passage, and then answer the questions that follow.

My grandfather and I are similar in many ways. For example, he sometimes calls me his "little librarian" because I like to read so much. But he enjoys reading, too. I sometimes call him the "giant librarian." After all, he has an entire room <u>packed</u> with books. Every shelf is crowded. I wish that I had one bookcase so full!

However, the books we like are mostly different. I enjoy lively stories and exciting tales of adventure. He likes to read <u>dull</u>, thick novels and history books. He says that one day I'll find his books interesting. We'll see about that!

1. What synonyms of the word <u>packed</u> can you find in paragraph 1? List two synonyms of <u>packed</u>.

_____

_____

HINT Which words does the narrator use to describe his grandfather's collection of books?

2. What antonyms of the word <u>dull</u> can you find in paragraph 2? List three of them.

_____

_____

HINT Which words does the narrator use to describe the books he likes?

 **DISCUSS** Some words don't have antonyms. For instance, no words mean the opposite of *tree* or *blue*. With a partner, come up with words that don't have antonyms, and share them with the class.

Coached Example

Read the passage and answer the questions.

Louis Comfort Tiffany was a gifted artist. He began his career as a painter. However, he is now known best for his work in the decorative arts. The decorative arts include things made for the home. They can be <u>practical</u> things, like furniture, or <u>ornamental</u> things, like vases.

Tiffany worked with all kinds of materials: metal, textiles, pottery. But he was a master at working with glass. His stained-glass windows were unlike any seen before. He learned how to make glass in new colors. He also learned how to blend colors in a single piece of glass. With his <u>brilliantly</u> colored glass, he made beautiful landscapes.

Tiffany is also known for his unique lampshades. The lampshades were actually dome-shaped, stained-glass windows. Lightbulbs lit up the lampshades from within.

---

1. Read this sentence from the passage.

    They can be <u>practical</u> things, like furniture, or <u>ornamental</u> things, like vases.

    If <u>practical</u> means "useful," then <u>ornamental</u> MOST LIKELY means

    A. boring.

    B. for decoration.

    C. sturdy.

    D. ugly.

    HINT The word *or* gives a clue that *practical* and *ornamental* are opposites.

2. Read this sentence from the passage.

    With his <u>brilliantly</u> colored glass, he made beautiful landscapes.

    Which word means the same as <u>brilliantly</u> in this sentence?

    A. smartly

    B. sharply

    C. quickly

    D. brightly

    HINT Replace the word *brilliantly* in the sentence with each answer choice. Which one makes the most sense?

Use the Reading Guide to help you understand the passage.

Reading Guide

When the narrator says she likes "the roar of the waves," what sound do you imagine?

Find the word *bored* in paragraph 2. What are some words you might use to say that you are not bored?

Read the last sentence of the passage. What size is a sky that "stretches in every direction"?

To the Mountains Again

Before summer vacation, many of my friends look forward to trips to the ocean. Don't get me wrong. I don't dislike the ocean. I especially like the <u>roar</u> of the waves. But in the summer, I don't really want to sit out on a hot beach in the bright sunshine. I'd rather sit in the shade of a pine tree and feel a cool mountain breeze.

Luckily, in the summertime, my family goes to the mountains. We rent a small cabin next to a lake. There's not much to do inside the cabin. For example, there's no TV. I'm not <u>bored</u> at all. On a sunny day, I might swim from morning until sunset. Or, I might go on a hike with my family. On rainy days, we <u>usually</u> go to the movies. Or, we might even go on a hike in the rain. I like to listen to the sound of the rain in the trees.

At least once during every trip to the mountains, my family and I wake before dawn. We pack lots of sandwiches and water in our bags. We put on <u>sturdy</u> boots. Our goal is to reach the top of a mountain before anyone else gets there. There is nowhere in the world better to be than the top of a mountain. We stand above the tops of the trees. The <u>enormous</u> sky stretches in every direction above our heads.

Answer the following questions.

1. Read this sentence from the passage.

   I especially like the <u>roar</u> of the waves.

   Which word means the opposite of <u>roar</u>?

   A. noise

   B. whisper

   C. laughter

   D. anger

2. When the narrator says that she is not <u>bored</u>, she means that she is

   A. tired.

   B. dull.

   C. lonely.

   D. amused.

3. When the narrator says that the boots are <u>sturdy</u>, she means that they are

   A. strong.

   B. ugly.

   C. big.

   D. rubber.

4. Read this sentence from the passage.

   The <u>enormous</u> sky stretches in every direction above our heads.

   Which word means the same as <u>enormous</u>?

   A. blue

   B. far

   C. cloudy

   D. huge

5. Read this sentence from the passage.

   On rainy days, we <u>usually</u> go to the movies.

   Write a synonym or antonym for <u>usually</u>. Tell whether your word is a synonym or antonym.

   _____

   _____

   _____

The following questions do not relate to a passage.

6. Read the word in each answer choice. Then match each word to its antonym on the right.

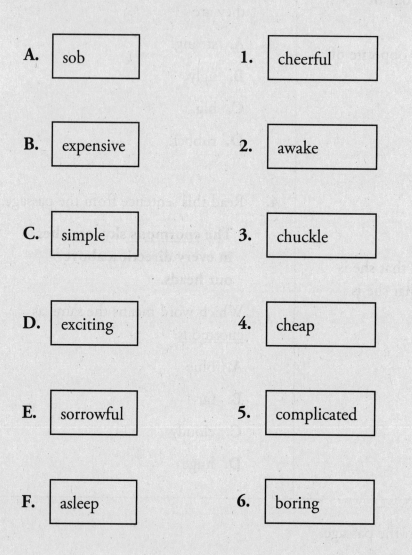

A. sob

B. expensive

C. simple

D. exciting

E. sorrowful

F. asleep

1. cheerful

2. awake

3. chuckle

4. cheap

5. complicated

6. boring

7. Choose all of the word pairs that are antonyms. There is more than one correct choice listed below.

A. dangerous—safe   F. waddle—run

B. exchange—keep   G. lovely—beautiful

C. retreat—go back   H. sweat—shiver

D. obey—listen   I. riddle—puzzle

E. silence—noise   J. perfect—wrong

8. Read this paragraph from a student report about desert plants.

> **Did you ever wonder how plants grow in the desert? Plants can grow so well there that one cactus can be as large as a tree. The giant saguaro cactus grows in the Sonoran Desert, which covers part of the states of Arizona and California and crosses into Mexico. Though it takes a long time to grow, the massive cactus can reach up to 60 feet tall. That's enormous for a cactus. Some grow as many as 25 branches, or arms, which make them seem more immense.**

Underline the words in the paragraph that mean the same as *big*.

30 Similes and Metaphors

Getting the Idea

Good writers use words in creative ways. They use figurative language. **Figurative language** does not mean exactly what it says. It is a way for writers to use words to paint a picture in the reader's mind. **Literal language** is language that means exactly what it says. Look at the difference between them.

Literal: Abril dances gracefully.
Figurative: Abril dances like a leaf in the wind.

Abril does not really dance like a leaf. The comparison to a leaf helps you understand how gracefully Abril moves.

This kind of figurative language is called a simile. A **simile** is a comparison of two unlike things using the word *like* or the word *as*. If you read a simile and think about what is being compared, you can understand and appreciate its meaning.

At the pool, Jerome swims <u>like a fish</u>.

Jerome does not actually swim as a fish would. But by comparing him to one, the writer emphasizes Jerome's skill as a swimmer. Read another example.

Darlene's suitcase was <u>as light as a feather</u>.

In this sentence, a suitcase is compared to a feather. You know how light a feather is. So you can imagine that the suitcase was very easy to carry.

Simile	Meaning
Nan's hair is like silk.	Nan's hair is soft and smooth.
By lunchtime, Dan was as hungry as a bear.	Dan was very hungry and wanted to eat lunch.
The cheetah ran like the wind.	The cheetah ran extremely quickly.

Like a simile, a **metaphor** compares two things in a sentence. The difference is that metaphors do not use the words *like* or *as*. A metaphor asks the reader to picture one thing as being another. It gives one thing the quality of another. Read the sentence below.

The <u>snow was a blanket</u> on the hills.

The snow is being compared to a blanket. When you think of a blanket, you imagine something thick and soft draping smoothly over a bed. Similarly, the snow provides the hills with a smooth white covering, hiding the frozen ground beneath. This metaphor gives the snow the qualities of a blanket. In that way, it helps you to picture the snowy hills in your mind.

Here's another example:

The king was cruel, and <u>his heart was a stone</u>.

The king's heart is compared to a stone. Stones are hard and cold, so the writer is expressing the idea that the king's personality has the same qualities. He is not open or understanding. The word *cruel* also helps you to understand the metaphor.

Metaphor	Meaning
Ravi is a volcano waiting to erupt.	Ravi will quickly lose his temper.
The baker is an artist when it comes to decorating cakes.	The baker creates beautiful designs with cake icing.
My bedroom is an oven.	The bedroom is very hot and uncomfortable.

Thinking It Through

Read the following passage, and then answer the questions that follow.

Bert woke up to the sound of a knock at the door. He opened the door to see a young boy standing in the rain.

"Would you like to buy a ticket for the Great Giveaway Raffle?" the boy asked. "It's my last one. You could win a new car. The car is as bright as a shiny red apple."

Bert bought the raffle ticket and went back to bed.

Later that day, Bert's phone rang. It was the Great Giveaway, telling him that he had won. Bert's mind was a blank slate. He had totally forgotten buying the raffle ticket that morning. Imagine his surprise!

1. What does the simile in paragraph 2 mean?

    _____

    _____

    _____

    HINT Look for two things being compared using the words *like* or *as*.

2. What does the metaphor in the last paragraph mean?

    _____

    _____

    _____

    HINT Bert has no memory of what happened that morning.

Coached Example

Read the poem and answer the questions.

The Big Game

The big game was here, and our team was ready,
<u>My knees shook like an earthquake</u>, but I held them steady.
I threw on my uniform and grabbed my baseball,
It was too late to run, too late to stall.

Mom said she'd be there, and Dad would be, too.
I got to the locker room, and <u>it was a zoo</u>!
The players ran around and panicked a lot,
But Coach said, "Don't worry; you've got a great shot."

1. The simile <u>my knees shook like an earthquake</u> suggests that the speaker was very

   A. cranky.

   B. excited.

   C. happy.

   D. nervous.

   HINT If your knees are shaking, how do you usually feel?

2. Read the following line from the poem.

   I got to the locker room, and it was a zoo!

   What two things are being compared in this metaphor?

   A. the locker room and a zoo

   B. a locker and a room

   C. the speaker and the locker room

   D. the speaker and a zoo

   HINT Try to imagine what the locker room looked like.

Use the Reading Guide to help you understand the passage.

Reading Guide

How is figurative language used in paragraph 2?

In paragraph 4, how does Jay describe himself to his dad? Is the description a simile or a metaphor? How do you know?

Notice how the descriptions of things, such as the ocean and the flashlight beam, help you picture the events of the story.

The Big Bass

Jay loved fishing. His dad had taught him all the basics. This included an important rule: if you don't plan to bring a fish home, you must return it to the water.

One day, after returning home from fishing with his friends at the canal, Jay saw his dad putting some line on a new fishing rod. Jay's dad fished for bass at night when the sky was as black as a crow's wing. Jay had always wanted to join him.

"How was fishing at the canal today?" his dad asked.

"I was a champion," said Jay proudly. "I caught five sea trout!"

"Not bad," his dad said with a smile. He continued working. The new fishing rod seemed to shine like glass. "What do you think?"

"Wow," Jay said. "It's really nice."

"I'm glad," said his dad, "because it's yours. You're big enough now to come bass fishing with me. Let's head down to the ocean after dinner."

That night at the beach, Jay and his dad waded out into the water. The ocean was a bottomless pit. They cast their lines. Suddenly, Jay felt a sharp jerk on his line. He managed to pull a large fish out of the water. The light from their flashlight shone as brightly as the sun as they took the hook out of the fish's mouth. It was an old fish—a king of the sea. At that moment, Jay decided to throw it back into the water. The entire night was as magical as a dream.

Answer the following questions.

1. What two things are being compared in the simile the sky was as black as a crow's wing?

   A. the color black and a crow's wing

   B. the sky and the color black

   C. the sky and a crow's wing

   D. the color black and all colors

2. What does the metaphor the ocean was a bottomless pit mean?

   A. The ocean was blue.

   B. All pits are oceans.

   C. The ocean was deep.

   D. All pits are bottomless.

3. The simile the light from their flashlight shone as brightly as the sun suggests that the light was

   A. very bright.

   B. very hot.

   C. yellow in color.

   D. gold in color.

4. Which sentence from the passage contains a metaphor?

   A. "The new fishing rod seemed to shine like glass."

   B. "At that moment, Jay decided to throw it back into the water."

   C. "'You're big enough now to come bass fishing with me.'"

   D. "It was an old fish—a king of the sea."

5. Read this sentence from the passage.

   The entire night was as magical as a dream.

   Is the sentence a simile or a metaphor? How do you know? What does the sentence mean?

   _____

   _____

   _____

   _____

   _____

The following questions do not relate to a passage.

6. Read each answer choice. Then match the underlined phrases to their meanings on the right.

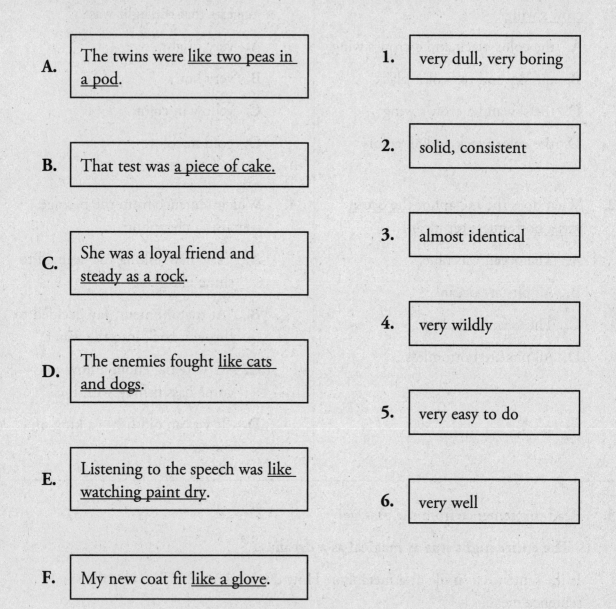

A. The twins were <u>like two peas in a pod</u>.

B. That test was <u>a piece of cake.</u>

C. She was a loyal friend and <u>steady as a rock</u>.

D. The enemies fought <u>like cats and dogs</u>.

E. Listening to the speech was <u>like watching paint dry</u>.

F. My new coat fit <u>like a glove</u>.

1. very dull, very boring

2. solid, consistent

3. almost identical

4. very wildly

5. very easy to do

6. very well

7. Read the paragraph and follow the directions.

> **The morning of the camping trip, Jason was sick as a dog. His head was pounding like a hammer. Jason knew he couldn't go on the trip, but he was so disappointed. He went back to bed and slept like a rock. A few hours later, he awoke with a clear head. He was happy as a lark that he felt better. Maybe he could persuade Mom to drive him to the campsite later.**

Underline the figurative language in the paragraph.

8. Read the paragraph. Then write the meanings of the underlined figurative language.

> **In some cities, you can sleep in hotels that are literally as cold as ice! The hotels are made from tightly packed snow, ice, and water. Some ice walls and "furniture" are <u>as clear as glass</u>. Guest rooms are <u>like the inside of a freezer</u>. The rooms have thermal clothing and animal skins that keep you <u>snug as a bug in a rug</u>. There are also areas that serve hot chocolate and other hot dishes to warm you up. Although ice furniture may feel as <u>hard as nails</u>, the hotel staff makes your stay so comfortable that you will <u>sleep like a polar bear</u>.**

_____

_____

_____

_____

_____

_____

_____

_____

_____

_____

_____

31 Idioms, Adages, Proverbs, and Allusions

Getting the Idea

An **idiom** is a phrase whose meaning is different from the individual words that make it up. Idioms are a kind of figurative language. They do not make literal sense, yet most people know exactly what they mean. Read this example.

> Mom told Jeff, "It's time to hit the sack!"

The idiom *hit the sack* does not actually mean to take a sack and hit it. It means "it's time to go to bed."

> "You're driving me up a wall!" the babysitter cried.

No one is traveling up a wall. This idiom means "you are annoying and upsetting me."

> Since the quiz is tomorrow, we're all in the same boat.

The idiom *in the same boat* means the whole class is facing the same thing.

When you come across an unfamiliar idiom, use context, or the words and phrases nearby, to figure it out. You can then **paraphrase** the idiom, or put it into your own words. For example, someone might say: "It's a surprise party for Kara, so *don't let the cat out of the bag*." You use the context to understand that the idiom means "don't let Kara know."

An **adage** is a statement that expresses some kind of truth about human nature, or how people behave. For example:

> Birds of a feather flock together.

This adage means that people with similar interests tend to spend time with one another.

Proverbs are very much like adages. A **proverb** is a saying that offers advice or instruction about how to live your life. Read these examples.

> Don't judge a book by its cover.

This proverb teaches that it's not fair to judge someone or something at first glance.

> Treat others as you would have them treat you.

This proverb teaches that if you want others to be fair and friendly to you, you must be fair and friendly to them.

You may also come across allusions in reading or speaking with others. An **allusion** is a reference to a person or event from literature, history, or mythology. Here are some allusions based on Greek myths.

Allusion	Meaning
Achilles's heel	Achilles was a great warrior whose only weak spot was his heel. Today, someone's Achilles's heel means his or her area of weakness.
Midas touch	King Midas had the power to turn everything he touched to gold. If someone has the Midas touch, it means what he or she does turns out well or makes money.
Pandora's box	Pandora had a box filled with all the evils of the world, like war, disease, and death, which she was forbidden to open. She eventually did open it, which is how those things came to be in the world. Today, a Pandora's box means a tempting opportunity that could be disastrous.
Odyssey	*The Odyssey* is a very long poem about Odysseus's journey home after the Trojan War. Today, the word *odyssey* means any long trip or adventure.

Thinking It Through

Read the following passage, and then answer the questions that follow.

Today was unbelievable! Troy, Gary, and I were just sitting on the school steps, telling jokes and <u>cracking up</u>. Suddenly, a car driving way too fast nearly hit a dog! The driver blasted his horn and leaned out the window shouting. Not just at the dog, but at us, too. And we hadn't done anything wrong!

We had an assembly lecture on traffic safety last week, and it was great. Maybe the adults in this town need to have a traffic safety lecture of their own. We all have to work together to be safe. It's like they say: <u>better safe than sorry</u>!

1. Is the phrase <u>cracking up</u> an idiom, an adage, or a proverb? Explain your answer and tell the meaning of the phrase in your own words.

_____

_____

_____

_____

HINT Use the context to help you. The writer and his friends were telling jokes.

2. What does the adage <u>better safe than sorry</u> mean? Paraphrase the adage in your own words.

_____

_____

_____

_____

HINT Think about what advice this adage offers.

Coached Example

Read the passage and answer the questions.

George was really excited about the class assignment: to create a new game. It could be a board game or a sport. That afternoon, George went home and brainstormed ideas. He thought about games for what seemed like hours. Finally, he realized he needed some help, so he called his friend, Louise. After all, George thought, <u>two heads are better than one</u>!

"Hello? Louise?" George said. "I'm working on that new project, and I was hoping you could <u>give me a hand</u>."

"Oh, I've started the project, too," Louise replied. "I've been sitting here forever trying to think of ideas! I'll be right over."

Together, Louise and George managed to come up with two great games. Teamwork, they agreed, was the best strategy.

---

1. What is the BEST paraphrase of the adage <u>two heads are better than one</u>?

   A. It's important to use your mind to solve problems.

   B. Thinking is the best thing you can do.

   C. Working together is better than working alone.

   D. It's always better to think about everything twice.

    Read the sentences around the phrase. What is George hoping to do?

2. What does the idiom <u>give me a hand</u> mean?

   A. Please help me.

   B. Please wash your hands.

   C. Handle with care.

   D. Think of using your hands.

   HINT George is having trouble coming up with ideas for his project.

Use the Reading Guide to help you understand the passage.

Reread the words in paragraph 4 that Jen's mom tells her to remember. Think about why Mom says this. What idea is she trying to express?

Jen's mother tells her to *take it easy* in paragraph 6. Is this an idiom or an adage? How do you know?

Allusions can refer to legends, stories, or real events. When Shawn says *the sky is falling* in paragraph 12, to what well-known tale is she referring?

Stage Fright

Jen could hardly believe it. She had let her friend Shawn talk her into trying out for the school play. Now it was the night of the show, and Jen was really scared! Jen was good at many things, but speaking in public had always been her Achilles's heel.

Jen's mother came into her room. "Hey, Jen," she said with a smile. "Ready for the big night?"

"Not really. I'm so nervous. Maybe I bit off more than I can chew."

"Oh, honey. I know it's hard. But remember: it's always darkest before the dawn!"

"Yeah, I guess." Jen frowned.

"Try to take it easy. I'm sure you'll knock their socks off!" She kissed Jen's head and left the room.

Jen wasn't so sure. What if she forgot her lines? What if no one clapped? Jen got up from her bed and stared into the mirror.

"Okay, Jen," she said out loud. "Cut it out! You can *do* this!"

With that, she grabbed her costume and walked out the door.

At school, Shawn gave her a big hug. "Jen," she said, "I know you're nervous. But you know what? I am, too!"

"You are?" Jen asked.

"Sure! Everyone gets a little stage fright," Shawn said. "But really, it's not like the sky is falling! Okay, Chicken Little?"

Jen laughed. With a friend like Shawn by her side, she knew she would do just fine.

Answer the following questions.

1. Read this sentence from the passage.

   "Maybe I bit off more than I can chew!"

   What does this idiom mean?

   A. to eat too much and feel sick

   B. to take on a job you can't finish

   C. to worry about starting something

   D. to avoid seeing your friends

2. Read this sentence from the passage.

   "But really, it's not like the sky is falling!"

   What is the figurative meaning of the sky is falling?

   A. The world is coming to an end.

   B. Everything is new again.

   C. You can accomplish anything.

   D. It's about to start raining.

3. What does the idiom knock their socks off mean?

   A. to make people undress

   B. to change someone's socks

   C. to disappoint an audience

   D. to impress and thrill an audience

4. The adage it's always darkest before the dawn means

   A. the sky is very dark early in the morning.

   B. try your best and don't be discouraged.

   C. things look the worst just before they improve.

   D. the sky is light before dawn.

5. In the passage, Jen feels that speaking in public has always been her Achilles's heel. What does this allusion mean?

   _____

   _____

   _____

   _____

   _____

The following questions do not relate to a passage.

6. Use your answer to Part A to answer Part B.

   Part A

   Choose the sentence that includes an idiom.

   A. The angry neighbor was a kind man who never hurt anyone.

   B. An avid marathoner, she was ready to go running at the drop of a hat.

   C. It is important to make sure you save money and not only spend it.

   D. He was very handy, so fixing the bike was an easy job.

   Part B

   Which definition of *idiom* BEST supports the answer to Part A?

   A. phrases with meanings that are different from those of the individual words

   B. phrases that express a truth about human nature

   C. phrases that offer advice or instruction

   D. phrases that reference a person or event

   E. phrases that reference classical mythology

7. Read the paragraphs and the directions that follow.

Ethan looked at the pile of money he had received for his birthday. What should he buy? As he thought, Uncle Howard came into the room. "You know, Ethan, <u>a penny saved is a penny earned</u>."

"But I want a new video game," Ethan said.

"Those are <u>a dime a dozen</u>," Uncle Howard said. "And they cost <u>an arm and a leg</u>."

"But there's a new one that looks so cool!" Ethan argued.

"<u>All that glitters is not gold</u>," Uncle Howard said. "You'll play it for a week and then be bored of it."

Ethan sighed. Maybe his uncle was right. Uncle Howard smiled and said. "It's your money, so do what you wish. Just remember that <u>a fool and his money are soon parted</u>."

Write whether the underlined phrases are idioms, proverbs, or adages. Then write the meanings.

_____

_____

_____

_____

_____

_____

_____

_____

_____

_____

_____

_____

_____

_____

This passage contains mistakes. Read the passage and answer the questions that follow.

Carmen Salva: Protector of the Land

(1) Carmen Salva is a teacher that grew up in a City called Tilcara in Argentina. (2) It has a rich history and wonderful views. (3) However, Salva felt troubled when she walked around Tilcara. (4) She knew that people were not giving the land the respect it deserved.

(5) On her way to school in the mornings, Salva saw trash nearly everywhere she looked. (6) She saw broken bottles and tin cans. (7) Old tires and bits of plastic. (8) Seeing this did not make Salva feel proud about where she lived. (9) But Salva did not <u>loose</u> hope. (10) Instead, she began to think. (11) She knew that with a plan, she could help make a difference.

(12) A lot of people did not understand the importance of clean water or caring for the land. (13) Many believed that someone else would take care of the litter problem. (14) But Salva knew that everyone needed to be responsible. (15) Salva <u>reviewed</u> her ideas and shared them with her students. (16) Most agreed that litter was a problem. (17) Salva and some of her students began volunteering. (18) A government program gave the students plastic large green trash bags and threw away the litter they collected. (19) Salva and her students started small. (20) They cleaned the area around their school first. (21) Then they moved to other neighborhoods. (22) From the first day, they saw what a difference they made.

(23) Salva created a youth environmental group. (24) She named this group *Esperanza de Vida*. (25) This means "Hope for Life" in English. (26) She knew that teaching people while they were still young was important. (27) There were many things Salva hoped to teach. (28) The country around them was a beautiful place. (29) It deserved to be protected. (30) These were all lessons Salva knew would last a lifetime.

(31) Salva has become a well-known person at her country. (32) Her group is always adding volunteers and working on new projects. (33) Many parents and other adults have become involved, too. (34) Slowly, the community changes. (35) Carmen Salva is proud of the progress that has been made. (36) As she says, It's never too early to start caring for the land you live in and grow up in.

1. Which word from paragraph 1 is NOT capitalized correctly?

   A. Argentina

   B. City

   C. However

   D. Tilcara

2. Which sentence is the correct revision of sentence 36?

   A. As she "says," It's never too early to start caring for the land you live in and grow up in.

   B. "As she says," It's never too early to start caring for the land you live in and grow up in.

   C. As she says, "it's never too early to start caring for the land you live in and grow up in."

   D. As she says, "It's never too early to start caring for the land you live in and grow up in."

3. The correct spelling of the underlined word in sentence 9 is

   A. lose.

   B. loos.

   C. luse.

   D. lews.

4. Which of the following is NOT a complete sentence?

   A. sentence 5

   B. sentence 6

   C. sentence 7

   D. sentence 8

5. What is the correct way to write the verb in sentence 34?

A. was changing

B. is changing

C. changed

D. will be changing

6. What is the correct revision of sentence 18?

A. A government program gave the students green large plastic trash bags and threw away the litter they collected.

B. A government program gave the students large plastic green trash bags and threw away the litter they collected.

C. A government program gave the students large green plastic trash bags and threw away the litter they collected.

D. A government program gave the students trash bags of large green plastic and threw away the litter they collected.

7. How could sentence 1 be corrected?

A. Change *that* to *which*.

B. Change *that* to *whom*.

C. Change *that* to *who*.

D. Change *that* to *she*.

8. What is the correct revision of sentence 31?

A. Salva has become a well-known person in her country.

B. Salva has become a well-known person of her country.

C. Salva has become a well-known person on her country.

D. Salva has become a well-known person with her country.

9. What is the prefix in the word <u>reviewed</u>? What does the word MOST LIKELY mean?

_____

_____

_____

_____

Read the passage and answer the questions that follow.

Pearly Whites

Amanda had a dentist appointment, and she was not happy about it. She did not want to go. Her mother, however, would not let her back out.

"It's been six months," Amanda's mom said. "You need to have a check-up."

"Come on, Mom," Amanda pleaded. "Can't I go some other time? My teeth feel fine."

Her mom shook her head and went back to making dinner. It was clear Amanda was not going to be convinced otherwise. Amanda's appointment was scheduled for that Friday after school. On Thursday night, Amanda stood in front of the bathroom mirror after brushing and flossing her teeth. She opened her mouth wide so she could inspect every tooth. She examined each one very closely. Moments later, Amanda's older brother Owen walked by and saw her.

"What are you doing?" Owen asked.

"Nothing, Owen," Amanda replied. "Mind your own business, please."

Owen smiled. He knew about Amanda's appointment, and he knew that she hated going to the dentist. He decided to have a little fun with his sister.

"It's no surprise that Mom is making you go to the dentist," Owen began. "You haven't been there in years."

"It's only been six months," Amanda said, annoyed that her brother was still standing there. "Plus, I brush twice a day. And I floss, too."

"I don't know," Owen continued, shaking his head. "Six months is a pretty long time. Think of how much can happen in six months. You might need to have some of your teeth pulled. Or, you might have a cavity. A lot of kids our age get cavities. If you have one, the dentist might have to use one of his instruments on you. Maybe an old, rusty drill!" Owen sighed dramatically. "I'm sorry, sis," he said. "It looks like you might be in big trouble."

Amanda tried to ignore her brother. Unfortunately, while he talked, she thought she saw something in the mirror—was that a tiny brown spot on one of her teeth? She scraped at it with a fingernail. She hoped it was a shadow, but she was uncertain. What if it was a cavity?

Ugh! When it rains, it pours. Maybe Owen is right, thought Amanda to herself. *Maybe the dentist is going to have to pull one of my teeth. Maybe I have a cavity, and he's going to use one of his old, rusty drills on me.* Amanda's heart sank.

The next day, Amanda sat in the backseat of the car after school. Her appointment with Dr. Boucher was at 4:00. The clock in the car read 3:45. Amanda's palms were sweaty. She could feel a lump rising in her throat. Her stomach ached as her mom drove. She considered asking her mom if she would cancel the appointment, but instead she sat there in silence. Owen's <u>words</u> from the day before rang in her ears.

"Hey, Mom," Amanda said. "How often does Dr. Boucher use his rusty drill?"

"What rusty drill?" Mom asked with a laugh. "Who put that idea in your head?"

Amanda's face became as red as a stoplight. "A little bird told me," she said with a frown. They arrived at Dr. Boucher's office right on time. Amanda was in the dentist's chair at 4:01.

Dr. Boucher spoke softly. He asked Amanda about school and quickly set to work on her teeth. For twenty minutes, Amanda waited for him to open a drawer containing a pair of pliers and a rusty drill. She imagined how she would look with false teeth like Grandpa's.

Before Amanda knew it, Dr. Boucher was finished. He removed his rubber gloves. Amanda wiped her mouth with a paper towel and felt her teeth with her tongue. They were all there. Amanda breathed a sigh of relief. Dr. Boucher smiled broadly.

"Great work, Amanda," said Dr. Boucher. "Now, if only your brother took such good care of his teeth."

10. Which sentence from the passage is a simile?

   A. "Amanda's face became as red as a stoplight."

   B. "They arrived at Dr. Boucher's office right on time."

   C. "Amanda was in the dentist's chair at 4:01."

   D. "Before Amanda knew it, Dr. Boucher was finished."

11. What is the best way to paraphrase the adage when it rains, it pours?

   A. The weather is always hard to predict.

   B. When things are bad, sometimes they can get even worse.

   C. Always be prepared for the worst.

   D. Nature is sometimes on your side.

12. What is a synonym for the word pleaded?

   A. begged

   B. asked

   C. requested

   D. discussed

13. Read this sentence from the passage.

   Owen's words from the day before rang in her ears.

   Which word would make the underlined word more precise?

   A. joke

   B. threat

   C. stories

   D. warning

14. Read this sentence from the passage.

   She opened her mouth wide so she could inspect every tooth.

   What does the word inspect mean? What context clues helped you figure out the meaning of this word?

   _____

   _____

   _____

   _____

Glossary

adage a statement that contains some kind of truth about human nature

adjective a word that describes a person, place, or thing

adverb a word that describes a verb, an adjective, or another adverb

affix a prefix or suffix that is added to a root word

agree to match in gender (male, female, or neither) and number (singular or plural)

allusion a reference to a person or event from literature, history, or mythology

antecedent the word a pronoun replaces

antonym a word that means the opposite of another word

apostrophe a punctuation mark used to create a contraction or a possessive noun

argument a written piece that states and defends an opinion

bibliography an organized list of resources used to write an article or a report

capitalization using capital (or uppercase) letters where necessary

cast of characters a list of characters who appear in a play

cause a reason why something happens

characters the main actors in a story. They can be people, animals, or other creatures.

character trait a quality possessed by a character

chart a graphic aid that uses columns and rows to organize information

chronological order the sequence in which events happen

claim a statement that something—an idea, event, or observation—is true

climax the part of a story where the conflict reaches its most exciting point

colon a punctuation mark used to introduce a list or an explanation in a sentence

comma a punctuation mark used to show a pause in a sentence or to connect ideas

compare to examine and consider the similarities between two or more objects, ideas, or people

complete sentence a sentence that contains both a subject and a verb

complex sentence a sentence made up of two sentences: one that can stand on its own and one that cannot

compound sentence a sentence that is made up of two sentences that can both stand on their own

concluding statement the closing statement in an argument

conflict a problem that the main character in a story must solve

conjunction a word that joins two complete sentences to make a compound sentence

context clues the words, phrases, or sentences around an unfamiliar word that help you understand its meaning

contraction two words joined to make one; an apostrophe takes the place of the missing letters

contrast to examine and consider the differences between two or more objects, ideas, or people

dependent clause a group of words that include a noun and a verb, but do not make sense on their own as a sentence

description descriptive words that help to paint a picture in the reader's mind

detail a specific piece of information

diagram a drawing with labels that shows the different parts of an object or how something works

dialogue the words characters say to each other

dictionary a book that lists words and their definitions

drama a play that is written in dialogue and performed on stage

editing correcting grammar, punctuation, and spelling errors in a piece of writing)

effect a result of a cause

evidence information used to support a claim

exclamation point a punctuation mark used to show excitement, surprise, or strong emotion

expert opinion the opinion of an expert or someone who knows a lot about a topic

eyewitness account a first-hand description of an event

fact a statement that is always true and can be proved

fiction writing that describes made-up people and events

figurative language language that does not mean exactly what it says; two examples are similes and metaphors.

first-person the point of view expressed by a narrator who is part of the story; uses the pronoun *I*

flowchart a graphic organizer that shows the order of events in a story from start to finish

formal style a writing style characterized by language that is proper and impersonal.

fragment a sentence that is missing either a subject or a verb

future progressive tense a form of a verb used to express an ongoing action that has not happened yet

genres forms or types of texts

glossary a section at the end of a book that lists alphabetically all the technical words and key words in the text with their definitions

graphic a visual tool such as a chart, graph, diagram, or timeline that is used to convey information

graphic novel a form of literature that tells a story using mainly graphics or art

heading a title in bold print at the top of a section of text or column of a chart that says what the section or column is about

homophones words that sound the same or similar, but have different meanings

idiom a phrase whose meaning is different from the individual words that make it up

independent clause a group of words with a noun and a verb that can stand alone as a sentence

inference an educated guess about a passage based on the author's clues and the reader's prior knowledge

informal style a writing style characterized by language that is casual or conversational

informational text nonfiction text that provides information about a topic

irregular verb a verb that has different spellings when used in different tenses

literal language language that means exactly what it says

main idea what a story or article is mainly about

metaphor a comparison of two unlike things without using the word *like* or the word *as*

meter the pattern of rhythm in a poem

modal auxiliary verb a verb such as *can, may, must,* and *will* that relates a possibility or necessity of an action

motivations the reasons for the ways characters act

narrative text a text that entertains the reader with a story

narrator the person who tells the story

nonfiction writing that describes factual information about people, places, and things

noun a word that names a person, place, thing, or idea

object of a preposition the noun or pronoun in a prepositional phrase

opinion a personal belief that cannot be proven true

outline a plan or "skeleton" of an essay in list form

paraphrase to restate information from a resource in your own words

past progressive tense a form of a verb that tells about an ongoing action that has already happened

period a punctuation mark used at the end of a sentence to show that it is a statement

perspective the attitude or feeling of the author toward the topic

plot a series of events that happen in a story

poetry a genre of writing that is separated into lines and stanzas, in which an author uses sound devices such as rhyme and rhythm to create meaning and evoke emotion in the reader

point of view the perspective, or view, from which the narrator tells the story

position statement a statement of the writer's opinion in an argument

possessive noun a noun that shows who or what owns an object

precise a word used to describe something that is specific or exact

prefix an affix added to the beginning of a root word

preposition a word that shows relationship in time or space

prepositional phrase a phrase that begins with a preposition and ends with a noun or pronoun; can act as an adjective or adverb

present progressive tense a form of a verb used to express an ongoing action that is happening now

primary source a source written at the time of an event by someone who was there

problem and solution a way of organizing a text by presenting a problem and describing how it is solved

progressive tense a form of a verb used to express an ongoing action without a specific end time

pronoun a word that takes the place of a noun in a sentence

prose a form of writing in which one sentence follows another, with sentences arranged into groups called paragraphs

proverb a short, well-known saying that often gives advice

publish to produce writing for others to read

punctuation the symbols used to organize sentences

purpose an author's reason for writing

question mark a punctuation mark used at the end of a sentence to show that it is a question

quotation marks punctuation marks used to show someone's exact words

reason why a writer thinks a certain way

relative adverb an adverb, such as *when, where* and *why*, that introduces a relative clause

relative clause a group of words that tells more about a noun

relative pronoun a pronoun, such as *which, that, who, whom,* and *whose*, that is used in a relative clause

research to gather information about a topic

resolution how the conflict or problem in a story is solved

resources print and online texts that provide information about a topic

response to informational text a written piece analyzing one or more informational texts

response to literature a written piece that analyzes one or more literature selections

revising deleting, reordering, and organizing sentences to make your writing better

rhyme words that end with the same sound

rhythm the pattern of stressed and unstressed syllables in a poem

rising action the events in a story that lead to a conflict

root the base, or main part, of a word

run-on sentence two or more complete sentences that are joined together without proper punctuation

scene a part of a drama

secondary source an account of an event that was not witnessed by the writer

second-person the point of view expressed by a narrator who speaks directly to the reader, using the word *you*

semicolon a punctuation mark used to join sentences that are related

sequence the order in which things happen

setting where and when a story takes place

simile a comparison of two unlike things using the word *like* or the word *as*

simple sentence a complete sentence that expresses one main thought

sources materials that provide facts, details, and other information about topics

stage directions instructions written in a play that tell the actors what to do

stanza a group of lines in a poem

subject the person or thing doing the action in a sentence

subject-verb agreement the use of a singular verb for a singular subject, and a plural verb for a plural subject

suffix an affix added to the end of a root word

summary a brief description of a longer work; a summary states only the most important ideas and details

supporting detail a fact, example, or other piece of information that strengthens or backs up the main idea

synonyms words that have the same or similar meanings

tense the time in which a sentence takes place

text structure the way in which an article or passage is organized

theme the central idea or message of a story, poem, or drama

third-person the point of view expressed by a narrator who tells the story without actually being in it

third-person limited the point of view expressed by a narrator who knows only the thoughts and feelings of a single character

third-person omniscient the point of view expressed by a narrator who knows all of the characters' thoughts and feelings

timeline a graphic organizer that shows the dates when important events happened

tone a writer's attitude toward his or her subject

topic sentence a statement of the main idea in a paragraph

transitions words or phrases that connect ideas to make writing flow better

verb a word that expresses an action or state of being

verse a group of lines in a poem

web a graphic organizer that shows the main idea of a story or article in the center and details in connected circles

word choice the words a writer chooses to convey his or her ideas

writing style a writer's unique way of writing; also called a writer's "voice"

Notes

Notes

Notes

Notes

Notes

Notes